Refugees Into Citizens

Refugees Into Citizens

Palestinians and the End of the Arab-Israeli Conflict

Donna E. Arzt

A COUNCIL ON FOREIGN RELATIONS BOOK

COUNCIL ON FOREIGN RELATIONS BOOKS

For further information on Council publications, please write the Council on Foreign Relations, 58 East 68th Street, New York, NY 10021, or call the Publications Office at (212) 434-9400.

Library of Congress Cataloging-in-Publication Data

Arzt, Donna E.
Refugees into Citizens : Palestinians and the end of the Arab–Israeli conflict / Donna E. Arzt
    223 p. cm.
    Includes bibliographical references and index.
    ISBN 0-87609-194-X
    1. Jewish–Arab relations—1949– 2. Refugees, Arab. 3. Palestinian Arabs—Rehabilitation. I. Title. DS119.7.A6863 1996
956.04—dc20   96–42112
                                                   CIP

96   97   98   99   PB   10   9   8   7   6   5   4   3   2   1

Contents

List of Maps, Figures, and Tables

IN MEMORY OF YITZHAK RABIN

We lost a great man, who made the peace of the brave with us. He was our partner.

—Yasser Arafat to Leah Rabin, November 9, 1995

Preface

One of the most difficult issues to be resolved in the Arab-Israeli conflict is the status of millions of Palestinian refugees dispersed throughout the Middle East, many of whom reside in refugee camps. Their origins, total numbers including living lineal descendants, current location inside and outside Mandate Palestine, and right to return "home," are all contentious matters, among others.

Working on the assumption that the Oslo Accord had broken new ground, the Council on Foreign Relations convened a study group to deal with this longstanding and complex problem. The study group held five meetings from November 1993 through June 1994. Discussions were spirited and often underscored the serious differences of analysis and evaluation permeating the issue. Constructive approaches were developed for an overall solution within the context of a comprehensive Middle East peace between Israel and the countries in which Palestinian refugees are located.

The study group participants were Odeh Aburdene, Fouad Ajami, Lamis Andoni, Musa Briezat, Burt Caine, Raghida Dergham, Alan Dowty, William Eagleton, Dennis Gallagher, Christopher George, Gidon Gottlieb, Malvina Halberstam, Hurst Hannum, Lou Henkin, Arthur Hertzberg, Neil Hicks, Paul Jabber, Basma Kodmani-Darwish, Daniel Kurtzer, Luke Lee, William Lee, Ann Lesch, Ian Lustick, Philip Mattar, Ted Meron, Judith Miller, Don Peretz, Trudy Rubin, Nawaf Salam, Gary Sick, Henry Siegman, Andrew Whitley, Ezra Zilkha, James Zogby, and Elia Zureik. The Project Director was Donna E. Arzt, of Syracuse University; the Coordinators were F. Gregory Gause III, and Richard W. Murphy, both of the Council on Foreign Relations; and the Rapporteur was Riva Richmond, of the Council on Foreign Relations. I served as the study group chair.

Although the present book by Professor Arzt was inspired by the study group, it neither represents the views of the group's participants, collectively or individually, nor that of the Council on Foreign Relations. It nonetheless encapsulates, in a succinct fashion, the complex and controversial issues of law and of history while proposing a theoretical solution to the problem of ending the refugee status of millions of Palestinians within the context of a comprehensive negotiated conclusion to the Arab-Israeli conflict.

Rita E. Hauser
The Hauser Foundation
New York, New York

ix

Foreword

Of the many images that I saw during the Palestinian *intifada* against Israeli rule, one stands out most strongly, and captures the essence of where we stand today in our attempt to resolve the Arab-Israeli conflict in a just and permanent manner. It was a television news story that showed a young Israeli soldier, bristling with high-tech weapons and communications equipment in his heavily armored jeep, passing an elderly Palestinian village woman who was walking home, with a very large head of cabbage balanced on her head. They exchanged heated words, and in her intense anger the Palestinian woman threw the cabbage at the soldier, shattering it into two large pieces on the ground. The soldier, obviously not trained in counter-cabbage tactics, seemed momentarily dumbfounded, but then reached instinctively, picked up the remnants of the cabbage, and threw them back at the lady.

And so here are we Palestinians and Israelis in the mid-1990s—one hundred years after the publication of Theodor Herzl's book *The Jewish State* in 1896 marked the birth of modern Zionism and the genesis of Zionist-Arab tensions in the Levant—hurling large, raw cabbages at each other, mutually flustered by our inability to fully defeat the other and to claim the land for ourselves. Our dispute has become a hundred years war, but it has not yet delivered a verdict about who owns this land, who will rule it, who will claim and savor its rich memories, and reap its bountiful harvests.

The Palestinian-Israeli war, and the wider Arab-Israeli conflict, has been about land, but not only about land. The land captures the importance of deeper issues and needs—of concepts of identity, community and nationhood, motivated by fierce, ancient and primordial forces of human dignity, protection and survival, and expressed in the modern vocabulary of sovereignty, statehood, and citizenship. The century-long span and modern brutality of the Palestinian-Israeli conflict are merely consequences that emanate from the core conflicting claims of a young Israeli soldier and an elderly Palestinian villager who passionately but irresolutely throw cabbages at one another.

Ending the modern Arab-Israeli conflict will require three basic elements: a fair and permanent resolution of the Palestinian refugee problem within the wider context of satisfying Palestinian national rights; the restoration of the territorial integrity and sovereign rights of all concerned Arab states; and the formal, official acceptance of Israel by the Arabs as a legitimate state in the Middle East, enjoying the security and sovereignty due to all countries. Such a comprehensive, durable peace requires tackling the complex moral, political, and psychological issues that Arabs and Israelis have long avoided. The election of Benjamin Netanyahu in May 1996 promises to put these issues under a stronger spotlight.

With the start in mid-1996 of the final status negotiations between Israelis and Palestinians, the days of procrastination are over, the moment of historical and moral reckoning is here. There are no more issues to prioritize or postpone, no more old documents to revise, no more old ideologies to argue. The frightening personal and national specters that have traumatized Arabs and Israelis for much of the past century must be faced and vanquished: Whose land is this? How can Israelis and Palestinians feel safe in this, their common ancestral landscape? Can Jews/Israelis or Palestinians living in other countries ever feel truly safe and secure without the protection and ultimate refuge of their own sovereign state?

The severe historical trauma of Israelis and Palestinians causes both sides to instinctively retreat into history, in order to find culprits, to pin blame, to point out the causes and justifications of their current political actions. But history is a bitter guide. Israelis and Palestinians both have credible moral, historical, and political claims for their own statehood in Palestine—but neither has a credible case to deny the right of sovereign statehood to the other. Both are compelled to recognize the legitimacy of the other if they wish to have their own legitimacy acknowledged.

Clearly, the single most important component of peacemaking always has been and remains today the status of the Palestinian refugees—not how to resettle them or find them jobs, but how to restore to them their full human rights and dignity within the context of their national community *as they define that community themselves*. In the past decade, the whole nature of the discussion of Arab-Israeli peacemaking has shifted toward more propitious diplomatic ground that recognizes the importance of addressing Israeli and Palestinian rights on equal terms. Peacemaking has moved ahead since 1991, even with many warts, bumps, and growls, essentially because the Israelis and Palestinians started to acknowledge and accept the demands of the other, *as defined by the other*. The imbalance in power in favor of Israel means that the Palestinians have had to make most of the compromises in the initial stages of the negotiations. This should not detract from the underlying process that is under way: a simultaneous and mutual re-humanization of the other by Palestinians and Israelis. The principal parties to this dispute can define their own identity and national aspirations, but they cannot dictate these to the other party. If I believe that Judaism is only a religion, but most Jews see themselves in terms of a nationality, race, sovereign state, or civilization, then I have to deal with Jews and Israelis in the terms in which they define themselves. Similarly, if Israelis see Palestinians as eligible only for self-rule in a fragmented, cantonal arrangement defined mainly by Israeli security concerns, but Palestinians see themselves as a national community deserving of statehood, then the Israelis must come around to accepting the Palestinians' self-definition of a future Palestinian national entity.

Donna Arzt rightly proposes a forward-looking strategy of politically realistic conflict-resolution and reconciliation that simultaneously respects the harsh yet often hazy facts of the past. She offers valuable starting points and milestones on the pathways that we shall have to negotiate successfully, if our aim of peace with justice in Palestine and Israel is to be achieved. She tackles an enormously difficult and contentious subject with an impressive combination of realism, fairness, and compassion. Her ideas will elicit disagreement and concern, as well as much praise and respect. Her proposals will not be fully accepted by any party to the dispute at hand, but they should cause all parties seriously to ponder the issues she raises and the options she suggests. I believe that she has exemplified the finest traditions of the American legal system—the triumph of the humanistic quest for realistic justice over the emotional tendency toward revenge and retribution.

The first and most important attribute of a peaceful Middle East—now glaringly missing—is justice. Donna Arzt offers impressive pointers toward that goal, especially as regards the rights and needs of the Palestinian refugees, as individuals and as a national community. Citizenship for the Palestinians will have to include some sort of sovereignty, even in a territorially truncated Arab Palestine. The point is not only the extent of the land The point is the humanity of the people, and their right never again to be invisible people.

Rami Khouri
Amman, Jordan

Acknowledgments

Many people contributed in a wide variety of ways to my ability to complete this book. It is not to be assumed that any of them concur with me on any particular point or points made in it. In fact, it is safer to assume that most of them disagree—vehemently. As I have learned, if the Arab-Israeli conflict is an explosive subject, the refugee issue is downright volcanic. Rather than striving to write "objectively," which is an unattainable, mythic position, I have instead endeavored to be as fair, balanced, and dispassionate as possible and to avoid accusatory and inflammatory forms of expression. Having at one point or another been called everything from "a naive American Jewish meddler" to "a Zionist stooge" and even a "supporter of terrorism" for the views I express here, I've learned to ignore the labels and instead try to keep my focus undeflected from what is indisputably my chief objective: jump-starting an imperative discussion about the refugees. I can only hope that more people read this book than have heretofore read my various law review articles!

For funding and sponsoring my efforts, I thank the Council on Foreign Relations and the Syracuse University College of Law. Special mention must go to Rita Hauser, chair of the Council study group entitled "The Shape of the Arab-Israeli Settlement: Humanitarian and Demographic Issues," for her personal encouragement, financial support, persistent commitment to Middle East peace, and patience in awaiting the completed manuscript. Council on Foreign Relations fellows Richard Murphy and Gregory Gause and staff members Riva Richmond, Nomi Colton-Max, and Shugu Imam provided integral assistance. Nomi's directional sense in Midtown is unparalleled.

At least five "generations" of research assistants at Syracuse University have rendered their dedication and service: Karen Zughaib, Jeanne Clark, Tara Verdonk, Tracy Zagroba, Mike Dufault, Tiffany Lee, and Kelly Aran. The staff at the Barclay Law Library, including Alissa DiRubbo, Bruce Hamm, Mike Poitras, Wendy Scott, and Jean Williams, have accommodated virtually every one of my nonnegotiable demands. Many other people gave me their time and suggestions either before or during research trips, including: Joe Alexander, Taisir Amre, Marina Barham, Dan Bitan, Rex Brynen, Shamay Cahana, Naomi Chazan, Ruth Gavison, Shlomo Gazit, Galya Golan, Mark Heller, Radi

Jarradi, David and Mary Ann Johnson, Ghassan Khatib, David Kretzmer, Leslie Lempert, Moshe Maoz, Nawaf Massalcha, David Michaelis, Gail Pressberg, Abbas Shiblak, Naser Tahboub, Salim Tamari, Jill Tansley, Shibley Telhami, David Viveash, and Elia Zureik. I especially want to thank William Lee of UNRWA for facilitating access to important data.

Numerous members and invitees of the Council on Foreign Relations study group, listed in the preface to this book, provided their time, thoughts, and reactions. I also thank Irwin Cotler, Mary Morris, Mehrzad Boroujerdi, and Stephen Marks for inviting me to speak on the book's topic at forums in Montreal, Haifa, Syracuse, and New York City. Alan Dowty, Galya Golan, Rita Hauser, Arthur Hertzberg, Neil Hicks, Ann Lesch, Moshe Maoz, Yaakov Meron, Richard Murphy, and Elia Zureik provided additional comments on an early version of chapter 4. The longer manuscript, in its various stages, also benefited from the expert copyediting of Debbie Manette, the capable editorial direction of Trisha Dorff and production help from Sarah Thomas, and the comments of Richard Murphy, Rita Hauser, Don Peretz, Judy Mayotte, and especially Rami Khouri, who reminded me that the personal is political (or is it the other way around?!), and Arthur Hertzberg, who asked the hardest questions, most of which I still cannot answer.

For giving me nourishment and/or a bed (or in some cases, a couch) in Israel, Jordan, New York City, and elsewhere during research trips: Eli and Sarah Presser; the Fishmans and Ioffes (whom I first met in Moscow in 1978); Avital and Noam Schlanger; the Kanter-Kepnes family; Burt and Shulamit Caine; the Aizenbergs and kibbutz Netiv HaLamed Hai; the Herolds (especially Avi, for removing the bullets from his room, twice); Rami, Ellen, Haitham, Raja, and Shaq, and the other Khouri cats; and my sister, brother-in-law, and nephew, Andrea, Walter, and Theo. Many others also offered much-needed encouragement: friends and colleagues Maggie Chon, Louise Lantzy, Hilary Josephs, Arlene Kanter, Patricia Hassett, Janis McDonald, Deb Kenn, Paul Lund, Wilhelmina Reuben-Cooke, Lynn Oatman, Daan Braveman, Chris Day, Red Schwartz, Brian Bromberger, Lou Kriesberg, and Pnina Lahav; former students Nancy Noonan, Michael Hovey, Sam Nelson, Susan Weinstein, and Lauren Austin; as well as Cindy Meeker, Carol Pope, David Kinsey, Joan Bornstein, and Elaine Reall.

Finally, I wish to thank my parents, Alvin and Lois Arzt, for allowing me to find my own peace, and Kasha, Duvey, and Misha Arzt, who kept me company during those frigid central New York days and nights in front of the laptop instead of the fire.

Donna Arzt
Ithaca, New York
May 1996

Introduction:
Principles of Peace

For Jews, the word is *galut*; for Palestinians, it is *ghourba*. For both, it means exile, a condition, both physical and spiritual, from which one longs to return to the Promised Land, the Homeland. Like the Jewish dream of returning to Zion, or of making *aliyah*, the Palestinian rendering of return, *el awda*, is similarly based on the self-image of a people living in "the world of the exile. The world of the occupied. The world of the refugee. The world of the ghetto."[1] For both peoples, history is equated with flight from disaster. Each has its own special term for the respective catastrophes of the 1940s that preceded their respective modern engagements with nationalism: for Jews, *Shoah*, the Nazi Holocaust; for Palestinians, *al-Nakba*, the catastrophe/dispersal in the 1948 war with Israel. It was exile and subjugation that made Palestinians Palestinian, just as it was the years of wandering in Sinai after slavery in Egypt that turned the Israelites into the People of Israel.[2]

Palestinians and Jews have so much in common that others, including even their adversaries, have implicitly treated them in parallel fashion. Compare, for instance, this hostile rejection of Palestinians as a traitorous community, made by a Kuwaiti official after the Persian Gulf War, with the classic anti-Semitic label, popular in Stalinist Russia, of Jews as "rootless cosmopolitans," a people "without honor, without character, without a homeland," the better-educated security risks suspected of "divided loyalties," who are "infected by the virus of truckling to everything foreign"[3]:

> [T]he Palestinians are treacherous peoples. They betrayed the hospitality and generosity shown them. They lived off the wealth of Kuwait and the Kuwaiti people. . . . The problem lies with the Palestinian people, who have no loyalty, unlike for example the Lebanese, Syrian and Egyptian peoples.[4]

Rejection, distrust, and vilification—not only of each other, but of each in the eyes of others—constitute a persistent subtext in the history of the Israeli-Palestinian conflict.[5] It is as if the two peoples have been looking at each other through a window that turns out to be a double-sided mirror, a mirror not only of their own fears, paranoia, obsessions, and prejudices and of the fears, paranoia, obsessions, and prejudices of others, but of their own similar passions, dreams, and needs.

Palestinian and Israeli identities are so caught up in each others' histories, their discourse so strewn with linguistically similar terms, their respective commitments to common values such as education and community so fierce, that it is patently obvious that they can resolve their mutual conflict only together. As stated by one of the Israelis who initiated the Oslo talks leading to mutual recognition between Israel and the Palestine Liberation Organization (PLO):

> We convinced the Palestinians that at the Israeli decision-making level there was a genuine desire to reach a settlement based on security, and an interest in helping the Palestinians to reach a strong, stable, and prosperous entity of their own. In return, the Palestinian negotiators convinced us that their leadership realized that terror and armed struggle would not bring them closer to their dream, and that the only solution was reconciliation and political dialogue.[6]

And as similarly stated by the chief Palestinian negotiator for Oslo II, the September 1995 Interim Agreement for the West Bank: "Their concern from the beginning was security. I said we understand, and I will support your needs for security. I want continuity of the land, I want to be sure the land will come later, even if in stages."[7]

Although each side expresses it differently, at the most critical level, the Arab-Israeli conflict is not about territory, not about religion and nationalism, but about defining the parameters of community, delineating the social and demographic boundaries and frontiers of each people's "control system."[8] In other, less academic, words, it is about the willingness to accept who one's neighbors are. What the rallying cry of "Jewish security" means for Israelis, "Palestinian dignity" means for Palestinians: the need for mutual acceptance as neighbors rather than as mortal enemies, a psychological state that is equally as essential to peace as is military, economic, or political stability.

*   *   *

The main thesis of this book is that a permanent and viable solution to the Arab-Israeli conflict must include the granting of citizenship to Palestinian refugees throughout the region of the Middle East. Only when all Palestinians have citizenship will the conflict be over, because only then would the refugees no longer serve as pawns or bargaining chips for the wider agendas of each of the parties to the conflict. Mutual acceptance of Israelis by their Arab neighbors and of Palestinians by Israelis and other Arabs can be achieved only when the Palestinian status and mentality of refugeehood is supplanted by permanent regional absorption, in the form of a combination of limited repatriation to Israel, the West Bank, and Gaza; integration into the Syrian, Jordanian, and even Lebanese communities where many Palestinians now reside; and resettlement of additional Palestinian families in other states of the Middle East as well as in Western states. Compensation for lost property and dual citizenship—symbolized in a "Palestinian national passport" in addition to citizenship in another state—must also be made available to those who do not repatriate.

While no formal position is taken here on either the exact final borders or the permanent legal status of the West Bank and Gaza, it is assumed that the establishment of a sovereign Palestine in those territories, either independent or confederated with Jordan, is more likely than any semi- or pseudo-autonomy plan to generate widespread Palestinian approval for compromises short of full repatriation to Israel.[9] In other words, in the absence of a Palestinian state, final resolution of the refugee question is highly unlikely.

Why should the replacement for refugee status be citizenship? Because citizenship symbolizes—and concretely cements—the indices of absorption and peace. The crux of permanent peace in the Middle East is regional stability, which depends on permanent absorption, which derives from citizenship. That is, citizenship not only in the formal, legal sense, but in the moral, political, social, and psychological senses as well, or what sociologist Rogers Brubaker has called "substantive citizenship," meaning an array of civil, political, and especially social rights and obligations.[10] In the words of the British sociologist T. H. Marshall, citizenship is: "the basic human equality associated with the concept of full membership of a community . . . the right to share to the full in the social heritage and to live the life of a civilised being according to the standards prevailing in the society."[11] What matters to the citizen is "the superstructure of legitimate expectations" she obtains by becoming a formally recognized member of a state.[12] The statement "I am a citizen" therefore signifies actual entitlement to an impressive "package" of obligations as well as rights.[13]

More than mere residence, citizenship is "an enduring personal status that is not generated by passing or extended residence alone and does not lapse with temporary or prolonged absence."[14] Because of that personal endurance, citizens can actually *participate* in civic life and in building the future of their state and society. They have a stake in their community's endurance. This civic ethos "is rooted in the dignity of humankind, in the need to respect every person for what he or she is."[15] Or as stated by Chief Justice Earl Warren in the

U.S. Supreme Court case of *Perez v. Brownell*: "Citizenship is . . . nothing less than the right to have rights. Remove this priceless possession and there remains a stateless person, disgraced and degraded in the eyes of his countrymen."[16]

When neighboring states grant their respective populations the permanent status of citizenship, regional stability through the reduction of interstate tensions and jealousies can emerge. Thinking specifically of Israelis and Palestinians and their joint future ushered in by the peace process, Israeli author Alouph Hareven has written:

> freedom of choice [has been] granted to both peoples, singly and jointly, to bring about the greatest turning point in their history: the emergence from the era of sacrifice into one where, instead of superiors and inferiors, one finds human beings and citizens who respect all people as people and as citizens, irrespective of their national language, faith, or opinions.[17]

But citizenship need not mean either assimilation on the one hand or ghettoization on the other. The perpetuation of a minority's distinct ethnic and cultural identity within the framework of an overarching national identity is not incompatible with a postmodern notion of statehood. Palestinians given citizenship in, for instance, Syria, need not be converted into a homogenized form of "Syrianhood" in order to assume the rights, duties, and loyalties of Syrian citizenship. International law requires that minorities be granted the right, in community with other members of their group, to enjoy their own culture, to maintain their own associations, both internally and with their corresponding groups across international frontiers, and to promote knowledge of their distinctive history, traditions, and culture through education. At the same time, minorities must be allowed to participate, both individually and as a group, in the political life of the state as a whole.[18] Promotion of this balance can be facilitated through formal measures such as dual Palestinian-Syrian or Palestinian–other Arab state citizenship, which has been suggested by Palestinians, even though dual citizenship has not before now been a common feature of the Arab world and is likely to be resisted by most Arab states.[19] (Issues of citizenship and minority rights are addressed in chapters 3 and 5.)

The first steps in the direction of Palestinian citizenship have already been taken through both the Madrid peace process and the Oslo peace process. (See chapter 1 for a description of the Madrid and Oslo peace processes involving Israel, the Palestinians, and other Middle Eastern and non–Middle Eastern states.) The Refugee Multilateral Working Group, a component of the Madrid process, was intended to undertake confidence-building measures focusing on improving the short-term living conditions of Palestinian refugees without waiting for political breakthroughs of a more long-term nature through the bilateral negotiation process. (See the documentary appendix for the texts of the opening Palestinian and Israeli remarks in this working group.) Similarly, the interim period before the Israeli-Palestinian final status negotiations were to begin in May 1996 was intended to build trust and explore avenues of cooperation. The very participation in these negotiations by the PLO and by Arab states such as Egypt and Jordan reflects a pivotal acceptance of the principle—which Arabs and especially Palestinians had rejected for the previous 44 years—that the refugees could improve their short-term quality of life without prejudicing their future rights and status either as refugees or returnees.

Brainstorming solutions to seemingly intractable problems is the most vital aspect of effective negotiation.[20] At this stage in the peace process, no one plan or proposal can either be ruled out or deemed definitive. The set of scenarios presented in this book is therefore intended only to offer new perspectives, to stimulate other ideas, and simply to generate dialogue on what is usually treated as virtually a taboo subject: the possibility of achieving negotiable compromises on the permanent status of the refugees.[21] Indeed, even the future of Jerusalem, that other ostensibly "intractable" issue, has been the subject of over 60 proposed solutions.[22] Not so the future of the refugees, whose potential return to their original homes has rarely been broached in any context other than the most uncompromisingly polemical: "All must return," from one side and "None. Never," from the other.[23]

This book is intended to provide policymakers and participants in the Middle East peace process, their national constituencies and the negotiations' cosponsors in the United States, Russia, Canada, Norway, and elsewhere, as well as readers with a general interest in refugees, in international relations, and/or in Middle Eastern affairs, with not only a forthright appraisal of the refugee components of the Arab-Israeli conflict but also with a confidence that the issues are ultimately resolvable. By emphasizing the present and future more than the past, the book attempts to present a forward-looking, balanced, fair, and practical framework for resolving the Palestinian refugee crisis and for implementing a permanent regional absorption plan. Avoiding the process of laying blame for who caused the original flight of the Palestinians in 1948, it takes as a given the existence of such refugees and concentrates, instead, on finding solutions that can be implemented as soon as possible within the context of Arab-Israeli peace.

The term "crisis" in the context of displaced persons is usually applied to acute dislocations caused by ongoing wars, systematic persecution, or natural disasters. The outflows caused by "ethnic cleansing" in Bosnia and Rwanda are recent examples of such crises. The shared objective of refugees and of the humanitarian and intergovernmental agencies administering aid to them is almost always to end the emergency as quickly as possible by finding permanent, even if less than wholly adequate, asylum.

Palestinian refugees, by contrast, have remained in their displaced status—many, in fact, in overcrowded, squalid refugee camps in Lebanon, Jordan, Syria, the West Bank, and Gaza since 1948 or at least 1967—much too long to still be counted as an "acute" dislocation. They are surely, however, one of history's oldest, largest, and most renowned populations of displaced persons; their prolonged predicament constitutes a crisis nonetheless. More ink (if not more blood) may have been spilled over their fate than over any other refugee group. That dubious distinction has in part been due to the notorious "intractability" of the Israeli-Palestinian conflict. Before the recent negotiations, however, it was also due to the deliberate policy of Palestinians themselves, with the certain connivance of Israel and Arab states alike, to perpetuate and politicize their refugee status by refusing any measures to be absorbed permanently in any place but Palestine. Three generations of refugees insisted that they remain in their squalid camps. In that sense they are virtually unique among refugee populations.

At the same time, the Palestinian refugee crisis is not so *sui generis* as to be insusceptible to influence and intuition culled from other refugee experiences. Traditionally, all sides to the Israeli-Palestinian conflict have treated the Palestinian situation as singular and exceptional—at least when considered politically expedient to do so, which was virtually always. But from the vantage point of the late 1990s and the perspective of an American scholar of international law, it seems part of a larger picture of global transformation in at least two respects: the mass displacements of people that result in redefinition of political borders; and reformulation of notions of national and ethnic identity in relation to citizenship and community. It would be myopic at this juncture to attempt to illuminate the options available for Palestinians without borrowing insights from refugee experiences in, for instance, southern Africa, Southeast Asia, and the Baltic region.

Part I of this book, titled "Past and Present" and consisting of three chapters, lays out the essential background to the historical, demographic, and legal aspects of the status of Palestinian refugees. While it acknowledges that each of these issues has been the source of protracted contention and violently charged rhetoric, it tries to avoid further fanning of the flames by pragmatically focusing on the data and the interpretations most conducive to reconciliation of the conflict.

Part II, "Present and Future," begins with chapter 4's proposed plan for permanent regional absorption to turn Palestinian refugees into citizens. It offers target numbers, timetables, priority rankings, and other suggested guidelines, all in an effort to help spark the refugee discussions in the final status talks. It also discusses what Western governments can do to facilitate a refugee solution, such as sponsoring a pledging conference to encourage states to resettle refugees and otherwise contribute to the absorption process. Chapter 5 then looks at a number of key legal and policy components in implementing such a plan, including citizenship issues, freedom of movement, and the human rights of minorities. It utilizes the lens of other refugee and minority experiences in other times and other places to suggest "norms of implementation" for Palestinians, Israelis, sponsoring governments, relief agencies, and other supporters of the peace process.

Finally, after a short conclusion, the reader will find an extensive bibliographical essay and an appendix containing excerpts from relevant international legal documents.

*   *   *

It is true that within the framework of the Arab-Israeli peace process, the refugee issue is not an abstract question easily extricated from the morass of other concerns, such as terrorism by both Palestinian and Jewish extremists, or other final-status topics such as borders, regional security, Jerusalem, water and trade, not to mention Jewish settlements and compensation for Jewish refugees from Arab states, all of which are beyond the scope of this book.[24] This truism, however, has often served as a convenient excuse for avoiding the difficult task of thinking and talking through possible solutions to the refugee question itself. Unless dialogue is initiated on each of these final-status subjects separately, the synergy, flexibility, creativity, and trade-offs needed to develop a comprehensive final settlement will never be generated. While this book is intended to facilitate discussions on one of the most sensitive aspects of the permanent settlement, Palestinian refugees, in order to move the entire process forward, it cannot deny that the other negotiation topics must also proceed at their own inherent pace.

Where, then, to begin? A good place is with a set of negotiation principles that are intended to encourage a practical yet equitable settlement. Even a subject so seemingly intractable as the refugee question, one so intimately connected to both peoples' self-identity and sense of justice and security, can be resolved if four basic principles are adopted:

- *Discussion of the refugee question must be forward, not backward-looking, so that age-old battles over fault and causes of dislocation will not be relitigated.* "Looking forward" does not mean *forgetting* the past; it simply means that the parties must *move on*. As put by Shimon Peres, one of the staunchest proponents of the Oslo process, when he was Israel's foreign minister, "The great thing is to divorce ourselves from the world of yesterday, and recognize the world of today."[25] This is easier said than done because concrete agreements must take into account concrete contemporary demographic figures, which all derive from the hotly disputed base figure, the number of Palestinians who left Israel during the 1948 war. It also requires a great amount of rhetorical restraint in use of politically loaded terminology such as "return," "expulsion," "transfer," or even "rights" and "refugees." The most strategic objective in this regard is to strive for permanence of solutions, such as actual absorption and acquisition of citizenship.

- *Wherever possible, obligations of the parties to the negotiations must be made reciprocal and regionally balanced.* The only pragmatic and fair resolution of the refugee question is through regional participation. Like all refugee crises, the problem is regional and therefore the solution must be.[26] This involves a fact that honest brokers must acknowledge: that a large percentage of Palestinians must be absorbed permanently either into countries of their heretofore temporary residence or into neighboring countries of the Middle East. As noted, compensation and a Palestinian national passport for those who do not repatriate should make this compromise palatable to many Palestinians. As a practical matter of economic and demographic stability, the West Bank and Gaza cannot absorb all the refugees, at least not in the short run. But if the costs and burdens of absorption are shared in a balanced fashion, the entire region can benefit.

- *The parties must recognize that each people, both Palestinians and Israelis, has equal rights to land, statehood, security, and survival.* These rights are both national and personal and must be considered established under law and God, in the eyes of history and of each other. "There should be recognition that every party has a legitimate right to safeguard its security. . . . Security cannot be approached as the exclusive right of any one party to be obtained at the expense of any other party, but security must be mutual and reciprocal."[27] The same is true of all other aspects of national self-determination. This principle, which derives from each people's fundamental humanity, means that the legitimate rights of one cannot be held hostage to the needs or demands of the other.

- *The standard to be achieved in the entire settlement must be international normalcy, the condition in which responsible, peaceful states and their citizens are expected to behave and interact with each other.* Normalization is not only the *goal* of peace, it is also the *standard* for peace. Normalcy was the dream of the founders of Israel, who wished to turn the Jewish people into "a nation like other nations," respected, secure, and proud. These aims are not so different from those of Arab states, which have long labored for dignity under the dread of Western domination. For refugees, normalcy means the replacement of "statelessness by identity, poverty by development, camps by neighborhoods, precariousness" by stability.[28] Normalcy also includes respect for human rights and nonpersecution of the ethnic minorities that will remain in Israel, Palestine, and all of the neighboring states. King Hussein of Jordan stated it best at the White House ceremony that ended the war between Jordan and Israel: "We are on our way now truly towards what is normal in relations between our peoples and ourselves."[29]

These four basic principles are a demarcation point for the rest of this book.

PART I

PAST AND PRESENT

Chapter 1

The Historical Framework

To set the stage for moving forward, an initial glance backward is critical. It would be foolhardy to proffer a future-oriented resolution without an understanding of what has already been tried, what facts are already "on the ground," as they are fond of saying in the Middle East, and what traditionally agreed-upon legal parameters exist within which a just solution is possible.

This chapter and the succeeding two offer snapshots of some of the relevant context surrounding the Israeli-Palestinian conflict in general and the refugee question in particular. The first of these contextual foundations is necessarily a historical one. Nevertheless, this chapter is not a history of how the Palestinians came to be a people, which has been discussed elsewhere.[1] It is only peripherally about how the Palestinians came to be refugees, which is the subject of new historiography and long-protracted controversy.[2] It is, instead, primarily a sketch of some of the many previous failed attempts, whether undertaken unilaterally, bilaterally, or multilaterally, to resolve their status. This limited topic is itself protracted, controversial, and convoluted enough so as to already have generated its own literature and counterliterature. In order to do it justice, this historical chapter is organized topically rather than chronologically. A sketch of the controversial history of the displacement of Palestinians is presented first, followed by descriptions of unilateral, regional, and then international proposals to resolve the demographic crisis. Finally, the question of the refugees is placed within the context of the most promising regional development of the 1990s, the multilateral negotiations known as the Madrid and Oslo peace processes.

"Magic Numbers": The Dispersals of 1948 and 1967

It is presumably a matter of simple historical fact that the U.N. General Assembly announced the partition of Palestine into a Jewish state and an Arab state on November 29, 1947, followed five months later by Britain relinquishing the mandate it had held over the area since the end of World War I.[3] Yet these events launched not only a state of war between Arabs and Israelis that effectively would last over 40-some years, but also a historical controversy that, unlike the state of war, will probably never be suspended. The controversy concerns two questions flowing from the partition and from Israeli independence, which was itself announced on May 14, 1948: first, how many Arab residents of Palestine fled the country at the outbreak of war, and second, why did they flee?

The actual number of Palestinians who became refugees as a result of the conflict is of more than mere historical importance, for it serves as the basis for establishing the number of Palestinian refugees who exist today and who are eligible for repatriation or resettlement, compensation, and other forms of relief. For that reason, the ever-disputed 1948 exodus figure is talismatic, a veritable "magic number." The estimated number has ranged from a low of 520,000 (the official 1948 Israeli figure) to a high of 900,000 to 1,000,000 (the figures used by various Arab spokespersons).[4] Middle-range estimates include 726,000 (the United Nations) and 810,000 (the British government).[5] Many of the "new Israeli historians," who have relied on recently declassified archives, set the number in the range of 600,000 to 760,000 and believe that they came from a total of about 370 different Arab villages.[6] Israeli officials discount these higher numbers by arguing that heads of Palestinian households as well as U.N. administrators frequently exaggerated the number of displaced persons in order to receive more relief funds.[7] Also at stake is the definition of who is a Palestinian: any non-Jew who resided in Palestine at the time of Israeli independence, or a narrower definition?[8]

According to the American political scientist Mark Tessler, the disagreements mainly derive not from how many Palestinians remained in their homes, but on the total number of Arabs who lived in Palestine before 1948. "Both sides concur that only about 150,000 remained inside Israel by the end of 1949, and thus, despite their differing totals, there is agreement that the overwhelming majority of the indigenous Arab population was removed from the area of the new Jewish state."[9] Many Palestinian and Israeli sources agree that the prewar total number of Arabs was about 1.2 to 1.3 million, with Jewish residents at that time numbering about 640,000 to 650,000 people.[10] That would mean that the percentage of Palestinians who fled ranges from about 43 to 83 percent. Using the middle-range U.N. figure on the number of refugees, it was approximately 58 percent.[11]

The 150,000 to 170,000 remaining Arabs eventually all became legal Israeli citizens.[12] Of these, anywhere from 25,000 to 32,000 were "internal refugees" who had fled their homes but remained within the armistice lines of Israel.[13] According to Tessler:

Although they had not left the country, [the internal refugees], too, abandoned their homes during or immediately after the war, and then either
were prevented from returning, allegedly for security reasons, or found
that their dwellings had been razed or occupied by Jews. As a result, they
either resettled in neighboring Arab villages or were obliged to occupy
the homes of others who had fled.[14]

The reason why the Arab residents of the new Jewish state fled has
its own contemporary consequence, given that the responsibility to pay
compensation is legally linked to causation. But the historical record
raises as many questions as answers. Did they flee voluntarily, at the request of the Arab Higher Committee, the representative body of the
Palestinians, or of the Mufti of Jerusalem, the area's quasi-political
Muslim spiritual leader, to join the invading Arab armies or in order to
clear the way, temporarily, for the military campaign to annihilate the
Jews, reconquer the land, and let the Arab residents return? Or was it
because of the collapse of their political institutions caused by the early
departure of the wealthier and well-educated Arab elites? Did they flee
because they were evicted as part of a scheme by Zionist leaders to secure Arab villages located in strategic transportation and communication lines or, more sinisterly, to readjust the population imbalance? Or
did they flee purely from fear that they would be massacred, or because
they heard that 254 Arabs were in fact massacred, at Deir Yassin, an
Arab village located in a predominantly Jewish area outside Jerusalem?
Did the Haganah (the semiofficial Jewish defense force) and Jewish terrorist groups such as the Irgun "encourage" them to leave or outright
conduct an "ethnic cleansing" operation by destroying their villages
and towns?[15]

Regardless of how one answers these questions—and the actual
response may turn out to be a variation on "all of the above"—a
few points can be agreed upon.[16] First, it is clear that "[t]he exodus
caused a disastrous complication and aggravation of the conflict,
and the refugee problem it created remains, even today, the major
obstacle in the search for peace."[17] Put in contemporary terms, because
it is historically, politically, psychologically, and legally at the heart of
the Arab-Israeli conflict, "[a]ny settlement that fails completely to solve
the refugee problem will not provide a realistic or durable settlement."[18] Perhaps this psychological component is most difficult for Israelis to grasp. The 1948 war uprooted Jews as well as Palestinians. In
addition to the new agricultural settlements such as those in the Etzion
bloc, old and established Jewish communities in the Jewish Quarter of
Jerusalem and in Hebron, for instance, were forced to relocate. And yet,
as articulated by Israeli journalist Danny Rubinstein:

> They, too, were dispossessed, but the State of Israel did not look upon them as refugees, and they did not nurture powerful dreams of returning to their ancestral homes and property. . . . No Jew can be a refugee in the land or the State of Israel. . . . [By contrast], [f]or the first generation of Palestinian refugees, the meaning of "homeland" was very simple, concrete, direct: a field, an olive tree, a veranda, a well. Hence, their loss was felt immediately, and deeply, as a great tragedy.[19]

A second, more concrete, point of almost universal concurrence is that whatever the cause of their having left, the Palestinians were not allowed to come back and their property was either looted and destroyed or turned over to Jews by the new state's acts of expropriation. In late 1948 and early 1949, after the termination of hostilities, new Jewish settlements were established on the approximately one million acres of "abandoned" land and newly arriving Jewish immigrants were settled in empty Arab housing.[20] Was this part of an official Israeli plan to further destroy "abandoned" Arab villages and fields, in order to ensure that the Arab residents would not return? Did Israel expel, or intimidate into fleeing, additional Arabs who were still living in border areas?[21] These, too, are contested questions.

However, it is indisputable that after the creation of the State of Israel, a series of legal measures were taken that served to institutionalize the blockage of Palestinian return. The Abandoned Areas Ordinance (1948), the Emergency Regulations Concerning the Cultivation of Waste Lands (1949), the Absentees' Property Law (1950), and the Land Acquisition Law (1953) operated to legalize the expropriation of some 3,200 to 4,600 square kilometers of Arab-owned land.[22] A portion of the requisitioned plots, especially agricultural lands, belonged to "non-absentee" Arabs—those who had not fled but had remained to become Israeli citizens. Although some of their land was returned in the years between 1949 and 1954, it was in the form of leases granted by the Custodian of Absentee Property rather than the restoration of title.[23] Among those few Jews who protested against these measures was the philosopher Martin Buber, who wrote in a letter to the Knesset speaker:

> We know well, however, that in numerous cases land is [to be] expropriated not on grounds of security, but for other reasons, such as expansion of existing settlements, etc. These grounds do not justify a Jewish legislative body in placing the seizure of land under the protection of the law. In some densely populated villages, two-thirds and even more of the land have been seized.[24]

By 1951, one-fourth of the Israeli population, then estimated at about 1.4 million, was housed on "abandoned" Arab property.[25] Golda Meir, who later became prime minister, had put the matter bluntly: "We used the houses of those Arabs who ran away from the country whenever we could for new immigrant housing. . . . We did not keep our refugees in camps."[26] Most of the immigrants in the first two years of the state were European-born Jews, survivors of the Holocaust. But between 1950 and 1954, Jews born in Arab or Muslim countries, including 140,000 from Iraq, 300,000 from Morocco, and 46,000 from Yemen, came in a series of migrations, some having been forced out, some brought and literally bought out by Israel.[27] Thus, one set of refugees replaced another.

Another group of Palestinian refugees was created in the wake of the 1967 war: those who fled from the West Bank of the Jordan River, mostly to the East Bank in the Kingdom of Jordan as well as Syria, or from the Gaza Strip to Egypt or Jordan. Most sources tend to agree that the total number was approximately 280,000 to 325,000 (although estimates range from 100,000 to 416,000); the figure consists of those who fled with the retreating Arab armies when Israeli troops occupied those areas as well as others, mainly women, children, and elderly, who moved voluntarily in the second half of 1967 in order to rejoin family members who had been working regularly in Jordan, and those such as students or travelers who were temporarily outside of these territories when the war began.[28] In addition to these Palestinians, about 17,500 Syrian Druze fled the Golan Heights to go deeper into Syria, and an indefinite number of Bedouins and Egyptian villagers in the Sinai fled across the Suez Canal to the center of Egypt.[29]

For ease in differentiating them from "the 1948 refugees," these groups are generally referred to as "the 1967 displaced persons." However, a disputed portion of them, perhaps 120,000 to 170,000, were persons who had *also* been refugees in 1948 and then fled *again* in 1967.[30] As in 1948, once they fled, they were prevented from returning by official Israeli policy, this time implemented by the Israeli Defense Forces in charge of the now-occupied territories. They, too, left property behind, approximately 106,000 acres in the West Bank and about 500 acres in Gaza, including almost 11,000 buildings, most of which have since been used by relatives of the owners.[31] Although over the years Israel has allowed a small percentage of the "1967 displaced" to return to the West Bank, it has also uprooted others from the territories through deportation and demolition of houses, ostensibly as punishment for terrorism.[32]

"Transfer" and Related Strategems

The demographic displacement of Palestinians by Jews did not begin in 1967 or even 1948. In 1880, when the first modern wave of Jewish *aliyah*, or immigration, to Palestine began, the extant Jewish population was approximately 24,000, living among about 470,000 Palestinians. By 1914 the respective figures were around 90,000 and 500,000.[33] Between the beginning of World War I and the end of World War II, Jewish immigration, both legal and illegal, would accelerate the differential growth rates of the two communities. While there was some Arab immigration to the area, it was primarily of a seasonal rather than of a durable residential nature.[34] Thus, while the permanent Arab population doubled between 1918 and 1945, it went from being ten times the size of the Jewish population to only twice the size. The number of Jews living in Palestine by 1948 was roughly equal to the number of Arab residents there in 1922, while the number of Arab residents in 1948 was approximately twice the size of the Jewish population there in 1922.[35]

"That this massive shift entailed enormous political and psychological consequences for both sides is self-evident," a historian has noted.[36] One consequence was the attempt to devise ways to transfer Palestinians out of the territory that was intended to become the Jewish state. Over 60 proposals would be trotted out in the period before 1948 alone.[37]

On one level, the early Zionist leaders were oblivious to the local Arab population, their concomitantly growing nationalism, and what might have been their reaction to the influx of Jews. Theodor Herzl, for instance, "tended to assume Palestine was a vacant land. . . . The Zionists failed to acknowledge the fact that the Arabs had their own national aspirations."[38] When Herzl did consider the indigenous population, after selecting Palestine as the actual location of a future Jewish state, he wrote in his diary: "When we occupy the land . . . we shall try to spirit the penniless population across the border by procuring employment for it in the transit countries whilst denying it any employment in our own country."[39] Herzl also had a plan for acquiring Arab property by paying high prices, retaining a repurchase option to avoid resale back to other Arabs, and, if necessary, offering housing, land, and transportation for the former owners outside of Palestine.[40]

Other Zionist leaders had their own ideas. While Ahad Ha'am, associated with Cultural Zionism, understood that Arab nationalism needed to be recognized, Revisionist leader Vladimir Jabotinsky "considered the Arabs to be of no political consequence and believed that an understanding with them was neither desirable nor possible."[41] Menachem Ussishkin, head of the Jewish National Fund, would express the wish that the Arabs, "go to Iraq . . . an Arab country and not [remain in] a Jewish country."[42] The socialist Labor leader (and later prime minister) David Ben-Gurion had suggested in 1936 that Palestinian farmers displaced through Jewish land purchases be settled in Transjordan, at Jewish expense. He later proposed a similar transfer to Syria. However, in both cases, he apparently meant voluntary transfers. Ben-Gurion had, in fact, in other contexts, recognized the right to self-determination of Palestinians, although he would later categorically reject proposals that the refugees be offered the choice between repatriation or compensation.[43]

These ideas about transfer, which were more in the nature of individual musings than actually planned Zionist programs, were not only the product of Jewish imaginations. A 1939 proposal to transfer several hundred thousand Arabs from Palestine to Iraq came from an unlikely source—U.S. President Franklin Delano Roosevelt—who would have financed the move with a fund contributed one-third from Jews, one-third from the British government, and one-third from the U.S. government. By the 1940s, Roosevelt's ideas became more extreme. He recommended that a barbed-wire fence be put around Palestine, which would be exclusively Jewish territory, and that "no Arabs should be [allowed] in it."[44]

By far the best-known proposal was that of the Peel Commission, appointed by the British government to investigate the causes of unrest following the 1936 Arab revolt. The commission recommended that Palestine be divided into three areas: a Jewish state from the border with Lebanon down to the Negev; an Arab state containing the rest of Palestine west of the Jordan River, together with Transjordan; and a British enclave consisting of the three cities symbolic to Christians: Jerusalem, Bethlehem, and Nazareth. Because 250,000 Palestinians were then living within the boundaries of the proposed Jewish state and 1,500 Jews were within the boundaries of the proposed Arab state, the commission called for "an exchange of land, and as far as possible an exchange of population."[45] Though the commission's report is a bit ambiguous, it appears that transfer of the Palestinians from the Galilee would be effected on a voluntary basis while transfer of those from the rest of the Jewish state, and of Jews in the Arab state, would be compulsory.

Reaction to the commission's recommendations were varied. Among the supporters were David Ben-Gurion and Golda Myerson (later Meir). Ben-Gurion favored the guarantee of maximal security and material conditions to the transferees, while Meir supported voluntary transfer and the guarantee of equal rights to Palestinians who remained.[46] Critics included writer Joseph Schechtman, who called the Peel proposal an unequal "one-way transfer of Arabs," while Colonel Josiah Wedgwood, a British Member of Parliament, labeled it a deportation, intended to "dump" the Palestinians away from their ancestral homes.[47] By December 1937, the commission's plan was moot because the British government issued a White Paper that, among other things, rejected the transfer plan.

Much later, of course, right-wing Israeli political parties such as Meir Kahane's Kach and Moledet (Homeland) would demand transfer of all the Palestinians in the occupied territories to other Arab countries. Although Kahane's party was eventually expelled from the Knesset, Moledet's leader, General Rehavim Zeevi, served in Yitzhak Shamir's cabinet in 1991.[48]

But lest it be assumed that only Palestinians were the subject of quests for transfer, it helps to recall that Arab rioting against Jewish newcomers to Palestine in 1920 and 1921, 1929, and 1936 was linked to the ebb and flow of Jewish immigration, or at least to rumors of massive invasions.[49] Moreover, virtually every PLO reference to the "liberation" of Palestine, from the 1960s at least until the organization's November 1988 implicit recognition of Israel, reminded Jews that they were intended for "transfer" not onto some other dry land but into the Mediterranean Sea. The 1968 Palestinian National Charter, for instance, stated (and continued to state, until its belated amendment on April 24, 1996): "Armed struggle is the only way to liberate Palestine. . . . Commando action constitutes the nucleus of the Palestinian popular liberation war."[50] Under the same charter, only the 24,000 or so Jews "who had normally resided in Palestine until the beginning of the Zionist invasion" in the 1880s would be entitled to remain in a "liberated" Palestine; but they would be considered "Palestinians," not Jews.[51] Others such as Egypt's President Gamel Abdel Nasser had unambiguously stated: "Our aim is to restore the national rights of the Palestinian people, namely, to destroy Israel."[52] Coupled with support for terrorism and with a continuing refusal to recognize Israel as a state, statements such as these could have only one meaning. The fundamentalist Palestinian groups Hamas and Islamic Jihad still use this language today and continue to act accordingly.

A fair overview of the issue of population transfer must also include mention of Palestinian and Arab resistance to resettlement efforts. With the exception of Jordan, none of the Arab states to which Palestinians had fled granted them citizenship or provided substantial material assistance to the refugees. Even in Jordan, Palestinians were often perceived as a demographic and political threat to the monarchy. (The relations between Palestinians and their host states are described more fully in chapter 2.) Moreover, all the Arab states assumed that "[a]ny compromise settlement of the refugee question, one not entailing large-scale resettlement, would mean that the last potentially effective measure short of coercion against Zionist-controlled Palestine was being given up."[53] Perhaps most significantly, the nature of exile and refugee camp life served over time to heighten Palestinian identity and intensify the longing for repatriation. Camp inhabitants in Lebanon would uproot saplings that had been planted, in opposition to even the most meager symbols of permanence.[54] Asked where he came from, a refugee would answer with the name of his original village in Israel, regardless of whether the village was still standing.[55]

The International Response

Although certain Zionist, British, and even American leaders had been considering the question of the Palestinian Arabs for some time before the establishment of Israel, the international community as a whole did not begin to focus on the Palestinians as a population unit until the middle of 1948. Count Folke Bernadotte of Sweden, serving as U.N. mediator on Palestine, and Ralph Bunche of the United States, on behalf of the U.N. Truce Commission, had spent the summer investigating methods of peacefully resolving the Arab-Israeli war, which had broken out in full force upon the declaration of Israel's independence on May 14.

Bernadotte's Progress Report of September 16, 1948, filed one day before he was assassinated by the Stern gang, a Jewish terrorist group, identified the rights of repatriation and compensation as two of seven basic mediation principles he recommended be followed: "[t]he right of innocent people, uprooted from their homes by the present terror and ravages of war, to return to their homes, should be affirmed and made effective, with assurance of adequate compensation for the property of those who may choose not to return."[56] He considered that the political, economic, and social rights of both Arabs in Jewish territory and Jews in Arab territory had to be guaranteed and respected. Israeli officials responded that "the return during the truce of [at least 300,000] displaced Arabs to the State of Israel which is still beset by enemy armies . . . would in fact gravely prejudice our rights and position."[57] Although he considered Israeli security concerns to be slight, Bernadotte recommended a temporary solution that excluded the repatriation of Palestinian men of military age.[58]

Bernadotte had also recommended that the United Nations supervise the process of Arab repatriation, resettlement, rehabilitation, and compensation, which the General Assembly proceeded to do three months later by adopting Resolution 194, including its well-known paragraph 11, a modification of Bernadotte's own words concerning return and compensation: "the refugees wishing to return to their homes and live at peace with their neighbors should be permitted to do so at the earliest practicable date, and . . . compensation should be paid for the property of those not choosing to return."[59] The General Assembly then created the Conciliation Commission for Palestine, composed of French, Turkish, and U.S. delegates, to make recommendations for final settlement of all aspects of the Arab-Israeli conflict and to undertake, among other functions, "to facilitate the repatriation, resettlement and economic and social rehabilitation of the refugees and the payment of compensation."[60]

Both Israel and the Arab states viewed the Conciliation Commission cautiously, in part due to suspicions about the ulterior motives of its members.[61] During the roughly 18 years of its active and semi-active operation, from 1948 through 1966, it managed to alienate all its intended constituencies equally at one point or another, thereby discouraging each of the players from agreeing to necessary compromises.[62] The commission came closest—if only fleetingly—to reaching a settlement on the refugee question during its conference in Lausanne in 1949. The United States strongly urged Israel to agree to repatriate from 200,000 to 300,000 refugees. After a series of commission negotiation efforts, in August of that year Israel reluctantly agreed to accept no more than 100,000 family reunification cases, screened to keep out security risks. It also insisted that the refugees return not to their original homes but to locations determined by Israel, where they would "not come into contact" with possible enemies of the Jewish state.[63]

The "100,000 proposal" was, in fact, fiercely opposed within Israeli political and popular circles and elicited a lukewarm international reception. It was also denounced by Arab delegations as a "less than token . . . propaganda scheme."[64] The proposal, which may have really been for admission of no more than 65,000 additional people, became snagged amid counterproposals concerning territorial compromises and frozen bank accounts as well as growing commission impatience with the parties' implacable negotiating styles.[65] Soon thereafter, Israel withdrew its reluctant offer.

After this early failure to achieve a negotiated agreement, the commission took the position that widespread resettlement was the most viable solution to the refugee issue and that Israel's payment of compensation would help facilitate Palestinian acceptance of this reality. Therefore, it concentrated on conducting a survey of estimated Palestinian property claims, which took many years to complete and satisfied none of the relevant parties. However, some of the insights it gained through its efforts in the 1950s still seem prudent today. For instance, the commission observed that "any attempt to go back to the origin of the conflict in order to determine the responsibility for the outbreak of the hostilities would have been . . . a step backwards."[66] It also recognized that a realistic approach to limited repatriation would require that it be set at a definite number and that the refugees be fully informed about what repatriation to a Jewish state would entail.[67]

In the meantime, the U.N. General Assembly had created the United Nations Relief for Palestine Refugees (which soon was changed to the United Nations Relief and Works Agency for Palestine Refugees in the Near East [UNRWA]) to provide food, shelter, health services, and training for Palestinians in the host countries to which they fled. Arab states had argued that the United Nations should create a special agency for Palestinians because they differed from all other refugees:

> In all other cases, persons had become refugees as a result of action taken contrary to the principles of the United Nations, and the obligation of the Organization toward them was a moral one only. The existence of the Palestine refugees, on the other hand, was the result of a decision taken by the United Nations itself with full knowledge of the consequences.... If the General Assembly were to include the Palestine refugees in a general definition of refugees, they would become submerged and would be relegated to a position of minor importance.... To accept a general definition ... would be to renounce insistence on repatriation.[68]

Therefore, even before the 1950 creation of the United Nations High Commissioner for Refugees, UNRWA developed its own working definition of who was eligible for its assistance, which was initially "a needy person who, as a result of the war in Palestine, has lost his home and his means of livelihood." This evolved into the more formal definition: "a person whose normal residence was Palestine for a minimum of two years immediately preceding the outbreak of the conflict in 1948, and who, as a result of this conflict, lost both his home and means of livelihood and took refuge in 1948 in one of the countries [Syria, Lebanon, Transjordan (now the West Bank and Jordan), and the Gaza Strip] where UNRWA provides relief," as well as his direct descendants.[69] To receive UNRWA assistance, a Palestinian must be registered with UNRWA, be living in an area where UNRWA operates, and be in need. During its first year of full operation, 1950, it registered just over 875,000 refugees.[70] Its number of registrants as of December 1996 was slightly over 3.2 million, an increase due to natural population growth and a self-acknowledged inability to record deaths accurately. Most of its over 20,000 current field staff positions are held by Palestinians.[71]

UNRWA as an agency was initially conceived to be short-lived, as was the unsettled status of the refugees. "Every three years, its mandate had to be renewed, by a vote of the General Assembly. Yet no one, since the early days, talked seriously of ending it. On the other hand, very few talked of making it permanent. The paradox is intrinsic to the Arab-Israeli conflict."[72] Dependent on irregular donor government contributions (predominantly from the United States), UNRWA has at times teetered on financial instability. Criticized by some for reaching beyond its formal humanitarian mandate to engage in political work and by others for treating the refugees in a paternalistic manner—failing, for instance, to consult parents on school curricula or to train its own Palestinian staff in budgeting techniques—UNRWA still has provided vital assistance in its routine health, welfare, and education operations. During the *intifada*, its staff stepped literally into the firing lines, serving as human rights monitors and advocates. Since the initiation of the peace process, it has launched the Peace Implementation Program, a major effort to improve educational and health services, emergency housing, and other infrastructure, and to offer small business loans in the camps and their environs.[73]

However, for most of the period both before and after the otherwise watershed 1967 war, international efforts to resolve the question of the Palestinian refugees were effectively stagnant, failing to budge either Israel or the Arab states from their irreconcilable positions on the question of repatriation. The world's attention was focused on Israeli occupation of the West Bank and Gaza, not on discussion of a permanent resolution of the refugees' fate. Even the 1978 Camp David Accords between Israel and Egypt said very little about the Palestinians, who were left out of the negotiations. The accords merely provided that the two countries would work with each other "and with other interested parties" to establish procedures for a "just and permanent implementation of the resolution of the refugee problem."[74] However, the subsequent Egypt-Israel Peace Treaty contained no such procedures, concentrating instead on withdrawal of Israeli armed forces and civilians from the Sinai and on freedom of movement from one territory to the other merely of the two states' nationals and their vehicles.[75] The Palestinians living in the Gaza Strip, which before 1967 had been under Egyptian administration, barely merited a mention.

Outside of these limited bilateral developments, the 1970s were not a fruitful era for the cause of Middle East peace. Politicization of the issue within the United Nations, from the General Assembly's 1975 "Zionism is Racism" Resolution,[76] to the infiltration of anti-Israel factions in virtually all corners of the Secretariat (as high up as its secretary-general, Kurt Waldheim)[77] only inflamed passions on both sides. A Palestinian scholar, Sami Hadawi, would write about the failure of the United Nations to solve the Arab refugee problem:

When the Palestine tragedy occurred in 1948, the conscience of the world was moved and prompt action was taken to bring relief to the victims. But through political obstruction inside and outside the United Nations, the injustice has been allowed to linger and the distress has been prolonged until now it is included in the category of problems that the world tends to accept as chronic. . . . Instead . . . meager relief is doled out to the victims in the hope that time will solve the problem.[78]

Ironically, however, as the Palestinian nationalist demand became more radicalized under more recent U.N. patronage, evolving from return of the refugees to outright self-determination for the Palestinian people, it laid a foundation from which peace could eventually be achieved.[79] This is because self-determination, meaning autonomy if not outright sovereignty, could substitute for comprehensive return to original Palestinian homes within Israel. "[E]very exiled Palestinian [would] now be able to consider the new Palestinian state as his home. The focus would no longer be on the specific house that was lost to him and his family" but to the homeland.[80] In other words, self-determination on the West Bank and Gaza could become a substitute for repatriation to—and the effective destruction of—Israel. A collective right could be substituted for an aggregation of individual rights.

Paradoxically, it would take developments such as the Persian Gulf War and the demise of the Soviet Union, the great champion of "collective rights" as well as the patron of the most anti-Israel Arab states, and the concomitant dominion of the United States, to effectuate this change.[81] Step one was achieved in 1988, when the Palestine National Council, the PLO's legislative body, declared the independence of the State of Palestine in "the territory of its homeland," implying the West Bank and Gaza but, for the first time ever, without insisting on Israeli withdrawal from its 1948 borders.[82] Step two would be the Arab-Israeli peace negotiations, begun in 1991 under the joint sponsorship of the United States and the then-extant but unraveling Soviet Union.

The Madrid and Oslo Processes

Named the Madrid Framework after the city where they opened, the negotiations were designed to operate under a two-track system: a bilateral track consisting of four sets of direct negotiations between Israel and four of its neighbors—Syria, Lebanon, Jordan, and the Palestinians (Egypt and Israel having already achieved peace); and a multilateral track of five committees attended by delegates from as many as 45 countries, Middle Eastern states as well as representatives from the wider international community, including Japan and the European

Union. The less publicized multilateral talks, covering water, the environment, arms control, economic development, and refugees, were intended to envision and help create the Middle East of the future while building confidence in the present among some of the regional parties. Viewing their accomplishments in October 1994, the U.S. Assistant Secretary of State for Near Eastern Affairs said of the multilaterals:

> They are building networks of Arab and Israeli professionals with similar interests. They provide mechanisms through which regional problems can be addressed. . . . The multilaterals are proving to be a catalyst for positive change and may be giving us a glimpse of what the region will look like when the countries of the area cooperate in an era of comprehensive Arab-Israeli peace.[83]

At a late 1995 multilateral meeting in Geneva, for instance, Israeli delegates were heard speaking Arabic to their Palestinian counterparts, who sometimes answered in Hebrew.[84]

The Refugee Multilateral Working Group, which is chaired by Canada, was specifically designed to undertake confidence-building measures focusing on improving the near-term living conditions of Palestinian refugees, particularly those outside the West Bank and Gaza, without either waiting for political breakthroughs of a more long-term nature through the bilateral process or prejudicing final status agreements on the political future of Palestinian refugees in their host countries.[85] This was, in and of itself, a significant development, as it meant that Arab states and Palestinians had accepted the principle— which they had previously opposed for 45 years—that the refugees could improve their quality of life without prejudicing their future rights and status as either refugees or returnees.

To this end, the members of the Refugee Multilateral Working Group agreed to undertake humanitarian projects in the areas of human resource development, vocational training and job creation, public health, child welfare, and social and economic infrastructural development, including housing rehabilitation. For instance, Germany, Turkey, China, and other countries announced plans for agricultural, business, and health skills training courses. The United States agreed to help develop housing facilities in Gaza, Syria, and Lebanon; schools in Jordan; and a refugee health center in Syria. Sweden is directing projects involving child welfare, and Italy is focusing on public health. In addition, member states have sponsored research projects, such as Canada's development of a database of existing information and material on the refugees and Norwegian surveys of the socioeconomic conditions of Palestinians living in Gaza and the West Bank, completed in

1993, and on Jordan, currently under way.[86] The concrete results in each of these areas have, to date, been less than stellar. But by discussing and funding projects that are outside the West Bank and Gaza as well as inside, the Refugee Multilateral Working Group has helped to reassure diaspora Palestinians that their needs have not been cast aside by the bilateral autonomy negotiations.

In terms of multilateral negotiations over movement of persons, the results have been even more modest. Israel agreed in 1993 to raise its annual ceiling on the number of family reunification cases it accepts from 1,000 to 2,000 (for a total of about 5,000 individuals); this involves the return to permanent residency status in the West Bank or Gaza of Palestinians who left in 1967 or later. Israel also agreed that the returning members of the Palestinian police force and their families would not be counted in the annual quota. Another 5,000 temporary residents of the territories have been allowed to remain permanently with their families, and up to 80,000 permanent residents of the territories who overstayed their permits to go abroad will be allowed back.[87]

By 1992, the global political and ideological changes brought about by the demise of the Soviet Union, the new coalitions formed during the Persian Gulf War, and the election of Yitzhak Rabin and his Labor Party coalition in Israel, would lay the groundwork for more explicit discussions of some of the most sensitive aspects of the Arab-Israeli conflict. The Gulf War had shattered both the myth of pan-Arab solidarity and the illusion that Arab military parity with Israel was achievable. Israelis were coming to see the peace process—and even its most taboo topic, refugees—as a component of security.[88] Israeli Foreign Minister Shimon Peres would therefore be able to announce in a speech to the U.N. General Assembly on October 1, 1992: "We should address the problems of refugees, not by threatening to destroy the existing demographic balance, but by exploring a range of possibilities for restoring the dignity of refugees and offering them a good life."[89] His deputy minister, Yossi Beilin, would state soon thereafter:

> For a whole generation the refugee problem has been perceived as insurmountable. The key to the solution is to understand each other's pain and [each] other's red lines. . . . In the very near future we will have to tackle sensitive issues left untouched for many decades. We must touch some delicate nerves; the brutalities of past wars, the missed opportunities and the regional "march of folly."[90]

The Declaration of Principles, ignited by "backdoor" negotiations in Oslo, Norway, and signed by the PLO and Israel in September 1993, contains only modest references to the refugees. Article V, paragraph 3, specifies that along with the issues of Jerusalem, settlements, security, borders, relations, and cooperation with neighbors, and other issues of common concern, the fate of the refugees will be negotiated during the permanent status talks, which officially were scheduled to begin in May of 1996. Article XII designates a quadripartite Continuing Committee composed of representatives of Israel, Jordan, Egypt, and the Palestinians, to "decide by agreement on the modalities of admission of persons displaced from the West Bank and Gaza Strip in 1967, together with necessary measures to prevent disruption and disorder," and other matters of common concern.

To date, the potentially most far-reaching result on refugees that has come out of the bilateral process arises from the Jordanian-Israeli Peace Treaty of October 1994. One of the six general principles of the treaty states that the two countries "believe that within their control, involuntary movements of persons in such a way as to adversely prejudice the security of either party should not be permitted."[91] In addition, Article 8, titled "Refugees and Displaced Persons," renewed the 1993 Declaration of Principle's call for a quadripartite committee to work toward the resolution of the matter of persons displaced from the territories during or after the 1967 war. Finally, in Article 24, Israel and Jordan agreed to establish a claims commission for the mutual settlement of all financial claims. The provision does not go into any detail, however, as to who can make claims, subject coverage, valuation of property, or sources of funding.

The quadripartite committee first met in Amman in early March 1995. The meeting produced only disagreement, entirely over the matter of numbers: Israel contended that the number of Palestinians displaced in 1967 was 200,000, while the Arab parties put the total number at about 800,000. Typically, UNRWA came out in the middle, at 350,000.[92] The discrepancy was mainly attributable to Israel's refusal to count spouses, siblings, and children of those who left in 1967.[93] With natural increase over 28 years, the middle-range 350,000 figure would have doubled to 700,000 by today. The rest of the disparity came from Israel's rejection of a few hundred persons involved in terrorism and those whose fate it seeks to have resolved in final-status talks: those from East Jerusalem, those whose hometowns have since 1967 become Jewish settlements, and those who are 1948 refugees who were displaced again in 1967. This latter category is certainly a significant percentage.

The Amman meeting was obviously a disappointment for anyone with idealistic expectations. But given that it was the very first, official face-to-face meeting on this subject, the virtual complete lack of progress was understandable. Because the issue of the 1967 displaced persons does not directly implicate the question of repatriation to Israel proper, an agreement on the mechanism for their future return to the West Bank is easily achievable, even before the final-status talks are over. Indeed, after the Amman gathering, the quadripartite committee met an additional four times in 1995 and twice in early 1996, achieving a breakthrough of sorts regarding the numbers and types of displaced persons.[94]

Although the September 1995 Interim Agreement between Israel and the PLO (Oslo II) does not advance the negotiations specifically as to the refugee question, its ambitious scope—400 pages covering elections, security and redeployment, legal issues, religious sites, water, economic relations, and more—seems designed to boost both morale and momentum so that the final-status issues can be tackled in an atmosphere of growing trust and cooperation.

A side effect of the direct bilateral process is that it has upstaged the work of the refugee and other multilateral working groups and, more significantly, obscured the issue of the refugees both by postponing the topic until the final-status negotiations and by redirecting the attention of Yasser Arafat and his deputies away from the Palestinian diaspora, where it had been focused primarily since the 1964 founding of the PLO, and toward the West Bank and Gaza. This redirection is particularly apparent since the January 1996 elections in the territories, which created a formal constituency to which the Palestinian Authority must now legitimately answer. In other words, Palestinian refugees, most of whom live outside these territories, have been lost in the shuffle of state-building. "The refugees perceive the Oslo [and Cairo] agreements as detrimental to their legal, national, and human rights. . . . [T]he absence of any reference to a possible solution to this problem reinforced their sense of dispossession and disenfranchisement, increasing their fears about their destiny."[95] At best, only those diasporan Palestinians who were displaced in 1967 stand to benefit from any Oslo-inspired short-term resolution of their residential status.

In addition to the matter of "the 1967 displaced," the fate of approximately three to four million other Palestinians (depending, of course, on the "magic number") who currently live in Jordan, Lebanon, Syria, elsewhere in the Middle East, and outside the Middle East still remains to be resolved. How many will eventually return? To where—the West Bank and Gaza? To within the Israeli Green Line, that is, the external borders of Israel before the territories were occupied in 1967? What will happen to those who remain outside of either Israel or the Palestinian territories? Who will receive compensation? How much and from what source? These are the questions that the remainder of this book attempts to address.

Chapter 2

The Sociodemographic Framework

A second perspective that is essential to understanding the complex position of the Palestinian refugees and to framing a permanent resolution to their predicament is the demographic and socioeconomic context. Numbers alone are insufficient to provide this understanding. This chapter attempts to convey not only the available estimates of how many categories of Palestinians reside in each location, but also what their communal circumstances in each of these locales are like, and how they got that way. In a sense, the chapter is an attempt to answer the question: Who is a Palestinian refugee today?

To date, no comprehensive field survey has been undertaken that attempts to analyze the future residential preferences (and therefore future development requirements) of Palestinian families or to determine which subcommunities are most urgently in need of attention. Because the available demographic data are woefully deficient, inferences must necessarily be drawn from what is presently known.[1] The most useful predictors are probably data that reflect (1) where the refugees came from originally and (2) their current living and working conditions as well as their legal and socioeconomic status.

To understand and to plan for future demographic movements in the region, data are needed about all Palestinians, not merely those who have been technically classified as refugees. It is also necessary to appreciate the problematic quality of the demographic data on Palestinians that currently exist. To begin with, there is little agreement on who is a Palestinian and who a Palestinian refugee. Moreover, the available information is typically overinclusive and/or underinclusive—and, it almost goes without saying, often partisan and polemical, as the numbers are assumed to represent the size of any eventual compensation payments. Moreover, because of the sensitivity of the issue, virtually all existing surveys have scrupulously avoided the central question: How many of the refugees actually continue to demand their full return to their original homes and how many would accept an alternative resolution of their status?[2]

Therefore, none of the demographic data presented in this chapter are warranted to be definitive. Estimates are presented solely for the sake of offering a starting point. Moreover, for planning purposes, it is assumed better to err on the high side of the full range of contested figures. See the "Note on the Quality of Existing Demographic Information" in the bibliographical essay for further caveats about the data.

It is also helpful to keep in mind that although many features of the Palestinian refugee issue are unique, or at least are considered by many to be *sui generis*, the Middle East has in fact had a long history of migration for religious, political, and economic purposes, beginning at least as early as the seventh century, with the rapid spread of Arab tribes carrying the message of Allah.[3] Contemporary economic, demographic, social, and political imbalances—such as the differing levels of economic development, jobs, fertility, education, and human rights in the Middle East—have produced their corresponding migration flows. Almost 20 countries in the Middle East and North Africa now contain close to 10 million refugees, fleeing from Afghanistan, Ethiopia / Eritrea, Iran, Iraq, Mali, Somalia, Sudan, Western Sahara, and elsewhere, in addition to Palestinians. Palestinian refugees are part of a complex pattern of population movements and concomitant structural change in the region.[4] Solutions to the crisis of the Palestinian refugees therefore must take into account the broader patterns of migration and change in the Middle East.

Historical Movements

Although this chapter concentrates on present-day demography, it is useful to begin by describing the overall structure and cultural characteristics of both the pre-1948 and post-1948 Palestinian communities and then to trace the directions in which Palestinian refugees migrated in 1948 and subsequent years.

Before the 1948 Arab-Israeli war, Palestinian society was "divided both horizontally and vertically. It was characterized by noticeable differences that distinguished northerner from southerner, hill-dweller from valley-dweller, nomad from permanent settler, urban-dweller from villager, and Christian from Muslim."[5] The overwhelming majority of Palestinians were Sunni Muslim; others were Druze, a secretive sect derived from Shi'a Islam, or Christians of a variety of denominations. Perhaps two-thirds of Palestinians were agricultural peasants. Families rarely left their original village for another one. When they did move, it was often to open businesses or pursue professions such as law or journalism in coastal cities such as Jaffa and Haifa. Thus, many of the urban refugees were themselves originally from rural areas in Gaza and the West Bank as well as present-day Israel.

"Most of the urban refugees, almost all of them Christians, and the members of the propertied classes from the villages never entered refugee camps at all. Instead, they rented houses in the suburbs of Gaza, Nablus, Beirut or Damascus."[6] It stands to reason, therefore, that those Palestinians who have survived for up to three generations in harsh refugee-camp conditions tend to come from more impoverished, less-educated backgrounds. They are more likely to have consciously fought assimilation and become politicized by militant movements such as Islamic fundamentalism or, earlier, Palestinian nationalism, in contrast to middle-class Palestinians, "who thought of themselves primarily as Arabs."[7]

Perhaps more significant, however, than the distinctions within Palestinian society are the distinctions between Palestinians and other Arabs in the Middle Eastern "host countries" in which they became exiled. Although to a Western eye, Palestinians do not seem to differ significantly in cultural or linguistic respects from other Arab peoples, subcultural differences in accent, food preparation, dress, and other customs were quite salient, especially in the early years. Palestinian society was shaped not by the desert and nomadic life but by "bustling towns and flourishing agriculture, by exposure to the West, and by the eminence imparted to it by the holy city of Jerusalem."[8] In addition, over time, "several factors have converged," according to scholar Laurie Brand, "to bind Palestinians more firmly together as distinct from other Arabs: the shared loss of homeland; the fact of having been unable to exercise the right to self-determination; the struggle to preserve and assert traditions and history despite the disruption of scattered exile; and the desire to return."[9]

"Isolated, the Palestinians were left to nurse a sense of betrayal, against both the West and their brother Arabs," in the words of writer Milton Viorst.[10] Palestinian specialist Rosemary Sayigh identifies a multitude of more specific factors that worked to set Palestinians apart from other Arabs, including:

- The trauma of the *hijra* [migration] and the exceptional hardships that followed it, their persistent refusal to believe in the finality of separation from Palestine, and finally, the mourning for lost homes, property and villages, the more paralyzing for peasants because these were the basis of their sense of identity. This loss made them draw in defensively.[11]

- Their poverty, markedly worse than they had experienced in Palestine ("they were disgusted at the animal-like conditions in which they were forced to live"),[12] and sense of "difference" as displaced persons, transients dependent on UNRWA rations and UNRWA schools, and as peasants forced to find work in cities, for which they were usually unskilled.

- The discrimination, brutality, exploitation, expulsions, and oppression they suffered at the hands of officials—in Arab states as well as the Israeli-occupied territories—and the contempt expressed by some host-country nationals. "It is said that the Sidonians [in Lebanon] used to call 'Ain al-Hilweh [refugee] camp 'the zoo' and that Lebanese children used to ask their parents to buy them a Palestinian, as a pet."[13]

- Their sense that they had fallen from a more advanced society—measured in higher levels of agricultural technology, crafts and trade, and especially educational achievement—into more provincial and backward ones. They translated this shock into a redoubled commitment to obtaining university educations, outside their host countries whenever possible.[14]

- The politicization process that, after pan-Arabism lost its appeal, included the call for armed struggle and revolution. According to Sayigh:

[P]ost-1965 Palestinianism has a mass basis that was completely lacking before 1948. . . . To be Palestinian, [especially] for very many camp Palestinians, means to be one who struggles and this "struggle-identity" radically changed their relationship to other Arabs, becoming like a political vocation, or pariah-turned-prophet, victim-turned-militant.[15]

Brand has similarly described this last factor: "[T]he historical experience of direct and continuing confrontation with Zionism and the resulting dispossession and statelessness have been the most basic factors that have shaped—not created—a Palestinian identity and nationalism as distinct and separate from other Arab nationalisms."[16] Naturally, over time, all of these distinguishing factors have become more pronounced.

Understanding the geographic connection between the refugees' areas of origin and their subsequent locales may help peace negotiators and repatriation planners predict which groups of refugees may be most interested in returning to their ancestral homes and where they might desire to relocate. Like migrating rural Russian Jews attracted to turn-of-the-century urban American neighborhoods where landsmen had already settled, villages and large family groupings of Palestinians tended to transfer to the same places of exile, even to the same section of a refugee camp. Generally speaking, most refugees took the following paths in 1948:

Area of Origin	*Relocation Site*
Ramla, Tiberias, and central region	West Bank, including East Jerusalem
Jaffa and southern coastal region	Gaza Strip and West Bank
Haifa, Acre, and Western Galilee	Lebanon
Lower Galilee and Beisan	Transjordan and West Bank
Safat and Upper Galilee	Syria and Iraq
Beersheva and	Gaza Strip
Negev	West Bank and Egypt

Estimates regarding how many people had reached each of these destinations by the end of the war can be stated only as ranges: Lebanon, 100,000 to 120,000; Syria, 50,000 to 80,000; Transjordan, 70,000 to 100,000; West Bank, 200,000 to 420,000; Gaza Strip, 190,000 to 220,000; Egypt, 7,000 to 10,000; and Iraq, about 4,000.[17] It is often overlooked that an unspecified number of Palestinians resided in the West Bank or Gaza before 1948 and remained there afterward, never becoming refugees.

Of the 160,000 or so who remained in Israel, another 25,000 to 32,000 Palestinians, it will be recalled, became "internal refugees," fleeing to areas that remained on the Israeli side of the Armistice lines. For instance, the Manasra family, whose entire village, originally located on a hill in the Jezrael Valley, evacuated itself to Nazareth, ten miles away, out of fear of Jewish revenge. The Manasras' village no longer exists, and its agricultural land has been taken over by a kibbutz. Other families moved only from one neighborhood in West Jerusalem to another in East Jerusalem. Still, to the Palestinians, this was exile.[18]

Most of these initial transborder movements are graphically summarized in map 2.1, which indicates flight routes, rough percentages, and round numbers, using U.N. estimates of the 1948 refugees.

Numerous secondary and tertiary migration waves complicate the picture further, with refugees moving back and forth across the Jordan River, to the Gulf states, Europe, North America, and sometimes back again. As summarized by Laurie Brand in 1988:

> Indeed, the post-1948 history of the Palestinians reads like a series of migrations and expulsions: 1950s, movement out of Jordan and Lebanon to the Gulf; mid-1950s, expulsions of Palestinian oil workers from the Gulf; early and mid-1960s, increasing movement from the West Bank of Jordan to the East Bank, and from Jordan in general to the Gulf; 1967, flight and expulsion of large numbers, many of them second-time refugees, from both the West Bank and Gaza to Jordan and Egypt; post-1967, migration from the newly occupied territories to the Gulf and to Jordan; 1970–71, the expulsion of the Palestinian resistance from Jordan to Lebanon; 1982, the massive destruction caused by the Israeli invasion of Lebanon, the exodus of Palestinian fighters by boat to all corners of the Arab world.[19]

Map 2.1   The Arab Refugees, 1948

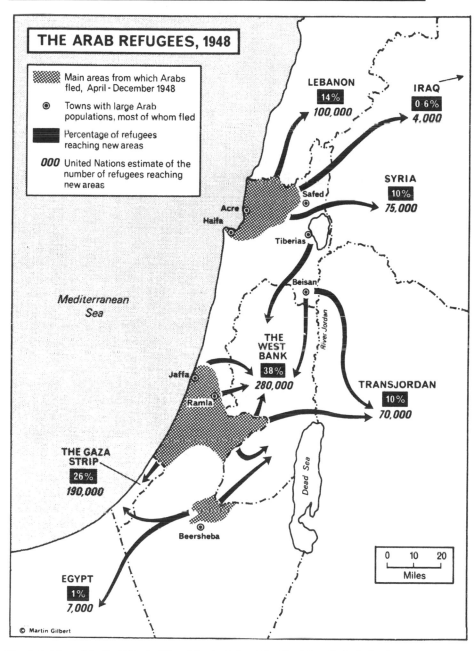

Reprinted from Martin Gilbert, *Atlas of the Arab-Israel Conflict* (New York: Oxford University Press, 1993), p. 47.

An updated summary would include the close to 350,000 who were expelled by Kuwait after the PLO announced its support of Iraqi President Saddam Hussein's invasion of that country in 1990. Most returned to their places of prior refuge, mainly in Jordan. As recently as late 1995, Libya expelled a few hundred of the country's 30,000 Palestinians; while many have been allowed to return, Qadaffi has declared it is only temporary, until the Palestinian Authority makes other arrangements for them.[20]

Inferences about future residential preferences can be drawn only tentatively from the movement of "displaced persons" in 1967. For instance, about 70,000 who followed the retreating Jordanian army to the East Bank were themselves "1948 refugees" who had been living in refugee camps near Jericho and might want to reestablish themselves there. But like the controversies over causation and the 1948 "magic number," even these movements are subject to complications and unanswered queries. How many of "the 1967 displaced" were merely joining family members who were already working in Jordan? How many were to be among the tens of thousands who, between 1968 and 1994, received Israeli permission to return to the West Bank as "family reunification" cases?[21] How many who were out of the region during the 1967 war have never been given Israeli permission to return? Perhaps most significantly, what is the extent of "intermarriage" among second- and third-generation refugees, such that an extended family's "place of origin" can no longer be identified with one or even two villages in Israel?[22]

More useful for present purposes, and to avoid further recriminations over issues such as causation, are data on where and how the refugees are situated today. It is presented here in four sections, corresponding to the four general areas of Palestinian residence: those in territories where UNRWA operates, that is, the West Bank (including East Jerusalem), the Gaza Strip, Jordan, Lebanon, and Syria; the Palestinians who are citizens of Israel; those in other Middle Eastern states, such as Saudi Arabia, Egypt, and Kuwait; and Palestinians outside the Middle East, including the United States. For each of these areas of present-day residence, the chapter offers relevant numerical estimates, descriptions of the refugees' legal and socioeconomic status, and an evaluation of their likely preferences for the future.

In UNRWA's Areas of Operation

A little over half of all Palestinians throughout the world today are registered UNRWA refugees. Recent UNRWA statistics for its population of registered refugees, as well as those in its refugee camps, in the five fields in which it operates—the West Bank, Gaza, Jordan, Syria, and Lebanon—are reported in columns 2 and 3 of table 2.1, which appears at the end of this chapter. As indicated there, in January 1996, UNRWA had a total registry of 3,246,044 refugees, approximately 33 percent of whom (1,061,351 people) still resided in the 59 UNRWA-organized refugee camps. The number of registered refugees living in camps as a percentage of the registered refugees is highest in Gaza (55.5 percent); the lowest percentage is in Jordan (19.3 percent). The percentages in the West Bank and Syria are 25.6 percent and 28 percent respectively, while in Lebanon the figure is just over half (53.6 percent). UNRWA also reports the distribution of registered refugees by seven districts of origin: Jerusalem, Ramallah, and Hebron; Gaza and Beersheba; Jaffa and Ramleh; Tulkarem, Nablus, and Jenin; Haifa; Nazareth, Bisan, Tiberias, Acre, and Safad; and "others." In each of the five UNRWA destination areas, refugees are recorded as coming from all seven districts.[23]

UNRWA's services are available to all registered refugees, regardless of whether they reside in the camps. These services include the provision of elementary and preparatory schools (education constitutes almost half of the agency's budget), vocational training, health centers, sanitation, emergency services when needed (such as during the *intifada* and the crises in Lebanon), shelter assistance and other forms of relief, and social services, such as facilities for women, youth, and the disabled, legal assistance, and a new income-generation program of low-interest loans to create jobs and economic stimulus. Relief included food rations until 1982 (1984 in Lebanon). Although UNRWA generally paves streets and collects trash in the camps, it is not legally responsible for administering, providing utilities for, or policing the camps; these functions are left to the host governments. Campsites are on a combination of state-owned and private land. Camps in the West Bank, for instance, established during Jordanian rule of the area, are on private land for which the Jordanian government continues to pay rent.[24]

The Occupied Territories Generally

Demographic data on Gaza and the West Bank (including East Jerusalem) are more extensive than on other Palestinian communities, due to a comprehensive survey of living conditions and attitudinal correlates conducted in mid-1992 by trained Palestinian data collectors working for the independent Norwegian Institute for Applied Social Science, known as FAFO.[25] (A similar survey of Jordan is currently under way.) Only the most relevant findings are summarized here.

Perhaps the most significant FAFO finding is that the proportion of young Palestinians in the occupied territories is quite large at present.

Forty-five percent of the population is below age 15, compared to 42 percent of non-Jewish Israelis, 31 percent of Israeli Jews, and, for an extraregional comparison, 19 percent of Norwegians. Close to 70 percent of Gazans, in particular, were born after 1967. Together with expected future fertility levels, this phenomenon gives rise to dramatic population projections for Palestinians in the West Bank and Gaza—nearly a doubling, in fact—over the next 20 years, if no significant changes occur.[26] It also means that almost three-quarters of the current population have spent their entire lifetime under occupation, while almost half have spent their formative years during the *intifada*, and the psychological impact of both has been devastating.

Also useful, for purposes of predicting whether families will seek to repatriate or to stay where they now live, are data on the birthplace of the father of current heads of households (usually meaning the grandfather or, increasingly, the great-grandfather, of the current generation of children). For the occupied territories overall, 30 percent of the fathers were born within the Israeli Green Line; by specific area, the figures are 59 percent for Gaza, 17 percent for the West Bank, and 15 percent for East Jerusalem. (These figures, naturally, are similar to the percentages of refugees per area.) The percentages of those whose fathers were born in the same village or city where the family currently lives are 40 percent for Gaza, 80 percent for the West Bank, and 62 percent for East Jerusalem.[27] From this and other factors one might conclude that many more Palestinians from Gaza than from the West Bank or East Jerusalem will wish to seek a new (or more accurately, former) residence than to become permanent residents of their present locales.

In both the West Bank and Gaza, employment rates vary considerably, depending on the agricultural season, whether Israel's borders are closed for security reasons, the number of work permits that Israel makes available, and the rate of household heads and sons being held in detention. In 1991, before serious peace talks began and while the *intifada* was still raging, 31.1 percent of West Bank workers and 38.8 percent of Gazan workers commuted to Israel. These percentages have risen steady in recent years, as the productive capacity of both areas has declined.[28] During open border periods over the last 25 years, official Israeli statistics have claimed unemployment ratios for the occupied territories as a whole ranging from 1 to 5 percent; in contrast, UNRWA estimates that the real figure is between 45 and 52 percent. FAFO's survey uncovered a 1992 unemployment rate of 7 percent (varying from 3 percent in the West Bank to 12 percent in Gaza), with unemployment defined as not working for one month or more within the previous year. However, these relatively low rates are tempered by the presence of many "discouraged workers" and much underemployment.[29]

The West Bank and especially East Jerusalem have a higher labor force participation among adult males than does Gaza, regardless of socioeconomic group. Female labor force participation is very low compared to the male rate, particularly in Gaza. As expected, employment is lowest in Gaza and in refugee camps. Urban refugee camps, in particular (the highest ratio of which are in Gaza), which are described by the FAFO report as "urban slum areas," lack an economic base independent of Israel.[30] For instance, Gazan manufacturers were, before autonomy, prevented from marketing their products outside of the Strip and Israel. Existing industries in each area are primarily small family businesses producing cement, textiles, soap, olive wood carvings, and mother-of-pearl souvenirs. The largest growth in recent years has been in construction jobs.[31] Gaza has a very small intellectual and professional class, as most such residents moved to the Gulf states in the 1960s.

Disposable income per person per year has consistently been twice as high for Palestinians in the West Bank as in Gaza, even though a greater percentage of Gazans over age 15 have had some high school or some college (53.1 percent versus 43.6 percent). Education in both areas was sporadic during the time of the *intifada,* when schools and universities were closed, and is only now becoming regularized again. Palestinian women in both territories are two and a half times as likely as men (29 percent versus 11.4 percent) to have had no schooling at all. There is a shortage of doctors in the territories because many Palestinians who study medicine abroad do not return. Yet there is also a surplus of engineers, most of whom cannot find work, while a great need exists for carpenters, blacksmiths, and mechanics.[32]

Despite the greater income levels in the West Bank, households there are somewhat less likely than Gazan households to have 24-hour electricity, indoor toilets, refrigerators, and telephones, although in both territories the appliances are usually old Israeli castoffs. Only 12 percent of households meet a decent infrastructural standard.[33] Because more West Bankers than Gazans live in freestanding houses, they have endured a greater percentage of housing demolitions as Israeli-imposed punishment for a family member's terrorism. A poll of Gaza and the West Bank conducted in the late summer of 1995 revealed that since the implementation of Palestinian autonomy in Gaza and Jericho, 44 percent of respondents feel their standard of living has worsened, 45 percent reported no change, and only 10 percent believe their living standards have improved.[34]

The West Bank

UNRWA reports that in January 1996, it had over 524,200 refugees registered in the West Bank (including East Jerusalem) and that another

470,000 persons living there were nonrefugee Palestinians. Until 1988, most West Bank residents automatically held Jordanian citizenship. After Jordan announced its Decision of Administrative "Disengagement" from the West Bank in July 1988, it began to regard the residents as non-Jordanians, continuing to issue them travel documents, but only for two years' duration. As other Arab states perceive the two-year paper as a refugee document only, many have refused to grant entry visas to its holders. In October of 1995, the Jordanian Department of Civil Affairs and Passports announced that under new regulations, West Bankers who had a Palestinian passport before July 1988 could replace their two-year documents with a regular five-year passport, even if they had lost their right to West Bank residency. However, the new passport will not serve to confer renewed Jordanian citizenship to West Bankers; the move is apparently just a humanitarian gesture on the kingdom's part.[35] Moreover, until the Palestinian Authority began issuing its own travel documents in November 1995, West Bankers who traveled abroad had to acquire permits from the Israeli civil administration; they lost their right to return if they overstayed their travel visas. Further, the legal status of spouses married to non-Palestinians and of family members who do not reside in the West Bank remains a complex, generally unresolved issue.[36]

The overall West Bank Arab population today is 96 percent Muslim and only 3 percent or 4 percent Christian, down from 20 percent Christian in the late 1930s, although Christians are believed still to constitute 15 percent of the 150,000 Arabs living in East Jerusalem.[37] Christian Palestinians in the West Bank have a higher literacy rate than Muslims (78 percent versus 69 percent) and also tend to have had more years of schooling.[38] However, in addition to a lower Christian birthrate, a discernible trend in out-migration of Christian Palestinians from their traditional West Bank population centers of East Jerusalem, Bethlehem, and Ramallah has been going on for most of the century, and particularly since 1967, possibly due to fear of Islamic revivalism. Muslims now make up a majority of the city of Bethlehem, the traditional birthplace of Jesus. Bethlehem's longtime mayor, Elias Freij, estimates that since 1917, about 45,000 Christian families have left Palestine for countries such as Chile, Venezuela, and Honduras as well as the United States, Canada, and Europe. They are not sending money or visiting and are now beginning to sell their properties as well.[39] "Venerable families with eight-hundred-year histories were among those who departed," according to an Israeli journalist. "The crumbling of the Christian-Palestinian community has weakened the moderate and Western-oriented elements in Palestinian society."[40]

East Jerusalem

The Arab population of East Jerusalem, estimated to be 150,000, deserves special mention. Of the three areas surveyed by FAFO, it ranks highest both in income levels and employment rates. Only two of the West Bank's 19 camps, Shufat and a small portion of Kalandia, are located within the city limits, although East Jerusalem's ratio of refugees to total Palestinians is about the same, 40 percent, as for the occupied territories as a whole. A higher percentage of Arab Jerusalemites, both Christian and Muslim, define themselves as "secular" than do those in Gaza and the rest of the West Bank. The ethnic, religious, and social diversity is higher in the city, and its occupants have access to a variety of Israeli social services such as national health insurance and social security. Moreover, the presence of Israeli military rule is less obvious in the city than in the rest of the territories.[41] Nevertheless, since 1967, Israel has built about a dozen new, rapidly expanding neighborhoods for about 150,000 Jewish settlers in what it has defined as East Jerusalem, by extending the municipal borders and seizing private property. Although the Arab population of the city is virtually the same size, its expansion is restricted by Israeli policy. Thus, much of the housing in Arab neighborhoods is, by necessity, "illegal."[42]

Since 1967, Arab Jerusalemites, all of whom have been issued Israeli identity cards, have been permitted to vote in citywide elections and to obtain Israeli citizenship. For years, few did either, preferring to maintain their Jordanian citizenship and thereby protesting Israel's annexation of the city. But since the signing of the Declaration of Principles in September 1993, which granted Arab Jerusalemites the right to vote for the Council of the Palestinian Authority, an odd event has occurred: between 3,000 and 10,000 have applied for Israeli citizenship, which comes with an international passport, greater freedom of movement within Israel, and the right to vote in national Israeli elections.[43] They may not have been aware that becoming Israeli would limit their rights as Palestinians, for according to the September 1995 Interim Agreement on the West Bank and Gaza (Oslo II), Israeli citizens (regardless of whether they are Jewish or Arab) are not entitled to participate in the elections for the Palestinian Council.[44]

The Gaza Strip

About 700,790 of Gaza's more than 900,000 Palestinians are registered refugees. The growth rate since the *intifada* began is reportedly as high as 5.2 percent per annum in the Gaza Strip, making it most likely the highest or second highest known rate of natural increase in the world.[45]

Due to concentration in one major urban seaport, Gaza City, plus eight refugee camps and nine villages, the population density of Gaza, an area just over twice the size of Washington, D.C., is extremely high (1,400/square kilometers [sq km], reaching 52,200/sq km in the typical camp) compared to the low density of the West Bank (135/sq km), which is spread across 11 medium-size urban centers and 430 separate villages.[46] Although pre-1994 Israeli policy restricted housing expansion beyond existing boundaries, new housing starts since Gaza achieved autonomy are intended to alleviate the overcrowding.

Except for an unknown and probably small number of Gazans with Jordanian or other citizenship, most Gazans are stateless. Between 1948 and 1967, all Gazans, whether registered as refugees or not, were issued *laissez-passer* travel documents by the administering power, Egypt, which continued to renew them even after 1967. However, when Kuwait expelled hundreds of thousands of Palestinians after the Gulf War in 1991, Egypt refused to recognize valid Egyptian-issued documents held by about 25,000 Gazans who had been working in Kuwait and out of the Strip for many years.[47]

After the Israeli occupation began, Gazan residents were required to have Israeli-issued identity cards, which could be revoked by the civil administration. Spouses and children of identity card holders (including those born in Gaza) who did not themselves hold such cards had to apply for family reunification in order to receive residency permits. Because few such applications were granted, many Gazan wives and children were living in the Strip illegally. Gazans seeking to leave Gaza needed *laissez-passer* documents from either Egypt or Israel. The procedure for international travel since autonomy began is unclear. But to travel to Israel or the West Bank, Gazans still need special work permits and magnetic identity cards.[48]

Because Egypt never annexed Gaza, the character of its institutions reflects more of a Palestinian identity than perhaps even the West Bank. Moreover, Gaza's population is 99 percent Muslim. (The 5,000 Jewish settlers constitute less than 1 percent of the total.) However, contrary to conventional wisdom, which associates Islamic fundamentalism with Gaza's refugee camps, FAFO discovered that:

> Islamicism is not particularly associated with Gaza refugee camps, nor indeed with Gaza at all, despite the long historical connection between Gaza and the Egyptian-based Muslim Brotherhood. Of the various types of localities surveyed, Gaza camps, along with Arab Jerusalem, seem to be the most secular. To the extent there is a regional concentration of Islamicist activism, it appears to be more associated with the towns and camps of the West Bank. Moreover, the general percentage of Palestinians who are secular, observant or activist does not vary with their refugee status.[49]

An indication of changing Gazan attitudes toward religion is the cloth-
ing worn publicly by women: more and more women since the early
1990s are going without the *hijab* (head cover) and some even wear
jeans, a previously unheard of phenomenon.[50] Nevertheless, the most
efficient social services in Gaza, including charity to the poor and out-
reach to youth, have been those run by Hamas, the Islamic Resistance
Movement. "Hamas clearly understands that under present conditions,
influence on the ground is first gained through social work, then
through religious work, and only in the end through political work."[51]
It remains to be seen what influence Hamas will continue to have under
the Palestinian Authority.

Jordan

Because the overwhelming number of Palestinians in Jordan are citizens of the state, and due to the relative openness of Jordanian society
vis-à-vis other Arab states, much is known about the Palestinian community there. Although there is some difficulty, not to mention political
sensitivity, in differentiating Palestinian Jordanians from non-Palestinian Jordanians, a fair consensus exists that the total number of Palestinians living there in 1993 (after the return of the expellees from
Kuwait) was approximately 1,850,000, of whom UNRWA had registered 1,140,199 as refugees; of these, 239,434 lived in Jordan's ten
refugee camps. Thus, the largest number (40 percent) of all Palestinian
refugees live in Jordan.[52] Since the return of over 300,000 Palestinians
from Kuwait in 1991, anywhere from 45 to 70 percent of all Jordanians
are Palestinian, meaning that they originated from west of the Jordan
River. (The kingdom has refused to reveal publicly the exact ratio of
East and West Bankers, as identified in the 1994 census.)[53]

Jordan granted full citizenship to all Palestinian refugees and their
descendants who were "habitually residents in 1954." It did not matter
whether they lived on the East Bank or West Bank, because in that era
Jordan had incorporated the West Bank and Palestinians drifted back
and forth fairly readily. Many families had branches and homes on
both sides of the river. However, once Israel took over control of the
West Bank, the situation became more confused, so in 1983 the Jordanian government created a dual system: yellow cards, which represented full residency and full citizenship rights for persons who had
left the West Bank for the East Bank before June 1 of that year; and
green cards, providing a renewable two-year Jordanian "passport" and
no right of residence for those who left the West Bank after June 1, 1983.
Green card holders can visit Jordan for only up to one month at a time.[54]
Thus, it is really no more than a travel document, of the type also issued

to Palestinians by Egypt, Syria, Lebanon, and Israel. As already noted, Jordan has recently announced that green card holders can apply again for five-year passports, but such a passport will not constitute full formal citizenship.

Full citizenship in Jordan for those Palestinians on the East Bank means full civil and political rights, including the right to vote and to be elected to office. The main category of Palestinians in Jordan who are not Jordanian citizens consists of those displaced from the Gaza Strip in 1967. They constitute approximately 70,000 persons. As noncitizens, they need official permission to work and then can do so only in the private sector. Their unemployment rate, at 40 to 50 percent, is higher than for Palestinian citizens. The noncitizens use Egyptian travel documents when traveling abroad and need return visas to get back into Jordan.[55]

In the early 1990s, the Palestinian community in Jordan had a 20 percent unemployment rate, comparable to the country's rate as a whole, as the economy was suffering badly. Unemployment increased immediately after the return of hundreds of thousands who had been expelled from Kuwait to 33 percent for the Jordanian population as a whole. Moreover, the returnees' families no longer receive the remittances of workers from the Gulf. Yet the expulsion from Kuwait has been a mixed blessing, as the returnees have boosted the economy through growth in consumption. The Jordanian government does, moreover, provide extensive social services and other public support for low-income refugees; it allots $300 million a year for refugee relief and far more than that for their education, health, and welfare services.[56] Although most Palestinians were purged from the civil service and the army after the king's violent "Black September" 1970 confrontation with the PLO, they continue to dominate the private sector. Palestinians are estimated to constitute 60 to 65 percent of the banking industry, 65 to 70 percent of the retailing field, and 75 to 80 percent of wholesale and import/export industries.[57]

If the concept of Palestinian-Jordanian "citizen refugees" seems anomalous, it reflects a decades-long tenuous relationship between two rival communities. The refugees perceived King Abdullah (assassinated by a Palestinian in 1951) as having betrayed them by acquiescing in the creation of Israel, annexing the West Bank, and either trying to force them to assimilate as Jordanians or accusing them of disloyalty. Although his grandson, King Hussein, has been more successful in cultivating the loyalty of the refugees, he also has been accused of selling them out in his rush to make peace with Israel. (Ironically, the 1988 disengagement of Jordan from the West Bank was considered as much a betrayal as was the 1948 annexation.) Even today, Palestinians complain of systematic discrimination in favor of native Jordanians. According to Milton Viorst:

> It is true that Palestinians never obtained top military and security posts in the Jordanian government, and suffered heavy-handed repression for political dissidence. . . . It is also true that the bulk of available development funds was spent on the East Bank rather than the West. Nonetheless, thousands of Palestinians became doctors, professors, engineers and bankers. Benefitting from education, hundreds of thousands gravitated to jobs in the Gulf, where many grew rich. . . . The King's policies helped, as much as anything, to transform the Palestinians from farmers and shopkeepers into a community prepared for leading positions in the modern economic culture that was spreading worldwide.[58]

Whether one's primary identity is as a "Jordanian citizen of Palestinian origin" or, simply, as a Palestinian whose stay in Jordan is considered temporary, seems to depend in great part on one's socioeconomic circumstances. Laurie Brand identifies four Palestinian-Jordanian groups in this regard: (1) refugee camp dwellers whose Palestinian identity is stronger, formed as it was primarily in opposition to Jordanian policy; (2) the middle class of small merchants and lower-level government employees, who have come to express loyalty to the king and some form of attachment to Jordan; (3) the bourgeoisie, who have achieved notable business success and who "tend to see no dilemma or contradiction in identifying themselves as both Palestinian and Jordanian"; and (4) those who went to the Gulf oil states, who see their Jordanian passports merely as a convenience; since their return in 1991, they have not become much more attached to the state.[59] Naturally, this continuum also reflects intentions concerning future residence, whether one will end up remaining in Jordan or seek to cross permanently back to the West Bank.[60]

Lebanon

Due to 15 years of civil war, invasion by Israel, and other patterns of violent attacks on camp residents, the size of the Palestinian community in Lebanon is subject to widely conflicting estimates. Lebanese Ministry of the Interior officials speak of 400,000 to 550,000, but UNRWA's list of registered refugees is closer to 350,000. There may, in addition, be another 38,000 or more nonregistered refugees in the country. About half of the refugees now live in the 12 official UNRWA-organized camps (three other camps were destroyed in the military conflicts), some of which have no electricity or running water. Unauthorized "shantytown" camps have been created but usually end up bulldozed, the inhabitants forced to squat somewhere else because the Lebanese government refuses to authorize new building projects. A large portion of the refugees in Lebanon have been displaced at least twice in their lifetimes; at least 20,000 may currently be homeless.[61]

The annual growth rate among the Palestinians in Lebanon is 2.3 percent, the lowest among all five UNRWA fields of operation. The community may have lost between 50,000 and 60,000 people in casualties and out-migration since the 1982 Israeli invasion and the "camps war" of the mid-1980s, which also produced almost 50,000 internally displaced persons and 5,900 squatters.[62] Moreover, about 12,000 PLO fighters were forced to leave, mainly relocating to North Africa; most had been expelled from Jordan earlier, in 1970. The PLO reported in early 1993 that as many as 100,000 camp residents and 15,000 noncamp refugees may have left the country, allegedly migrating to the United States, Canada, Australia, Germany, Sweden, and Denmark.[63] This exodus remains unconfirmed.

About 60 percent of the Palestinians in Lebanon live below the U.N. poverty line, making it the poorest of the communities in the UNRWA orbit.[64] This situation is partly due to steep inflation in the Lebanese economy, a high unemployment rate (according to UNRWA, 33 percent in the early 1990s, although others say 90 percent), a decline in international aid to the refugee community there, and the legal status of the Palestinians, who since 1962 have been classified as foreigners. Under a 1964 decree, no foreigner may work, either for pay or unpaid, without permits from the Ministries of Labor and Social Affairs.[65] Priority is given to Lebanese citizens as well as to foreign workers from Syria and Asia, over Palestinians. Palestinians are also prohibited from entering government hospitals and the secondary school system.

As a result of years of war, the illiteracy rate is high among adult Palestinians in Lebanon and may be rising as increasing numbers of refugee children drop out of school. Even Palestinian lawyers and engineers are forbidden to practice their professions, while doctors and pharmacists are able to practice only in Palestine Red Crescent Society clinics; unlicensed clinics and pharmacies have been shut down. Many Palestinians, particularly women, therefore work illegally at black market jobs such as housecleaning for wages far below the officially sanctioned minimum wage and without any benefits.[66] Palestinians who leave Lebanon for employment purposes risk losing permission to return and to reside there. In fact, the government decided in late 1995 that all Palestinians, even those holding Lebanese travel documents, would henceforth require visas to exit and reenter the country. About 25,000 Palestinians who have managed to obtain non-Lebanese passports are said to have been denied residency altogether.[67]

Between 1950 and 1972, approximately 3,000 Palestinian families were given Lebanese citizenship. These were undoubtedly cases of Christian Palestinian women marrying Christian Lebanese men (not the reverse) or of wealthy Muslims who "bought" citizenship. Other Christians and the rare Shi'ite Palestinians became citizens as part of the 1989 Ta'if Accord, which ended the Lebanese civil war. By a 1925 law, the naturalized wife retains her citizenship after the death of the husband; however, Lebanese jurists are divided over whether the underage children of such a deceased father are accorded citizenship. The exact number of naturalized Palestinians is unknown but is probably in the neighborhood of 30,000.[68]

Lebanese officials have on more than one occasion expressed an intention to expel all Palestinians, who are predominantly Sunni Muslims, at the earliest possible occasion, claiming that their integration in the country would upset the country's "delicate sectarian balance," in which Shi'ite Muslims have a slight majority over a dwindling number of Maronite Christians. "Opposition to their resettlement is one of the few issues that unites the Lebanese government and public opinion across most of the sectarian communities," particularly since the 1989 Ta'if Accord.[69] The Beirut-based anthropologist Rosemary Sayigh states that the two publicly declared Lebanese policies toward the Palestinians—reestablishment of state control over them and refusal of *tawtin* (naturalization)—have been supplemented by a third, undeclared one: "encouraging Palestinian emigration through the intensification of various pressures."[70]

Indeed, rumors occasionally are heard that the Lebanese government intends to demolish all the camps and replace them with sports stadiums and the like. Responding to reports that some Palestinians expelled from Libya would attempt to return to Lebanon, a cabinet minister reportedly responded that his country would not be a "dump" for "human garbage."[71] As Palestinian American author Fawaz Turki, who grew up in Beirut, responds: "The Lebanese had made it clear that I would never be at home there. I returned the favor by never feeling any loyalty to Lebanon."[72] Despair about the future is probably greatest among Palestinians in Lebanon, most of whom do not believe that the Palestinian Authority will ever achieve the dream of a sovereign Palestinian state.[73] Because of these attitudes and the generally dismal conditions of their refuge in Lebanon, there may be few Palestinians who would like to stay permanently, even if given citizenship. And because most come from the Galilee, they are the most likely to continue to seek repatriation to Israel.

Syria

Of all the areas within the UNRWA orbit, the least amount of information has been published on Palestinians in Syria, perhaps as a reflection of the difficulty of conducting research in such a closed society. UNRWA itself reports that most of the 342,507 registered refugees of Syria live in the greater Damascus area, mostly in camps that are, in fact, fairly well integrated into regular housing in the city rather than segregated as in other UNRWA fields of operation. Other refugees live in northern towns such as Aleppo or south near the Jordanian border. Perhaps another 10,000 to 30,000 Palestinians in Syria are nonrefugees. In the early 1990s, the Palestinian community there had an 8.4 percent unemployment rate, the lowest in UNRWA's five fields of operation.

Syria officially treats Palestinians "like Syrians by origin in Syria, in all matters pertaining to . . . the rights of employment, work, commerce and national obligations and by keeping their nationality of origin."[74] They also have full, unrestricted access to government schools and universities. However, unlike Jordan, Syria does not grant citizenship to Palestinians, unless they are women married to Syrian men (but not vice versa) or had Syrian citizenship before 1948. Instead, Palestinians are issued Palestinian travel documents. It is estimated that fewer than 3,500 of the 350,000 refugees have Syrian citizenship.[75] Syria prohibits Palestinian residents of the newly autonomous areas of Gaza and Jericho from entering the country, even for short visits. The government has also refused to cooperate with the Palestinian Authority itself; it is perhaps the only Arab state that does not recognize the travel documents that the authority has recently been issuing.[76]

Although it can be said that Palestinians in Syria are, indeed, treated like Syrian citizens "in all but name," that must be understood within the context of Syria's notorious human rights record. Hundreds of Palestinians are reportedly languishing in Syria's appallingly overcrowded prisons, many held without trial, others with sentences as long as 12 years, for crimes such as spying for the PLO, trying to emigrate without permission, traveling to Israel, or no known grounds. Reports of torture have been corroborated by human rights organizations. Some Palestinians claim that family members traveled to Syria, often to study, and then disappeared, as long as 20 years ago.[77] It has also been reported that since the 1960s, between 90,000 and 120,000 Syrian Kurds have had their citizenship revoked.[78] In that sense, Syrian citizenship, at least in its current guise, is not such a valuable form of protection, even if the government was readily willing to grant it to Palestinians, which is doubtful.

*   *   *

These snapshots of Palestinian life in the various UNRWA fields of operation are too varied to draw generalizations, except to note two points: First, 80 percent of Palestinians live within a 100-mile radius of pre-1948 Palestine, yet fewer than half of them have citizenship of any kind, which results in the denial not only of the security of permanent residence but also of dignity, civil and political rights, and even "the crucial criterion for respect and status in Arab society—ownership of land."[79] Second, those in Jordan live under the best conditions, those in Lebanon and Gaza the worst, with the West Bank and Syria falling in the middle. By a very rough equivalence, this continuum may also reflect differing degrees of readiness to settle permanently in the country of refuge or to acquire a new residence.

The Palestinians of Israel

If it can be argued that the Israeli-Palestinian peace process has all but disregarded the Palestinian diaspora, then it has totally ignored a subpopulation at one time considered to be "the bridge of peace": the Palestinian citizens of Israel. This is ironic, because they constitute the one major group that "thus far supports the [Declaration of Principles] with few doubts."[80] They hope it can free them from disabilities they have suffered since 1948: discrimination, segregation from the Jewish majority, and suspicion of dual loyalty. Although this is probably the most unique of Palestinian communities, it personifies the closest attempt to achieve coexistence with Israelis and therefore deserves closer attention.

The precise number of Palestinians living within Israel's pre-1967 borders is not known, because the Israel Central Bureau of Statistics, which conducts census surveys on the basis of religion rather than nationality, does not recognize the category "Palestinian." In November 1995, approximately 1,064,000 people, or 19 percent of the 5,600,000 total population counted in the Israeli census, were reported to be non-Jewish, with 14.4 percent reported as Muslim, 2.9 percent Christian, and 1.7 percent Druze and others. Palestinians are either Muslim or Christian, but depending on the definition, they may or may not include additional Muslim tribes and sects, such as Bedouins, Druze, and Circassians.[81] Israel's population also includes Armenians and other non-Arab Christians. Virtually all of the non-Jews are Israeli citizens, although only Druze are drafted into the Israeli army; by mutual consent, the other Arabs are not, but Bedouins and Circassians often volunteer to serve. In a country that places such an honor on military service, awarding economic benefits to veterans and defining many jobs as requiring "prior army service," this distinction is significant.[82]

Despite frequent claims that Israel is in danger of "losing its identity as a Jewish country," the percentage of Arabs to total population is virtually the same now as it was in May 1948, that is, 19 percent, because the higher Arab birthrate tends to be offset by Jewish immigration.[83] Due to Israeli policy, Arab immigration is virtually nil and the rate of Arab emigration from Israel is minimal, given the Palestinians' attachment to the land and fear that their property also would be appropriated if they left.[84] A reasonable estimate, extrapolated from a 1988 official Israeli figure of 850,000, is that at the present, the Israeli Palestinian community consists of about 990,000 persons.[85] But since this figure includes the Arab population of East Jerusalem, annexed by Israel in 1967, Palestinians themselves would probably subtract 150,000 from it, for a total of 840,000.

Most of the Israeli Palestinians live in rural villages in northern Israel, in the "Big Triangle" centered around the city of Nazareth (population 65,000) in the lower Galilee. Smaller concentrations live between Tel Aviv and the Green Line in the villages of the "Little Triangle," and in the cities of Acre, Tel Aviv/Jaffa, Haifa, Lod and Ramla, as well as East Jerusalem.[86] The nomadic Bedouin primarily live in the Negev desert in the south; however, most have been relocated to seven officially designated settlements. About 50,000 of the state's Arab citizens live in 120 illegal, "unrecognized villages" established near the site of villages demolished in the 1948 war.[87] There is only one cooperative Arab-Jewish town in the entire country, the experimental Neve Shalom/Wahat Al-Salam between Tel Aviv and Jerusalem, which operates a School for Peace and the country's first bilingual, bicultural kindergarten and primary school. Although Arabs do attend Israeli universities (there are no Arab universities in the state, while the occupied territories have six), the country's primary and secondary schools are segregated—and decidedly unequal.[88]

The State of Israel was created with the understanding that it would protect the interests of its minority population. The 1917 Balfour Declaration by the British government, which was subsequently incorporated in the Preamble to the League of Nations Mandate for Palestine, stated that the establishment of a national home for the Jewish people shall do nothing "which may prejudice the civil and religious rights of existing non-Jewish communities in Palestine."[89] Israel's Declaration of Independence, issued May 14, 1948, similarly states:

THE STATE OF ISRAEL will . . . ensure complete equality of social and political rights to all its inhabitants irrespective of religion, race or sex . . . it will safeguard the Holy Places of all religions. . . .
    WE APPEAL—in the very midst of the onslaught launched against us now for months—to the Arab inhabitants of the State of Israel to preserve

peace and participate in the upbuilding of the State on the basis of full and equal citizenship and due representation in all its provisional and permanent institutions.[90]

Officially, only three Israeli laws treat Arab citizens differently from Jews: the Law of Return and the Nationality Law, which arguably are akin to affirmative action policies designed to implement Israel's status as a refuge for Jews, and an emergency regulation extended from the British Mandate period, which required military permits for Arabs traveling outside their villages.[91] This latter regulation was suspended in 1966. Moreover, at least two new provisions of the Basic Laws, components of the evolving constitution, implicitly apply to protect the property and equal employment rights of Arab citizens of the state.[92]

Nevertheless, the socioeconomic disparity between Jewish and Arab Israelis is glaring. In 1992, Arab unemployment was double that of the Jewish population; 42 percent of Arab university graduates, compared to only 15 percent of similarly educated Jews, remained unemployed.[93] In the early 1980s, only 12.7 percent of Arab households had telephones, compared to 65.6 percent of Jewish homes; 32.9 percent of Muslim homes crowded more than three people per room, compared to only 1.3 percent of Jewish homes.[94] True, Arab family life revolves around the extended family, the *hamula*, in close proximity, and the standard of living of Israeli Palestinians is generally higher than that of their counterparts elsewhere in the Middle East.[95] But the gap between Arab and Jewish lifestyles is due not only to private market forces or cultural reasons; municipal services are also distributed on a distinctively unequal basis. For instance, in the mid-1980s, per capita government grants were 1:5 people in the Jewish sector and 1:50 in the Arab sector.[96] Until recently, many Arab towns and villages had no proper sewage or electrical systems and few community centers, parks, or paved roads.

Beginning in 1992, under the Rabin government, municipal budgets were adjusted upward, municipal boundaries expanded to alleviate some overcrowding, and industrial zones and housing developments were established in Arab centers. Many Arabs drive new Volvos and display other signs of the Israeli economic boom, such as the ubiquitous cellular phones. A government commission is even proposing that some of the 1948 "internal refugees" be allowed to return to their original homes. And not a single Israeli Arab serves as a political prisoner. Still, there are almost no Israeli Palestinians in senior decision-making positions in the government bureaucracy, and no Arab has ever served in the cabinet.[97] The state is unlikely to give up its flag containing a Jewish star or replace the reference to "Jewish souls" in the national anthem. And, during the Rabin and Peres administrations, the Israeli right continued to attack the Labor government's one-vote majority in the Knesset because it was achieved with the help of five votes from Arab political parties, as if that mattered in a democracy.[98]

Yet even if Israel is a flawed democracy, it is a democracy nonetheless, unlike any government in the Arab world. As put by Walid Sadek, an Arab Knesset member: "It is our land and our government, and we are fighting for the view that Israel is a nation of all its citizens, not just of all its Jews."[99] Moreover, with but rare exception, any protest activity on the part of Israeli Palestinians has been nonviolent and within the bounds of the law.

Perhaps the most salient factor determining the future residence of Israeli Palestinians is their sense of national identity. The term "Israeli Palestinian" is itself problematic. The label one uses—whether "Palestinian," "Arab," "Israeli," "Palestinian Israeli," "Israeli Arab," or other variations—can be an indication of ideology and one's attitude toward the State of Israel.[100] It can also reflect an identity confusion. Yet there is nothing inherently wrong with feeling both Palestinian and Israeli. Moreover, it should not be considered treasonous for a Palestinian Israeli to support politically, or even financially, the establishment of a sovereign Palestinian state and express solidarity with Palestinians elsewhere. After all, diaspora Jews in democratic countries engage in activity in support of Israel and their fellow Jews who may be oppressed elsewhere.

Yet many Palestinian citizens of Israel, such as the novelist Anton Shammas, who writes in Hebrew rather than Arabic to prove "that there is something called 'Israeli' that is not necessarily Jewish," have stated publicly that they would not move to a Palestinian state.[101] In fact, many are tired of being asked about it. "When people ask me if I will move to live under the Palestinian authority, it reflects a critical misunderstanding of my situation," explains the publisher Muhammad Ghanaim. "I want to be an Israeli citizen and I'll fight it to the end. Not out of love or hate for one or the other. But I was born here as a citizen, and I don't want to be a precedent for anything else."[102] In other words, living in the West Bank and Gaza, even under Palestinian sovereignty, would not necessarily be preferred over living in the original homeland—as equal citizens of Israel.

In Other Middle Eastern States

Close to 450,000 Palestinians currently reside in the rest of the Middle East, beyond Israel, the occupied territories, and the other three UNRWA fields of operation. Estimates by the U.S. Bureau of the Census indicate the following numbers of Palestinians may currently be living in these other Middle Eastern and North African states: Algeria, 4,661; Bahrain, 2,174; Egypt, 40,063; Iraq, 29,922; Libya, 27,530; Oman, 6,636; Qatar, 30,995; Saudi Arabia, 205,840; and the United Arab Emirates, 47,374. In Kuwait, perhaps 311,742 Palestinians resided there before the Persian Gulf crisis.[103] Other sources estimate the precrisis figure at closer to 400,000 Palestinians in Kuwait, about 70,000 of whom held Israeli-issued travel cards while the rest held Jordanian passports.[104] Somewhere between 250,000 and 350,000 Palestinians were expelled from Kuwait and other Gulf states in 1990 and 1991; most returned to Jordan, with smaller numbers going to Lebanon, the West Bank, and Gaza, leaving only about 20,000 to 30,000 in postwar Kuwait.[105]

Like Kuwait, many of the Gulf states are secondary and tertiary migration destinations for laborers from as close as the next-door state and as far away as Southeast Asia. Foreign workers—or more descriptively, given their work contracts, indentured servants—today make up 40 percent of the workforce in Bahrain, 70 percent in Kuwait, 42 percent in Libya, 81 percent in Qatar, 75 percent in Saudi Arabia, and 80 percent in the United Arab Emirates. The Arab workers tend to be male engineers or construction workers and the Asian ones, female housekeepers.[106] But unlike the workers from Morocco, for instance, or for that matter the Philippines, most Palestinians have no national embassy to turn to when in trouble. Only a small handful of the wealthy or "those who rendered outstanding services to the developing of oil states in the Gulf" or in Egypt were granted citizenship.[107]

Additional information is available about Palestinian communities in only some of these "outer Middle Eastern" countries. In general, virtually none of the Palestinians there have citizenship of any kind, except for those who had resided in Jordan earlier.

Kuwait

Although only a small number of Palestinians live in Kuwait today, it is important to understand what happened to them there, both because it may foretell what may unfold in other Arab states and because Palestinians may wish to return there in the future. Attracted by the new oil-exporting industry, Palestinians migrated voluntarily to Kuwait in a steady stream after 1948, with an increased wave after the June 1967 war. Most of them held Jordanian passports, but many were stateless. Men arrived first, followed later by wives and children. By the time the Palestinian community reached 200,000 people in the late 1970s, its size was over 50 percent of the total of Kuwaiti citizens, a status limited to an elite few.[108] Along with Lebanese immigrants, well-educated Palestinians, such as the Cairo University–trained engineer, Yasser Arafat, held key positions in both the public and private sector, fulfilling a critical need for technological and managerial skills. "They played the most crucial role in building the modern Kuwaiti state, being widely represented in banking, the technical services, education and the various industries," including oil and defense, as well as the civil service, and constituted about 40 percent of the medical profession.[109]

Despite this important role in the economy, Palestinians in Kuwait always led a precarious existence. Their residency was revoked if they were unemployed for 15 days, left the country to study, retired from work, or engaged in public political activity. Only 10 percent of spots at Kuwait University were open to foreign students, regardless of whether they had been born in Kuwait. No foreigner could own land or more than a minority share in a business.[110]

Although the Kuwaiti government had traditionally been the most generous financial backer of the PLO, allowing it to organize the local Palestinian community and, for a time, to operate its own schools, that relationship began to change after events related to the Lebanese civil war produced repercussions in Kuwait[111] and even more dramatically in 1990, when the PLO supported Saddam Hussein's invasion and reports surfaced of Palestinians aiding the Iraqi occupying force. "Despite instances of support for the [anti-Iraq] resistance and many heroic efforts to save Kuwaiti lives and property, the Palestinians were rejected as a community of traitors."[112]

Almost all foreign workers fled Kuwait after the Iraqi invasion on August 2, 1990. However, once the country was liberated, Egyptians and some other Arab communities were allowed to return, along with newly imported Asian workers. But not the Palestinians.[113] Those few who had remained were primarily holders of Egyptian travel documents who left Gaza before 1967 and therefore were excluded by Israel from returning. Egypt also refused them entry, ostensibly due to the same suspicion of their pro-Iraqi leanings. The human rights group Middle East Watch reported in 1991 that the Kuwaiti government had committed atrocities against Palestinians and was attempting to deport as many of them as possible, despite their lack of an alternative place of asylum.[114] A steady stream of the remaining Palestinians has been leaving since then, many to Iraq. Kuwait has recently announced that it will not permit the return of those who left during the Gulf War.[115]

Saudi Arabia

Although Saudi Arabia now has the largest concentration of Palestinians outside of the UNRWA host region, very little is known about the community there. While some Gazans worked in Saudia Arabia in the

1950s (many to be deported after they went on strike), most Palestinians did not begin to arrive there until the 1960s. In 1970, when the number of Palestinians approached 31,000, about 7,000 served as teachers, a role they often played in other Middle Eastern states.[116] Professionally, the community is thought to resemble the highly skilled, pre-1990 group in Kuwait, with a heavy concentration in the oil industry. However, foreign workers' rights are even more heavily constrained. No visas are granted unless a person is sponsored by the government or a company or institution that can be held responsible. Therefore, the community consists primarily of men without their families, in contrast to Kuwait, where foreign workers' families can live. In 1957, an agreement between the Saudi government and American oil companies gave priority in employment to citizens of Arab League states, thus excluding the vast majority of Palestinians, who were stateless.[117] Palestinians also left Saudi Arabia during the Gulf War, although not as many as those who left Kuwait. Since 1991, the country has not admitted more Palestinians, even those with foreign passports.

Egypt

Unlike Kuwait and Saudi Arabia, Egypt is a place of primary as well as secondary migration for Palestinians. Moreover, except for a historical fluke, it too might have been one of the UNRWA host states.

Fleeing Jaffa in 1948, about 3,000 Palestinians went to Egypt by boat. Others arrived by crossing the Sinai. Wealthy refugees found housing in Cairo, and a few were able to purchase Egyptian citizenship. Many others were sheltered in a refugee camp on the Sinai side of the Suez Canal; soon, however, most were transferred to camps in Gaza or to other Arab countries that would take them. Because Egypt did not request U.N. assistance, the few thousand refugees remaining in the country were not eligible for UNRWA registration or relief. Instead, they received aid through the World Council of Churches and the U.S. development assistance agency, USAID.

Although Egypt was responsible for the military administration of the Gaza Strip between 1949 and 1967, Palestinian migration from Gaza to Egypt proper was kept to a minimum, with an exception only for foreign university students, who were given government scholarships. During the 1967 war, members of the Gazan police, the Palestinian Liberation Army, and their families retreated with the Egyptian army, thereby doubling to about 33,000 the number of Palestinians in Egypt.[118] Since then, the borders have been kept generally closed to Palestinians. For instance, when Libya began expelling several hundred of its 30,000 Palestinians in the fall of 1995, Egypt refused to let any enter, instead busing those with Jordanian passports to Jordan. Currently, only Palestinian university students are being admitted.[119]

Beginning in 1949, the Egyptian government issued either Egyptian identity cards or All-Palestine Government (APG) travel documents to Palestinians in both Egypt and Gaza. The short-lived and rather ineffective APG had been formed in 1948 to serve as a representative body for the refugees. Its travel documents provided only for one year's residency and forbade the bearer from working. These documents were replaced in 1960 by United Arab Republic (U.A.R.) travel papers, but they, too, were little more than symbols of nationalistic pride. They required frequent renewal, sometimes granted only when financial security could be demonstrated. But the 1950s had seen President Gamal Nasser's and the Egyptian people's growing support for the Palestinian national cause, which translated into free health care for the refugees, access to government schools, and permission to own land and to work as doctors, veterinarians, midwives, and dentists and in the import/export business. In 1962, the year the U.A.R. disbanded, Palestinians were also authorized to work in public sector jobs and to send their children to government schools.[120]

These mild privileges came to an end, however, when Palestinian students and the PLO demonstrated against Anwar Sadat's 1977 trip to Jerusalem and the organization and other Arab states "froze" their relations with Cairo. The status of Palestinians in Egypt was downgraded from "residents" to "foreigners," who must pay hard currency to obtain permission to remain. In the words of Laurie Brand:

> Gone were the days of the relatively free movement of members of the Palestinian resistance movement in and out of Egypt and the days of generalized feelings of solidarity and sympathy for the Palestinians among average Egyptians. The media gradually succeeded in convincing many Egyptians that it was Palestinians who were responsible for Egypt's involvement and sacrifices in four wars; that Palestinians were living in Egypt like kings; and that the resistance was corrupt. Most devastating, the Egyptian media adopted and popularized one of the favorite Zionist myths: that the Palestinians had sold their land prior to 1948 and therefore did not deserve Palestine.[121]

Although relations have improved somewhat under Hosni Mubarak, the Palestinians' educational, health, and employment privileges have not been restored. However, the government has recently announced its intention to naturalize the Palestinians who currently reside there.[122]

Libya

Most of the approximately 27,000 to 30,000 Palestinians in Libya are persons who were displaced from the Israeli-occupied territories by the 1967 war and attracted to the North African state because of its liberal entry and foreign worker policies and vocal support for the Palestinian cause. Mainly teachers and skilled workers, with some physicians and engineers among them, the majority have no other place that will take them in—a fact demonstrated by the refusal of Egypt, Lebanon, and Israel to admit the hundreds who had been expelled in late summer 1995. Although Qadaffi's avowed purpose in trying to expel them was to demonstrate his dissatisfaction with the Palestinian-Israeli peace accords, his true motive may have been the deteriorating Libyan economy, which has been aggravated ever since April 1992, when the U.N. Security Council ordered a blockade to punish the state for refusing to turn over suspects in the Pan Am 103 Lockerbie bombing. As of mid-January 1996, about 200 of the expelled Palestinians were still residing in temporary camps on the Egyptian border, due to expired, lost, or inadequate travel documents, to fear of retaliation, or for other reasons.[123]

*   *   *

Few conclusions can be reached as to what the Palestinians in the outer Middle Eastern states might wish to do after the end of the Arab-Israeli conflict. It is unclear what percentage would seek to remain if given citizenship, an expansion of economic and political rights, and other forms of encouragement, and how many would prefer to move back to the West Bank, Gaza, or Israel. Given that most migrated for economic reasons, they may need to remain for the near future, at least until economic opportunities in areas closer to home improve. As their fate has so often depended on political relations between the temporary host state and the PLO, the prospect of permanent peace and stability between Israel and the Palestinians should affect the willingness of Arab states to treat their Palestinian residents as welcome potential citizens and not merely as political or economic pawns.

The Wider Palestinian Diaspora

Precious little information is available about the Palestinian communities of the West and other countries outside the Middle East and North Africa, despite the rapid growth of Muslim and Arab populations there.[124] This is in part due to the reluctance of many democratic countries to procure or report census data on the basis of nationality or religion. (Arabs are reported as Caucasian in the U.S. Census, for instance.)

Moreover, like immigrants from other nondemocratic regions, who tend to distrust government agencies, Palestinians may be more likely than native-born citizens to ignore census forms, so the data that exist may be skewed. Immigration statistics, from which demographic data can be derived, would be unlikely to identify "Palestine" as a country of origin. Rather, Palestinians would be classified together with other Arabs as coming from Jordan or Lebanon as well as with non-Arabs arriving directly from Europe or Israel.[125] Finally, political reasons may, at least in the past, have discouraged some organizations from revealing how many Palestinians have voluntarily left the Middle East and made lives elsewhere.

A May 1991 estimate, reported by the U.S. Bureau of the Census, the Institute for Palestine Studies, and others, gave a figure of 325,000 Palestinians living in "non-Arab states," including 150,000 in the United States.[126] The Washington-based Center for Policy Analysis on Palestine has reported a higher estimate of 450,000 in the "rest of the world" for the same period, 1990 to 1991. This latter calculation explicitly rejected as too low the data compiled by the PLO's own Economic Department-Central Bureau of Statistics, which had reported only 280,846 Palestinians lived outside Israel and the Arab world in 1986.[127]

While Palestinians are dispersed as far as Australia,[128] Brazil,[129] Canada, and Denmark, the largest community may be found in the United States. Palestinians have been arriving as immigrants in the United States since the end of World War II, constituting the largest group in the "second wave" of Arab immigration, which has also included Egyptians, Jordanians, Lebanese, Syrians, Yemenis, and Iraqis. Arab Americans in general are among the fastest-growing immigrant groups in major metropolitan areas such as New York City and northern New Jersey; Detroit and Dearborn, Michigan; Chicago; and the greater Los Angeles area. Over 140,000 Arab immigrants moved to the United States between 1980 and 1988, ranking them as a group above British immigrants and just below Laotians and Cubans.[130] Although Palestinians and other Arab Americans are frequently subject to discrimination, stereotyping, and antiterrorist hysteria—during the Persian Gulf War and after the World Trade Center bombing, for instance—as a whole, Arab Americans have a higher educational achievement level and a higher representation in managerial, professional (especially health care–related), and sales positions than other American ethnic groups. Palestinians have tended to work in scientific or academic jobs and in business.[131] It is not known exactly how many have U.S. citizenship; however, there is no objective reason why they would be ineligible to obtain it.

The most comprehensive analysis of Palestinians in the United States comes from a 1990 Arab American Institute study based on data from the 1980 U.S. Census.[132] In it Palestinians are estimated to constitute only 3.2 percent of the total Arab American population of 2 to 2.5 million, compared to the 44.9 percent who are Lebanese, the largest subgroup. That would yield a Palestinian American population in the range of 64,000 to 80,000, smaller than the 150,000 in the above-noted estimate. These distinctions depend, of course, on the definition used, which can depend on generational factors. Older Arab Americans might refer to their homeland as "Lebanon" or "Greater Syria," the geographical designations of an earlier era, when in fact their village may have been located in what is now known to Palestinians as Palestine or to Israelis as Israel.[133]

While no survey has ever been conducted that reflects the preferences of these "wider diasporan Palestinians" in regard to repatriation to Palestine, it can be assumed that most are well integrated and are doing well financially, having had the necessary capital and skills to have been admitted to these countries in the first place. Although they are likely to visit the Middle East frequently and may intend to invest in new Palestinian businesses and industries, few may wish to return as permanent residents. On the other hand, in the words of Palestinian American author Fawaz Turki:

> America is a means to get an education, make a fortune, establish a name, acquire a passport. [Palestinians] do not go to America to become American. . . . I predict that these [Palestinian] children, who grew up American, cut from the same cultural cloth as other American children, will one day return to their roots, to their culture, to the land of their birth. . . .[134]

Summary

Table 2.1 and figure 2.1, which appear at the end of this chapter, supply summary statistics, adapted from UNRWA and other sources, on the estimated number of Palestinians by present location, type of residence, citizenship or lack thereof, and year of displacement. As already noted, these figures are not offered with the guarantee that they are definitive. As this and later chapters demonstrate, comprehensive and accurate demographic information is needed so that a peace settlement can be implemented and also planned for in advance

To avoid more of the age-old, protracted numerical debates, any census that is undertaken should be conducted by a neutral party, such as the Canadian or Norwegian governments, or a nonpartisan research foundation such as FAFO, in a noncoercive environment. Yet in ad-

Table 2.1 Estimated Palestinian Population Breakdown

	I. Total Palestinians	II. Registered UNRWA Refugee	III. In UNRWA Camps	IV. With Citizenship	V. Percent in Camps of Total	VI. 1967 Displaced Persons
West Bank	1,200,000	524,207	133,886	7,500 + Israeli[a] stateless	11%	N/A
Gaza	880,000	700,789	389,035		44%	N/A
Jordan	1,832,000	1,328,768	256,977	1,762,812	14%	696,340
Lebanon	372,700	349,773	186,006	30,000	50%	unknown
Syria	352,100	342,507	96,447	3,452	27%	17,500 plus descendants
Israel	840,000	N/A	N/A	840,000	N/A	N/A
Other Middle East	446,600	N/A	N/A	mostly stateless	N/A	unknown
Non-Middle East	452,400	N/A	N/A	unknown	N/A	unknown
Totals	6,375,800	3,246,044	1,061,351	2,643,764 plus?	17%	713,840 plus ?

[a] Until 1988, when Jordan cut its ties, most West Bank residents had Jordanian citizenship. At least 7,500 East Jerusalem residents have taken Israeli citizenship. This figure is only 5 percent of the total in East Jerusalem but may be growing.
SOURCES: The second and third column figures are from UNRWA General Information Sheet (January 1996). Other columns are author's estimates derived from averaging multiple sources.
N/A = "not applicable."

Figure 2.1.   Distribution of Palestinians in 1991

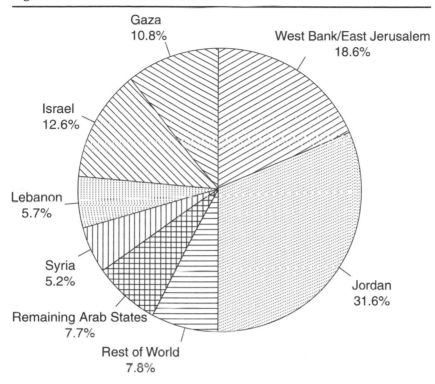

SOURCE: Center for Policy Analysis on Palestine (1992).

vance of a final settlement of all the outstanding negotiation topics, it will be difficult to ascertain the true preferences of refugee families concerning repatriation or resettlement. (Most would be unwilling, at this time, to concede that complete and comprehensive repatriation is not their sole individual or collective objective.) Nevertheless, it would be tragic if the peace process were to be stalled due to the lack of a propitious moment to conduct such a census. As explained more fully in chapter 4, individual Palestinian preferences can be expressed in a post-treaty application process, if it is designed to provide informed consent regarding all available residential choices and compensation packages.

But numbers tell only one part of the story and provide only part of the backdrop to a negotiated resolution to the five-decades-long crisis of the Palestinian refugees. It would be a mistake to assume that predictions as to where individual Palestinians intend to live in the future, or as to who will have the greatest difficulty adapting in residential transitions, can be made entirely on the basis of a rational, cost-benefit analysis. The image of the homeland after three generations of communal life in *ghourba* (exile) is too abstract, too spiritual, to quantify in the manner of an economist or even a demographer. Palestinian identity has been sustained for almost 50 years as a form of deliberate resistance to the abandonment by and hostility of not only their Israeli usurpers but also their Arab brothers and sisters. "Who is a Palestinian refugee?" is now more a matter of ideology and self-identity than geography and demography.

Chapter 3

The International Law Framework

The third set of considerations that forms the foundation for resolution of the refugee issue is that provided by international law. Much scholarly and polemical writing in the last 28 years has raised the question of the international legality of the Israeli occupation, including deportation of Palestinians and creation of Jewish settlements in the West Bank and Gaza.[1] That question, while politically absorbing, is not directly relevant to this inquiry. For instance, if Palestinians are owed compensation for property left behind when they fled in 1948 or 1967, the question is not affected by the legality or illegality of Israeli settlements in the West Bank and Gaza after 1967.[2] Moreover, if Palestinian rights are dependent on the legality of the occupation, then at best only the two million Palestinians living inside the territories—and not the over three million living outside—would be entitled to exercise their right to return and to self-determination there.[3]

It should therefore be obvious to any observer of Middle Eastern affairs that another legal treatise on the subject of the military occupation will not further the cause of reconciliation or facilitate the negotiation of permanent peace. As an Israeli diplomat recently put it: "International law, as applied to the Middle East, has for far too long taken the shape of forensic debates—an exercise that may have provided us lawyers with many hours of professional satisfaction, but was intrinsically sterile."[4]

By contrast, the international law of freedom of movement offers some important definitions and guideposts for resolving the refugee aspects of the peace settlement. After all, it will be through the mechanism of transborder movement—of goods as well as people—that peace will be realized. The legal aspects of return, expulsion and transfer, refugee status, compensation, and nationality and statelessness are particularly relevant. The following text describes both the "hard" international law, the legally binding treaties and the generally and consistently recognized customary norms, and the "soft" law, the less widely accepted principles derived from nonbinding declarations of international organizations, such as the U.N. General Assembly. How-

63

ever, there is sufficient ambiguity even in the "hard" law terminology so as to conclude that existing international law will not by itself resolve all conflicts between the parties. New norms of international law will inevitably be made in the course of the Arab-Israeli peace process, norms that will then be available to help settle future conflicts, both in the same region and elsewhere.[5]

The Concept of "Return"

So much of the rhetoric surrounding the Arab-Israeli conflict has centered on the apparent "right of return" of the Palestinian refugees that the concept calls for close examination. In fact, whether there is a right to return in international law is a question with a rather ambiguous and inchoate answer. The Universal Declaration of Human Rights, adopted by the U.N. General Assembly just one year after the same body adopted the plan to partition Palestine into a Jewish state and an Arab state, provides: "Everyone has the right to leave any country, including his own, and to return to his country."[6] But what if, at the time of initial departure, one's own country did not exist? And could one's descendants, who had never themselves lived in it, "return" a few generations later? It is not certain that the drafters had considered these questions, or that they had intended the provision to cover the mass movement of refugees as opposed to the travel rights of individuals under "normal" conditions.

The Universal Declaration language was later modified in its treaty form in the International Covenant on Civil and Political Rights, to read: "No one shall be arbitrarily deprived of the right to enter his own country."[7] While avoiding the more restrictive term "return," which would seemingly require an initial presence and then a departure, this formulation retains the ambiguous language about one's "own country." Because contested repatriations are so rare, this provision has never formally been implemented or subjected to definitive construction. The word "arbitrary" in this context has been said to prohibit illegal and discriminatory denials, such as denials on the grounds of race, religion, or nationality. But it also implies that in certain circumstances there can be lawful and nonarbitrary deprivations of the right to return, such as those based on national security and public order.[8] Moreover, wouldn't this nondiscrimination principle protect only those minorities whose country it is in the first place, that is, citizens?

Perhaps the phrase "one's own country" should be interpreted liberally, to include a homeland with which one has ancestral, religious, and cultural if not geographical and political ties.[9] After all, international law does require that human rights treaties be interpreted in their fundamentally humanistic rather than technical connotation. And such a broad conception of "homeland" is the policy behind Israel's Law of Return, which allows any Jew, without regard to prior residence, to become a citizen upon immigrating.[10] But this version of "return" is a self-proclaimed right, not strictly a principle of international law. If the Israelis have proclaimed it, why cannot another people, such as the Palestinians? If every Jew can return to Israel, why cannot every Palestinian return to Palestine?

Nonetheless, in its most widely accepted meaning, international law can be said to provide only a right to enter a preexisting country on the part of an individual whose country it always was. This is a far cry from authorizing a collective return to specific homes or land in the State of Israel on the part of non-Israelis. It may be reflective of the general perplexity of this issue that of the three regional human rights treaties, the European, the Inter-American, and the African, only the latter provides a right to return, which can be restricted on national security and other grounds.[11]

In the particular context of Palestinians, the most relevant evidence of "soft" law is the much-cited U.N. General Assembly Resolution 194(III), adopted on December 11, 1948, one day after the Universal Declaration of Human Rights. Resolution 194 created the Conciliation Commission for Palestine, which was authorized to assist in achieving "a final settlement of all questions outstanding between" the various parties, including economic development, the Holy Places, and the administration of Jerusalem.[12] The resolution is best known for its paragraph 11, which, as already noted, resolved:

> that the refugees wishing to return to their homes and live at peace with their neighbors should be permitted to do so at the earliest practicable date, and that compensation should be paid for the property of those choosing not to return and for loss of or damage to property which, under principles of international law or in equity, should be made good by the Governments or authorities responsible.

A second subparagraph of 11 gave related instructions to the commission, including the facilitation of refugee "repatriation, resettlement and economic and social rehabilitation," terms that contemplate absorption in third states as well as in Israel.[13] Unlike the "hard" treaty law on return, Resolution 194 does refer specifically to "homes" and to loss of property.

As some Israeli commentators are wont to point out, however, nowhere does the paragraph use the word "right" in relation to "return." In fact, the term "should"—as opposed to the mandatory "shall"—connotes at most a moral but less than a legal obligation. Moreover, the term "refugee" is not limited to "Palestinians" and therefore, with the reference to multiple "Governments or authorities," might include Jewish refugees from Arab states, as well. (Israelis often note that well-known Security Council Resolution 242 similarly refers generically to "refugees" and uses the phrase "a just settlement" rather than the legal term, "right.")[14] Perhaps most significantly for purposes of the Middle East peace process, paragraph 11 attaches the modifying phrase, "and live at peace with their neighbors," to the qualifications of those who would be permitted to "return to their homes."[15]

Over the decades, hard-line Palestinian commentators have based the right of Palestinian return not on Resolution 194 but on both the alleged illegality of the creation of the State of Israel and the existence of three presumptively uncontested facts: the distinctive historical traditions, cultural traits, and genetic lineage of the Palestinian people; the geographic and historic tie of Palestinians to the whole of the land in question; and their attempt to exercise their right to self-determination there.[16] This view implied the literal replacement of Israelis with Palestinians, either through transfer or annihilation, as described in chapter 1. The more moderate and contemporary Palestinian view places Palestinian return in a more accommodationist, less rejectionist context: it recognizes Israel's right to exist within its pre-1967 borders and accepts the possibility that religious minorities—presumably Jews—might remain within the future sovereign territory of Palestine.[17]

Given all its caveats, not to mention Resolution 194's implicit recognition of Israel's right to exist, it is understandable why Arab states initially rejected the resolution and why, for a brief time in 1949, Israel accepted it.[18] Nevertheless, the General Assembly has reafffirmed Resolution 194 virtually every year (usually over Israeli and U.S. objections, occasionally employing the additional words "right" and "self-determination").[19] Given the ambiguity of the "hard" law on the question of return, the resolution remains the one international articulation that is most specific and most relevant to the question of Palestinian refugee return.

Where does all this jurisprudential commentary leave the question of Palestinian return to within the 1967 borders of Israel? Apparently, not with much of a solid legal justification. If Israel were to admit any number of refugees—such as the 75,000 that are proposed in chapter 4—it would do so as a matter of sovereign discretion, not by international legal obligation. Moreover, because it has the right under international law to protect its national security and public order, Israel could limit the maximum number and select which individual refugees it would admit, on which particular basis (for instance, family reunification), and over what particular frame of time. If Palestinians have the *right* to return to anywhere, it would only be to a sovereign state of Palestine, wherever that will someday be established. That is why establishment of a Palestinian state in the West Bank and Gaza is so central to a fair and pragmatic resolution of the refugee problem.

Mass Expulsion and Transfer

The inverse of the right to return is the right not to be expelled against one's will. International law permits the deportation of individual aliens only in very limited circumstances, such as for serious crimes or violation of immigration regulations, temporary military necessity, or endangering the national security, public health, or public order. Due process must always be provided to those expelled.[20] By contrast, the expulsion of masses of aliens is absolutely prohibited by international law. The 1945 Nuremberg Charter made wartime mass deportation a crime against humanity, and the 1949 Geneva Convention Relative to the Treatment of Civilians in Time of War also prohibits deportations and forcible transfers, mass or individual.[21] Although no international treaty expressly prohibits mass expulsion of civilian populations in peacetime, scholarly opinion and regional human rights treaties covering Europe and Africa clearly indicate that the principle is widely accepted.[22]

Despite the prohibition, recent human history is replete with examples of expulsion, from the forceful ejection of Asians from Uganda in 1970 through the expulsion of illegal immigrants from Nigeria in 1983 and 1985 right up to this decade's "ethnic cleansing" of the former Yugoslavia and Rwanda. Examples in the Middle East include the Iraqi expulsions of Iranians in 1979 and its own Kurdish citizens in 1991, or as described in chapter 2, the Kuwaiti expulsion of close to 350,000 Palestinians during the Persian Gulf War. On the latter action, a Palestinian has commented:

> You can call it deportation, you can even describe it as population transfer. But I call it the third catastrophe after 1948 and 1967. Imagine what would happen if Israel deported 300,000 people. The whole world would be up in arms. But when an Arab deports or kills his Arab brother, it's all right, nothing happens.[23]

Not all of history's expulsions have been unilateral, however. Bilateral "transfer" and "protection agreements," such as those between Greece and Turkey and between Greece and Bulgaria after World War I, as well as the New Delhi Accord between India and Pakistan after

World War II, were negotiated in order to return ethnic minorities to majority population states. International law permits such multilateral transfers only if they are conducted in an orderly and humane fashion, if compensation is offered for abandoned property, and if they are truly voluntary, that is, if the transferees are given the individualized option to remain on their native soil and no direct or indirect force is involved.[24]

Within the context of the Arab-Israeli conflict, extremists on all sides have called at times for "transfer," "relocation," "liberation," and other euphemisms for expulsion. While it is conceivable that the parties to a settlement might negotiate an orderly, humane, and voluntary "transfer" or "protection agreement" that might, for instance, exchange Palestinians for Jewish settlers in the West Bank and Gaza, a settlement that is consistent with human rights norms would have to contemplate the possibility that significant minority populations might choose to remain on each side of the international borders. (Guidelines for the treatment of such minority populations are discussed more fully in chapter 5.)

Another group that must be freely granted the option whether to leave or to remain is the community of Palestinians living predominately as noncitizen refugees in Lebanon, where government leaders have on occasion announced the intention to expel them.[25] The rationale often given by Lebanese officials, that due to its history of civil strife the state needs to "maintain its delicate sectarian balance" between Muslims and Christians, is not one sanctioned by international law. Moreover, states such as Libya, which in September 1995 expelled hundreds of Palestinians as punishment for their leaders' making peace with Israel, should be censured for violating the prohibition on expulsion.[26]

The Concept of "Refugee"

In ordinary discourse, the word "refugee" has a rather broad meaning, referring to someone fleeing from intolerable conditions. Where a refugee is presently located, where she intends to go, and the particular reasons for her flight, do not usually matter in common usage.[27] We tend to consider as refugees anyone fleeing natural disasters, severe economic distress, or international or civil war zones, as well as those fleeing political and racial persecution.

The definition of "refugee" under international law, by contrast, is much more technical. To qualify for that designation and for the international protection afforded to such individuals, a person must satisfy four conditions established by the 1951 Convention Relating to the Status of Refugees: (1) she must be outside her country of nationalilty or her country of "former habitual residence"; (2) she must be unwilling or unable to avail herself of the protection of that country; (3) her un-willingness or inability must be attributable to a "well-founded fear of persecution"; and (4) the persecution must be individualized and based on reasons of race, religion, nationality, membership in a particular so-cial group, or political opinion.[28] "Persecution" in this context usually means "a deliberate act of the government against individuals, and thus excludes victims of general insecurity and oppression or systemic economic deprivation."[29] Victims of war and armed conflict are not considered refugees under this definition *"unless* they are subject to differential victimization based on civil or political status."[30]

International and national agencies, such as the United Nations High Commissioner for Refugees (UNHCR) and the U.S. Immigration and Naturalization Service, which administer this de jure or "convention" definition, must make determinations as to each of these four criteria for each individual applying for refugee status. Therefore, in most parts of the world, persons fleeing war zones or natural or economic disasters are not, under international law, classified as refugees.[31] They are some-times referred to as de facto or "humanitarian" refugees, as opposed to de jure or "convention" refugees. If they have not crossed the borders of their country, they are known as "internally displaced persons."

Under this technical juridical definition, most Palestinians—includ-ing those who fled Palestine in 1948—are not refugees because they can-not meet all four criteria. First, in the West Bank and Gaza, Palestinians may not be "outside" their country of origin or, more broadly, their for-mer habitual residence, depending on how either Israel's or Palestine's borders are delineated. Second, they may be unable, due to Israeli law and policy, to avail themselves of Israel's protection, but they are *not un-willing* to return there. Indeed, Palestinians are unique among refugees "in their desire to return to their country of origin while the general po-litical conditions that caused them to become refugees persist."[32] Third, they may be unable to show that they had a "well-founded fear of per-secution" on account of their being Palestinian if they had fled because it was a war zone, particularly if they left voluntarily or due to encour-agement. Fourth, even if they can prove their flight was due to fear of massacre by Israeli military forces, it would be difficult to prove they feared individualized persecution when thousands of other Palestinians remained to become Israeli citizens.

However, these criteria are not dispositive because UNRWA has its own operational definition of who is a Palestinian refugee: a person

whose normal place of residence was Palestine during the period 1 June 1946 to 15 May 1948 [that is, for two years preceding the outbreak of the conflict in 1948] and who lost both his home and means of livelihood as a result of the 1948 conflict, and took refuge in 1948 in one of the five countries or areas where UNRWA provides relief. Refugees within this definition and their direct descendants are eligible for UNRWA assistance if they are: registered with UNRWA; living in the areas of UNRWA operations; and in need . . ."[33]

Due to long-term usage by UNRWA and through numerous U.N. General Assembly references to "Palestinian refugees," this definition has come to have a legitimacy of its own. It is thus considered a special category of refugee, for Palestinians who would otherwise not meet the convention definition.

It must be noted, however, that under international law, refugee status is not accorded to persons who have committed crimes against peace, war crimes, crimes against humanity, serious nonpolitical crimes outside the country of refuge, or acts contrary to the purposes and principles of the United Nation, such as persecution or other human rights violations.[34] It has never been determined whether this exclusion from the convention definition of refugee applies to Palestinians who otherwise qualify under the UNRWA definition. Whether terrorism is a political or nonpolitical crime, moreover, is a question not likely to be resolved easily, although Israel can make a strong case that national security reasons justify denial of a terrorist's right to return. In other situations, such as in Pakistan and Somalia, governments have objected to the extension of UNHCR resources to persons who have served as "instruments or aggression and disruption," but the international community as a whole has not disapproved.[35]

A reasonable interpretation is that the exclusion would apply to individual Palestinians but was not intended to apply as a blanket restriction for all persons who may have cooperated with invading Arab armies in 1948 by fleeing the area. Thus, only those Palestinians who themselves engaged in unlawful acts, such as war crimes or terrorism, could be denied the benefits of refugee status, such as compensation for lost property or the ability to return to their original homes. Just as return is an individual rather than a collective right, limitations on the right to return can be applied only on a case-by-case basis.

Persons who are granted de jure refugee status are entitled to certain rights enumerated in the 1951 convention. The most significant is the right to *non-refoulement*, that is, not to be expelled or in any other manner returned (*refouler*) to the frontiers of territories where their life or freedom would be threatened on account of race, religion, nationality, membership in a particular social group, or political opinion. Other rights include access to courts, to freedom of movement within the country, to own movable and immovable property, and to housing, association, public education, and employment.[36] Refugees are also entitled to documents, valid for one to two years, that permit them to travel outside the territory of asylum and return to the country of issue. All state parties to the convention must recognize such refugee travel documents.[37]

In most of its rights provisions, the convention establishes a standard of treatment "as favorable as is accorded to nationals" of the country, or "the most favorable treatment accorded to nationals of a foreign country in the same circumstance." The right to public education is an example of the former, employment of the latter. As noted in chapter 2, Palestinians do not have the right to work, to own property, or to public education in some of their host countries, notably Lebanon. Jordan, Syria, and Lebanon, the three Arab states where UNRWA operates, have not ratified the 1951 Refugee Convention or its 1967 protocol. (Nor, for that matter, has Kuwait, where many Palestinians lived before 1991.) In fact, in the Middle East and North Africa, only Algeria, Egypt, Israel, Morocco, Tunisia, and Yemen are parties to either treaty.[38]

The Right to Compensation

Although it has rarely if ever been addressed, let alone exercised in the context of mass population relocations, the right of refugees to receive adequate compensation for property left behind is a basic principle of customary international law. It derives from three even more established and fundamental principles: first, that states are responsible for injuries caused by acts within their control; second, that remedies are required for any deprivation of rights; and third, that the adequacy of compensation is determined by its purpose, which is to restore the claimant to the position enjoyed before the deprivation occurred.[39] Thus, the obligation to pay compensation is owed—by the state that caused its citizens to become refugees—to those refugees who do not otherwise have their preflight status restored through voluntary repatriation.[40] The kinds of property for which reparation is due can include real and personal property confiscated by either the state or private individuals, as well as both movable and immovable property that has been destroyed.

While the compensation principle is usually thought to apply only to de jure or "convention refugees"—that is, those persons who have been persecuted individually rather than to masses fleeing war or economic disaster—the U.N. General Assembly has historically identified compensation as integral to conciliation of "the situation in Palestine." Renowned paragraph 11 of Resolution 194 of December 11, 1948, had resolved that "compensation should be paid for the property of those choosing not to return and for loss of or damage to property which, under principles of international law or equity, should be made good by the Governments or authorities responsible."[41] It then instructed the Conciliation Commission to, among other tasks, facilitate payment of compensation. The General Assembly has reiterated the principle of compensation numerous times, not only in the specific context of Palestinian refugees but in the more general context, as well.[42] Moreover, as the UNRWA definition of Palestinian refugee, quoted earlier, turns on the loss of "homes and means of livelihood" as a result of the 1948 conflict, it is logical to infer that compensation was intended to replace the value of lost homes and income-producing property.

Although Israel has on occasion stated its willingness to pay compensation for real property left behind by the refugees (conditioned on Palestinian resettlement in neighboring states), the offer has been criticized as a backhanded method of legitimizing the land seizures.[43] Moreover, Arab governments and Palestinian economists never accepted the Conciliation Commission's estimate of the total value of Palestinian property for which compensation was due.[44] The commission determined that over 80 percent of Israel's territory after the 1948 war represented abandoned Arab land. While three-quarters of it was semidesert or otherwise not cultivable, a significant portion of former Arab land proved valuable in the growth of the young state. For instance, of the 370 new Jewish settlements created in the first five years of Israel's existence, 350 were on the site of former Arab villages. Moreover, at least a third of Jewish immigrants in those years, who themselves were predominantly refugees from Nazi Europe or Arab states, were housed in both urban and rural areas abandoned in 1948 by Palestinians.[45] According to Don Peretz, an American specialist on the subject of Palestinian refugees, "[i]t is questionable whether Israel would have been able to bring in so many new immigrants so rapidly [in the years 1948 to 1953] had it not taken over and used abandoned Arab property."[46]

While mere de facto refugee status is thus not a barrier to compensation for Palestinians who left property behind when they fled in 1948 and/or 1967, another complication arises in reference to compensation for Palestinians: Who should be responsible for paying? The obligation to compensate is said to rest "upon the countries that directly or indirectly *force their own citizens* to flee and/or remain abroad as refugees."[47] Just as the formulation "return to . . . one's own country" poses problems for those whose "own country" did not exist at the time of flight, if the Palestinians who fled in 1948 and 1967 were not citizens of the country that forced them to flee, then technically, no country owes them compensation.

More notably, compensation is contingent on causation. This again raises the endlessly contested historical question as to why approximately 720,000 Palestinians fled Israel in 1948: voluntarily, because Arab states wanted temporarily to clear the area before annihilating its Jews, or forcibly, as part of a Zionist plan to alter the population balance? Due to fear of being massacred, or to facilitate the massacre of others? Significantly, paragraph 11 of Resolution 194 refers in the plural to payment "by the Governments or authorities responsible," rather than singling out Israel.

In 1957, Dr. Elfan Rees, an advisor on refugees for the World Council of Churches, had this to say about resolving the compensation claims of the Palestinians:

> I believe there is a three-fold debt owing to these refugees. There is the debt owed to them by the State of Israel, there is the debt owed to them by the international community, and I think it is not unfair to say that there is a debt owed to them by the Arab States themselves . . . the debt that men of the same language, the same faith, the same social organization should at any time in history feel due from them to their fellows in distress, the debt which in simple terms would involve regarding these people as human beings and not as political footballs.[48]

Rees also expressed hope that the international community would bear its share in contributing to a fund that would clearly be beyond the financial capabilities of Israel by itself.

Like the concepts of "return" and "refugee," the legal principle of compensation is conducive to resolution of the Palestinian refugee question only to the extent that it is not used to relitigate old battles, to reopen old wounds, and to allocate unilateral blame. Compensation should be made available to facilitate acceptance by individual Palestinians of the reality that they will not all be able to return to their original homes. The compensation aspects of a plan to absorb the refugees permanently are outlined more fully in the next chapter.

Nationality, Passports, and Statelessness

A final topic of relevance to the international legal status of Palestinian refugees is citizenship (usually referred to as "nationality" in international law contexts) and its inverse, statelessness. As described in chapter 2, of all the Arab "host states" where Palestinians reside, only Jordan has granted them citizenship on a wide scale. In addition to the Palestinians who are citizens of Israel and an unknown number in some Western states, only small numbers of Palestinians are citizens of

Lebanon, Egypt, and Syria. Moreover, the status of those West Bank Palestinians now holding two-year Jordanian travel documents is unclear, but it is something less than full citizenship. With a worldwide population of 6.3 million, over half of whom are stateless, Palestinians surely constitute the world's largest concentration of stateless persons. They are thus rightfully concerned that any final peace settlement include the comprehensive granting of citizenship.

In the Middle East, statelessness is not a problem only for Palestinians but also for others in Syria, Lebanon, Bahrain, and, in particular, Kuwait. Yet the right to a nationality, to change one's nationality, and not to be arbitrarily deprived of one's nationality are all fundamental principles of international law, pursuant to Article 15 of the 1948 Universal Declaration of Human Rights. In general, public international law does not prescribe how nationality is to be acquired or who is a national of particular states, because these are primarily issues of domestic jurisdiction. However, it does set limits on the involuntary termination of nationality, requiring that a state's rules be reasonable and not invidiously discriminatory. For instance, states are forbidden to discriminate on racial or ethnic grounds in the enjoyment of the right to nationality.[49]

States have traditionally recognized two involuntary methods of acquiring citizenship that operate by force of law at the time of birth: *jus soli*, which confers the nationality of the state where a child is born, regardless of her parents' nationality; and *jus sanguinis*, which confers the nationality of a child's parents, regardless of where she is born. The former was the traditional process in common law countries, the latter the customary method in civil law countries. Presently, a large and increasing number of states, including England, France, and the United States, apply combinations of *jus soli* and *jus sanguinis* principles; for instance, in France, citizenship is acquired automatically at age 18 by all children born in France of foreign parents, so long as they have resided there for five years and have no criminal record. On the other hand, Germany still adheres exclusively to *jus sanguinis*, conferring citizenship (upon immigration) on ethnic Germans born outside the country, but denying the same to even the German-born children and grandchildren of Turks, Greeks, Spaniards, and other guest workers.[50] Most Muslim states determine nationality on a patrilineal *jus sanguinis* basis, that is, only if the father—but not if only the mother—is a national.[51] Thus, only where a Palestinian woman has married a national of, for instance, Syria would her children be considered Syrian nationals, even if they had been born there.

A third form of acquisition of citizenship is by naturalization, initiated by a voluntary act on the part of the individual, such as marriage or a declaration of intent. It can be discretionary, granted only on a case-by-case basis by the state, or by right, in which the state is obliged to grant it to those who meet particular conditions established by legislation. Naturalization is essential to any society that seeks to integrate immigrants and refugees within the first generation of their arrival. Indeed, "obstructing the laws for naturalization of foreigners" was one of the grievances that the American revolutionaries addressed to King George III in the 1776 Declaration of Independence. In the well-known case of Nottebohm (Liechtenstein v. Guatemala), the International Court of Justice held that in the context of diplomatic protection, naturalized citizens must have a dominant or "genuine and effective" connecting link with the state of nationality, usually demonstrated, at a minimum, by continuity of domicile there.[52] Traditional Islamic law has a similar rule for naturalization of Muslims in the yet to be achieved ideal Islamic state.[53] Two other traditional methods of granting citizenship, by territorial annexation (usually in military subjugations) and territorial cession (usually by peace treaty), are no longer considered compatible with the status of international relations.[54]

Perhaps the most basic principle of the traditional theory of sovereign statehood was that states are the sole subjects of international law and individuals are its objects. Accordingly, an individual could exercise her international rights and duties only through and at the discretion of her state of nationality. As a corollary of this doctrine, it was assumed that an individual could have only one nationality and owe allegiance to only one sovereign.[55] Although today most countries that reject dual citizenship do so more for practical than conceptual reasons,[56] many countries such as France, Italy, Greece, Canada, the United States,[57] and the United Kingdom in fact recognize it and do not require dual nationals to elect one nationality over another unless there is a direct conflict in allegiance. Under English law, for instance, a dual national is not considered to be "half one nationality and half another" but two complete nationalities; the coexistence of British and enemy alien nationality is even possible.[58]

While Latin American countries often enter into bilateral treaties that encourage dual nationality, before the dissolution of the Soviet Union, many East European states were parties to agreements intended to eliminate dual citizenship cases. Armenia, among other former Soviet republics, explicitly refuses to recognize dual nationality. However, one of the United Nations' conditions for the recognition of Bosnian sovereignty in 1992 was, in fact, that dual citizenship be permitted within the new state's constitutional structure.[59] In general, it is fair to state that the number of people who are dual (or even plural) citizens is increasing and will undoubtedly continue to grow.

Dual citizenship, as a Palestinian and, for instance, a Syrian or Jordanian or, for that matter, an Israeli, would be a sensible solution to the problem of Palestinians who are unable to live in a future state of Palestine. In addition to acquiring dual nationality at birth (caused by the simultaneous operation of *jus soli* and *jus sanguinis* principles), individuals can obtain a second nationality by marriage, by naturalization, and by other means, including the transfer of sovereignty.[60] Among other rights, dual nationals may legally possess passports issued by both countries, and use of either one does not divest them of nationality in the other state.

However, Muslim-majority states have traditionally looked askance at the notion of dual citizenship, particularly between two Muslim states. For instance, Libya's 1951 Constitution explicitly forbade anyone from simultaneously holding Libyan nationality and another nationality, while both Egypt and Turkey have objected to the acquisition of American citizenship by their own citizens without the consent of the Egyptian or Turkish governments.[61] Although King Hussein has proposed that Arab states grant dual citizenship to Palestinians, to share the burden of supporting unemployed refugees, Jordan has traditionally allowed its citizens to hold simultaneously only American citizenship but not, for instance, Syrian.[62] This situation does not bode well for the possibility of dual Palestinian and other Arab state citizenship, which Palestinians have recently been proposing.

The main reason that international law regulates, if only to a limited extent, the law of nationality, is to avoid—or at least to reduce—widespread statelessness, the condition in which a person is not considered a national of any state. "To avoid citizenship vacuums, international standards have been developed that impose an obligation on states to grant citizenship to stateless people who are not recognized as citizens of any other state."[63] Article 1 of the 1961 Convention on the Reduction of Statelessness provides that a state "shall grant its nationality to a person born in its territory who would otherwise be stateless." Both the Convention on the Rights of the Child[64] and the International Covenant on Civil and Political Rights require that every child have the right to acquire a nationality, regardless of whether her parents have a nationality. Indeed, in 1949, only one year after the Arab-Israeli war, the U.N. Economic and Social Council called for universal acceptance of the principle that everyone should acquire a nationality at birth and that no person should lose it unless she has acquired a new one.[65] Like the 1951 Refugee Convention, these treaties and resolutions attempt to encourage states to facilitate the integration and naturalization of nonnationals on their soil.

While being stateless precludes a person from invoking diplomatic protection, traditionally the chief means by which individuals exercise rights in international law, it does not mean that the person has no rights. The 1954 Convention on the Status of Stateless Persons provides stateless persons with special protection from expulsion and free access to courts, employment, housing, public education, and social security.[66] International law also provides that stateless persons be accorded rights similar to those accorded refugees, such as liberty and security of the person and freedom of speech, religion, and association. As already noted, few of the Arab states where Palestinians reside have ratified either the 1951 Refugee Convention or the various treaties on statelessness. Nevertheless, to the extent that these rights reflect the norms of customary international law, it is obvious that Lebanon, Kuwait, Libya, and possibly other such states have been in egregious violation of the rights of Palestinians.

Perhaps the most important privilege of citizenship is the international passport, which allows people to exercise the fundamental right to leave their country—and to return to it—as well as to travel easily between countries, not only for pleasure trips but for employment opportunities, as well. Between 1924, when their Ottoman nationality lapsed under the Treaty of Lausanne, and 1948, when the British Mandate ended, many Palestinians held passports issued by the High Commissioner for Palestine that were titled "British Passport, Palestine." Under the League of Nations Covenant, "A" level mandates such as Palestine (as well as Iraq, Lebanon, Syria, and Transjordan) were to have their own nationalities; thus, holders of these documents were not considered British subjects but "citizens of Palestine" who were accorded British diplomatic and consular protections when outside Palestine. But because the state of Palestine was not created when the mandate ended, the status lapsed, as did the privileges attached to the passport.[67]

Although the Arab League's own 1945 charter speaks of cooperation between its member states in the field of passports and visas, it was not until 1952, four years after hundreds of thousands of Palestinians became refugees, that the league addressed the need for a standard passport to facilitate refugee travel. "Such a document was not to be viewed as an acceptance of the political status quo nor was it intended to diminish in any way the refugees' separate identity or rights as Palestinians."[68] Nevertheless, even after three subsequent league resolutions (which are nonbinding) calling on host governments and other Arab states to issue travel papers to Palestinian refugees, this appeal was largely ignored. According to Brand:

> No country wanted to be perceived as accepting the status quo and no country but Jordan had any desire to lay the groundwork for the permanent incorporation of the Palestinians. Probably just as important, none of the people involved in the decision-making process had any first-hand experience or were concerned about what it meant in practice—in terms of travel, residence, educational and employment opportunities, access to health care and the like on a daily basis—to be a stateless Palestinian.[69]

No uniform travel document was ever created for the refugees. Moreover, although the Arab League urged its member states to allow separated Palestinian families to reunite in the country where the family head resided, it explicitly decreed that its members not grant citizenship to Palestinian refugees, so as not to preempt their claim to Palestinian nationality.[70]

Instead, due to a mélange of regulations in different states, the travel documents that most Palestinian refugees do possess vary greatly according to their place of refuge, the date they arrived there, their marital status, their wealth and general ability to "purchase" citizenship (or merely to show a monetary reserve necessary for a transit pass), whether they renewed their documents on time or not, and other conditions. Many of these documents fail to provide even the right to live in or reenter the country where the Palestinian was born if the document expires while she is outside its country of issuance—regardless of whether she has the right to reside anywhere else. Moreover, many Arab states refuse to grant entry visas to Palestinians unless their travel documents indicate they have permission to return to the state that issued it.[71] Thus, it is not only Israel that has placed deliberate limits on the freedom of travel of Palestinians.

At the end of 1995, the Ministry of the Interior of the Palestinian Authority had begun issuing Palestinian passports to residents of the West Bank and Gaza that at least 41 countries, including Israel, the United States, Jordan, China, Egypt, Canada, Norway, Brazil, South Africa, Russia, and the United Kingdom, had agreed to recognize.[72] Eventually, if these or similar documents are issued to Palestinians living outside the West Bank and Gaza, they will serve not only as a symbol of Palestinian national identity but also as a document permitting travel in and out of the territory of Palestine, creating conditions analogous to that of diaspora Jews who travel to and from Israel.

Summary

The message of this chapter is best summed up by international legal scholar Antonio Cassese, who serves as president of the International Tribunal for the prosecution of war crimes in the former Yugoslavia:

Admittedly, the "response" of international law to complex problems such as the one under discussion is unsatisfactory. On the other hand, one cannot demand from legal standards more than they can realistically offer: a set of general guidelines that must be pragmatically and realistically applied by all the parties concerned, taking into account—in the case at issue—not only the wishes of the population concerned but also the host of non-legal problems that beset Arab-Israeli relations.[73]

While legal disputes over the various treaties, resolutions, and other texts ostensibly relevant to the Arab-Israeli conflict will undoubtedly continue, at least they provide a general framework for facilitating a permanent peace agreement, namely, the need to balance individual rights to freedom of movement with realistic limitations for public order and security. Step one, laying out the legal principles and standards that should apply to the status and treatment of Palestinian refugees, is close to completion. Step two, implementing and ensuring compliance with those principles, has hardly even commenced.

PART II

PRESENT AND FUTURE

Chapter 4

From Refugees to Citizens

This chapter outlines the basic components of a plan for permanent regional absorption of Palestinian refugees that is intended to result in a mutually agreeable division of responsibilities among all of the parties to the peace process. It is offered as a proposal, not a formal blueprint, so that participants in the negotiations can borrow some parts, reject other parts, improve on those for which future fact-finding may shed more light, and be prompted to generate other possible solutions. Chapter 5 elaborates on some of the major components of the plan by examining similar efforts in other countries or regions of the world and suggesting relevant legal standards to facilitate implementation within the Middle East.

The plan develops from the assumption that because the conflict is regional, the solution must be regional. Accordingly, it can best be worked out within the context of the multilateral rather than the bilateral negotiation process (even if, like most of the post-Oslo agreements, it is initiated in bilateral discussions).[1] The collective approach is more suitable because it recognizes that refugees are not merely individuals residing in isolated enclaves but also members of a regional community that transcends national borders. Because of its roots in the post–World War II era, much of the preexisting framework for resolving refugee crises has been grounded in the ideology of individualism.[2] Yet a postmodern refugee framework appropriate to the 1990s and the 21st century requires a collective perspective: a mutually satisfactory solution to a jointly shared, regional problem.

No plan to resolve the refugee question will work without a comprehensive, viable, and bona fide peace that can be carried out in good faith. Realistically, Syria, Lebanon, Israel, and other states are not likely to grant citizenship to Palestinian refugees unless such a commitment is preceded by, or offered concomitant with, a final settlement of the entire Arab-Israeli conflict. But that only proves that the refugee question is ultimately inseparable from the underlying cause of the decades-long conflict: the failure to accept the reality that Israelis and Palestinians, Arabs and Jews, live together in the same neighborhood. Thus, only when the burdens and benefits of peace are distributed in a regionally balanced fashion will all the parties be willing to come on board.

Components of the Plan

A common denominator of the plan's basic components is the underlying premise that only through the granting of citizenship to Palestinians, wherever they will eventually reside, both within and without the Middle East, will a permanent and viable solution to the Arab-Israeli conflict be achieved. The international refugee regime has traditionally posited three "durable solutions" to the global refugee crisis, each of which is a form of permanent absorption. In descending order of generally accepted preference, they consist of *repatriation*, or voluntary return to the country of national origin or state from which the refugees fled; permanent *integration* in the locale of asylum; and *resettlement* in a third country that has agreed to take them. Given the nature of most refugee flows and of global conditions, the first two solutions have rarely been achieved. Voluntary repatriation has been unlikely when refugees are unwilling to reexperience the persecution that caused their flight originally. Moreover, asylum countries, which are usually contiguous to the country of origin, are often too poor and unstable themselves to absorb a large new population. And given the reluctance on the part of wealthier, more stable states to absorb poor and racially or culturally divergent masses, even resettlement is becoming less viable an option.[3]

All three of these obstacles have, until recently, been reflected in the Palestinian refugee crisis. Comprehensive repatriation, although desired by the Palestinians, was impossible while the ongoing "cause" of their flight—the fact that Israel existed on the land that was considered to be Palestine and refused to recognize Palestinians as a distinct people—continued. Moreover, the neighboring countries of the Palestinians' asylum were either too poor (Jordan), too unstable (Lebanon), or too anxious to use the refugees as political pawns in a long-term regional conflict (Syria). Although the Palestinians were not so culturally divergent from the peoples of the wealthier, more stable Arab states (Kuwait and Saudia Arabia, for example), these countries also followed the "pawn strategy," refusing to absorb the refugees because, as they refused to recognize the reality of Israel, they insisted that full repatriation—as the sequel to Israel's destruction—was the only possible resolution.[4] Yet even as early as 1950, the U.N. General Assembly was recommending that either "repatriation *or resettlement*" be employed as a means of absorbing Palestinian refugees "into the economic life of the Near East."[5]

The Madrid and Oslo frameworks have altered all these barriers, because Israel's right to exist has now been acknowledged by all the participants, including the Palestine National Council, and Israel has likewise acknowledged the Palestinians to be a people. Therefore, while no one of the three durable solutions is viable or realistic in itself, it is possible to devise a strategy that uses all three in as balanced a manner as is feasible and fair. To paraphrase the late U.N. Secretary-General Dag Hammarskjold, such a strategy would treat the Palestinian refugee question not as a regional liability but as a net, and mutual, regional asset.[6] Each party to the Arab-Israeli conflict, whether it be Israel, the Palestinians, the neighboring asylum countries, or the wider group of Middle Eastern states, will lose a little and gain a little more, which can add up to a regional boon in economic development and political maturity.

The plan consists of four structural components:

- *Absorption Targets*. Each of the Middle Eastern parties participating in the final peace treaty negotiations—which will include Israel, the Palestinian Authority, Jordan, Egypt, and, it is hoped, Syria, Lebanon, and other Arab states, as well as any Western states that offer to participate—will absorb an optimal ("target") number of refugee families that will not be demographically, politically, or economically disruptive to it or to neighboring states.[7] This caveat is particularly important in the West Bank and Gaza, the stability of which would be undermined by an overly rapid flood of immigrants. The refugees will be absorbed on a gradual basis over a seven-year period commencing after the final peace treaty is adopted, which is supposed to be no later than May 1999. (Specific target figures are proposed and explained in the next section and in table 4.1.) During this necessary transitional period, in which the refugees will move in gradual waves rather than in one large-scale rush, housing, jobs, and infrastructure can be readied and disorder avoided.

  After the seven-year period is over, population changes will occur naturally, within the standard of "normalcy" that the peace settlement strives for. In other words, no attempt will be made to destabilize a neighboring state by drastically altering one's own population, nor to attack the legitimacy of a neighbor's immigration or other demographic policy, especially given that both Israelis and Palestinians will continue to conceive of their territories as places of refuge for their respective peoples.[8]

- *Choice, Compensation, and Palestinian Passports*. All refugees will be offered a fully informed, written choice of available residential and compensation options, including absorption in a state in the region, return to the Palestinian territory (regardless of its legal status) in the West Bank and Gaza, or, if qualified (according to criteria to be described), return to their ancestral home in Israel. Each family will, in writing, rank its residential preferences. In accordance with international law norms, no one will be forced to reside anywhere against her will.[9] As Dag Hammarskjold noted in 1959: "No reintegration would be satisfactory, or even possible, were it to be brought about by forcing people into their new positions against their will. It must be freely accepted, if it is to yield lasting results in the form of economic and political stability."[10]

In addition to receipt of compensation (either in the form of a "reintegration allowance" or real property, as will be outlined) for those who are eligible but who do not return to Israel, all Palestinians, no matter where they reside, will be offered a Palestinian passport that will declare their Palestinian nationality and enable them to visit and/or work in the West Bank and Gaza if they choose. (Employing Palestinians with specialized job skills living in Israel and Jordan, states contiguous to the West Bank and Gaza, may be needed and probably preferred over the option of importing non-Palestinian specialists.) This is consistent with the 1988 Independence Declaration of the Palestine National Council, meeting in Algiers, which called Palestine the state of the Palestinians, "wherever they may be."[11] In other words, every Palestinian will be able to consider the new Palestinian entity, no matter what its final legal status, and no matter where she and her family reside, as her home. Such a national passport "would express for every holder the emotional and symbolic bond that unites the Palestinian people."[12]

- *Citizenship and Rehabilitation.* In addition to Palestinian passports, the refugees will be offered citizenship and full protection of their human rights in each of the absorption states, including Israel, to which they go. Thus, anyone who does not become absorbed in the West Bank or Gaza will be eligible for dual nationality (or dual citizenship, if the territories become an independent sovereign state), both as Palestinians and as citizens of their country of residence.[13] The value of possessing a state's citizenship was amply demonstrated during the Persian Gulf War, in the contrasting treatment of the Palestinian citizens of Jordan and the expendable and expellable Palestinian workers of Kuwait.

The resettled refugees also will receive rehabilitative services, including health care, education, and job training, in order to encourage their full social, political, and economic integration. Given that Palestinian refugees have, for three generations, refused absorption in most of the places they have resided, this support will play a crucial role in the process of transition to true citizenship. The rehabilitation services will be supported by development funds awarded to the countries on the basis of their willingness to absorb optimal target populations and administered with the assistance of the respective specializing U.N. agency and relevant nongovernmental relief organizations.

- *Temporary Decision-making Bodies*. In order to facilitate the process of deciding on target numbers, residential selection options, and compensation awards—and to ensure that such selections and awards are made fairly—four new bodies will be established: a joint population commission, a compensation tribunal, a repatriation committee, and a repatriation tribunal for appeal of the committee's decisions. (See figure 4.1.) When all of the decisions, selections, awards, and appeals are finalized, which may take about a decade, these institutions will be phased out. Claims to property or compensation will also be extinguished, so that closure on the refugee issue can be achieved.

Target Populations

The main feature of the proposal is an adjustment in the demographic distribution of Palestinian refugees in the region. The recommended "target figures" are meant as approximations of optimal conditions and not as strict quotas in the sense of either a floor or a ceiling. Yet they are stated as specific numbers in order to facilitate planning and resource allocation.

Perhaps the best way to explain and illustrate the plan's "target absorption" aspects is graphically. The left side of table 4.1 repeats from table 2.1 (found in chapter 2) the estimated current population of Palestinians by country or territory and the most recent figures for those still residing in UNRWA camps, which are identified because they represent the top priority for resettlement. These constitute the "from" side of the proposal. The right side of table 4.1 corresponds to the "to" side. It presents optimal population figures for the year 2005, approximately seven years from the date of the permanent peace agreement. Included in the far right-hand column are approximations of the percentage of target Palestinians vis-à-vis the country's or territory's total (Palestinian refugee and non-Palestinian refugee) population.

Working from a projected total worldwide Palestinian population of 8,265,000 for the year 2005, each proposed target figure in table 4.1 is based on the following assumptions:[14]

Table 4.1   Proposed Palestinian Population Absorption Targets

	"From"		"To"	
	Estimated[a] Total Current Palestinians	Total[a] in UNRWA Camps 1996	Proposed Targets for Year 2005	Proposed[b] Percentage Pales. to Total Pop.
West Bank	1,200,000	133,886	2,400,000	98%
Gaza	880,000	389,035	450,000	99%
Jordan	1,832,000	256,977	2,000,000	40%
Lebanon	372,700	186,006	75,000	1.8%
Syria	352,100	96,447	400,000	16%
Israel	840,000	N/A	1,000,000 + 75,000	19%
Other Mideast States	446,600	N/A	965,000	—
Non-Mideast States	452,000	N/A	900,000	—
Totals	6,375,800	1,061,351	8,265,000[c]	—

[a] These columns identical to columns I and III in Table 2.1 (Source: UNRWA General Information Sheet, January 1996).
[b] BASIS: Proposed Targets for 2005 as percentage of projected total populations for 2005 of 5,000,000 (Jordan); 4,200,000 (Lebanon), 18,400,000 (Syria) and 5,600,000 (Israel). Percentages for West Bank and Gaza assume a small percentage of Jewish settlers will decide to stay.
[c] SOURCE: U.S. Bureau of Census projection for year 2005. See Don Peretz, *Palestinians, Refugees and the Middle East Peace Process* (Washington DC: United States Institute of Peace Press, 1993), p. 16.

West Bank

The target population is 2,400,000 Palestinians. This target doubles the current population of 1,200,000, which is enough to cover natural population growth, the return of the approximately 350,000 displaced persons from 1967, plus others (mainly from Gaza and Lebanon) who urgently need permanent homes.[15] Assuming that housing starts and development keep pace in the period up to the year 2005, this target number should not overburden the economy or infrastructure.

Gaza

Target population is 450,000 Palestinians. This figure cuts in half what would have been the projected natural growth for 2005, based on the current figure of 880,000. Although Gaza currently has one of the highest densities of anyplace in the world, most of it is confined to a small portion of the entire strip, which means that there is room for the 450,000 who would remain there to disperse more comfortably.

Except for a small number of family reunification cases and 1967 displaced persons, no new refugees will be absorbed in Gaza during the seven-year transition period.

Jordan

The target population is two million Palestinian refugees (as distinct from the long-term Palestinians of Jordan who are not refugees). This target is only 168,000 more than the current Palestinian population of 1,832,000 and less than the projected natural growth. Most Palestinians who now live in Jordan are already citizens; most, particularly those with thriving businesses and other means of earning a living, probably will stay. Perhaps only a small number of the 13 percent who are still in Jordan's refugee camps will seek to move elsewhere. Because Jordan has already supported a disproportionate share of refugee resettlement needs, it will not be expected to absorb additional refugees from other areas, except for a small number who may have family reunification needs.

Lebanon

The target population is 75,000 Palestinians, a figure much reduced from the 372,000 current figure. Although Lebanon has expressed the intention to expel all but a few thousand Palestinians currently residing there, doing so would be a violation of international law. Many of the refugees probably will prefer to resettle in Jordan, the West Bank, or northern Israel, where their families originally lived. The figure of 75,000, which is identical to the number proposed for repatriation to Israel, is essentially symbolic: if Israel can be persuaded to allow the return of 75,000 Palestinians, Lebanon can also be expected to grant citizenship to and permanently absorb that many refugees.

Syria

The target population is 400,000 Palestinians. Because most of the 352,000 Palestinians currently in Syria have been integrated into the society in all but formal citizenship, it is assumed that when they are granted that status, most will remain. The target is based on projected natural growth, plus the resettlement of some refugees from Lebanon, and the departure of a portion of the 96,447 who were still in camps as of 1996.

Israel

The target population is 1,075,000, which is composed of 1 million Palestinians who have been Israeli citizens since 1948 (based on projected natural growth from the 840,000 of the mid-1990s and on the assumption that few will seek to move to the West Bank) and another 75,000 Palestinians who will be permitted to return and be offered Israeli citizenship. (Because this target requires a more elaborate explanation, it will be described below after the final two target locations.) The offer of citizenship is important so as not to drive a wedge between the new returnees and those who remained after the 1948 war.

Other Middle Eastern States

The target population is 965,000 Palestinians. This target is based on half a million newly resettled Palestinians on top of the natural population growth from the 446,600 who currently reside in these other Arab states (some of whom may opt to move to the West Bank, Israel, or elsewhere). It is hoped that once Syria signs onto the peace process, other Arab states, particularly the sparsely populated Gulf countries such as Saudi Arabia, Iraq, and Kuwait, will also see it in their interest to participate, which will include a commitment to absorb refugees. (Of these latter states, the participation of Iraq is most in question.)

Non-Middle Eastern States

The target population is 900,000 Palestinians. This target doubles the current figure of 452,000, most of whom are in Western states such as the United States. It assumes that they are rather well integrated in these states and that only a small portion will seek to return to the Middle East. While Western states may prefer to contribute development and compensation funds to the peace process rather than absorb additional refugees, they may be willing to participate in a pledging conference like that undertaken in 1979 for the Indochinese boat people, which was more successful in locating absorption spots than even its sponsors had anticipated.[16] The close to half a million Palestinians already living very productive lives in Western states should encourage these countries to agree to absorb more.

Further Assumptions Concerning Israel

Although there is currently much popular opposition in Israel to the idea that even a single Palestinian refugee should return to live within the Green Line, this sentiment can be overcome when it is presented as part of a reciprocal and regional framework for resolving the Palestinian refugee question and obtaining a full-scale peace. Israel's decision to accept Palestinian refugees could be described, instead, as the same process of "absorption" that the Arab states would concomitantly be undertaking, rather than as the oft-feared acknowledgment of a Palestinian "right" to "return." Moreover, because there will be a top limit of 75,000 returnees, Israel need not risk being overwhelmed by a massive influx of non-Jews. At least three additional reasons exist for this seemingly optimistic belief in a change of popular heart.

First, the target number of Palestinians in Israel, composed of existing citizens with but a small addition of newly absorbed former refugees, will be only slightly over one million in the year 2005, compared to the projected Israeli Jewish population at that time of over four million. (These figures compare to the combined 2005 target of just under three million Palestinians in the neighboring West Bank and Gaza, although the relative ratios may later change depending on birth and death rates, immigration, and out-migration.) Moreover, there is a historical precedent for Israel's agreement to absorb more Palestinians, namely, the 1949 Lausanne Conference described in chapter 1, during which Israel agreed to accept 100,000 Palestinian returnees. Given the small number of Jews living in Israel at that time, 100,000 was a much greater relative percentage then than 75,000 would be to Israel's Jewish population in the year 2005. Similarly, 100,000 was a greater percentage of the total Palestinian population of 1949 than 75,000 is of the projected 2005 population.[17] Therefore, 75,000 additional Palestinian citizens will not unduly endanger Israel's demographic stability.

Second, each Palestinian who seeks to return to—or "be absorbed by"—Israel will be required to meet certain criteria to be agreed upon in the final peace treaty, such as the following:

a. They must be able to prove original residence before 1948.

b. They must have close family members (a term that would have to be defined) who have been citizens of Israel since 1948.

c. They must agree, by written contract, to comply with the condition in General Assembly Resolution 194 to "live at peace with their [Israeli] neighbors." If, after running a security check, Israel has substantial evidence (such as proof of prior terrorist activity) that the would-be returnee is not likely to comply, it can veto the return.[18] However, it would be a rebuttable presumption, to be resolved by an impartial tribunal set up under the final peace agreement.

A population subgroup very likely to seek return, and which would be most likely to satisfy this third criterion, is the oldest living generation of Palestinians, the ones who retain personal memories of life before 1948.

Finally, it should be understood that Israeli agreement to this rather small and symbolic target of 75,000 persons is essential to facilitating the final peace agreement, because only when the Arab states see that Israel at least partially recognizes Palestinian claims for return (regardless of the terminology employed) will they themselves be willing to grant citizenship to and permanently absorb their own target numbers of refugees. It also will facilitate mutual acceptance of peace if Israel accepts full Palestinian self-determination. In other words, Israel would make a pragmatic decision to exchange partial, symbolic return of Palestinians and the establishment of a Palestinian state in the West Bank and Gaza for the Palestinian and Arab state acceptance of less than full Palestinian return and less than the complete territory they originally sought. As explained by Palestinian author Ziad Abu Zayyad, many Palestinians have come "to view their return as the acquisition of national independence and dignity, and not necessarily as a literal return."[19] Israelis would do well to recognize their own advantage in such a compromise resolution and to express their commitment to truly being part of a *regional* absorption plan that will lead to greater regional stability.

Current Needs and Preferences

The traditional discourse concerning Palestinian refugees has tended to divide them into categories based on where they lived before 1948 and 1967, when they left, and why they left. Because there will never be full or even partial consensus on the "magic number," this kind of discourse can never lead to a negotiated settlement. Moreover, the "numbers game" is inherently retrospective and blame-ridden. As time passes, the categories—whether 1948 versus 1967, voluntary versus involuntary—blur and become harder to distinguish anyway. Therefore, the most pragmatic, not to mention humanitarian, method of resolving the refugee question is by focusing not on past causes but on current needs, by paying attention to the most vulnerable Palestinian populations, that is, those who most urgently need permanent solutions to their residential, legal, political, and social status.

Most observers would probably agree on a priority ranking that looks something like this, in descending order of urgency:

1. Any refugees in temporary housing, such as those expelled from Libya in late 1995 who were living in tents on the Egyptian border;

2. Given Lebanon's oft-stated intention to expel them, residents of the most vulnerable refugee camps in Lebanon, and those expelled from Kuwait in 1990 who were never able to be reabsorbed into Jordan;

3. The residents of the most overcrowded and unsanitary refugee camps in Gaza;

4. All other refugee camp residents in Jordan, Syria, Lebanon, the West Bank, and Gaza;

5. All other refugees, including Palestinian residents of other Middle Eastern states, most of whom are stateless.

The actual list of need-based priorities would be set by a joint population commission (composed of representatives of the signatory parties to the final peace treaty, with a majority of seats held by Palestinians) that will function much like the joint commissions that have operated in other instances of bilateral population transfer.[20] The commission will then supply each family with written and oral explanations of their available residential and compensation options. (See figure 4.2 as an example of available options.) To ensure that the decisions are made under conditions of informed and free consent, a set of commission-generated guidelines, such as those used or proposed in other contexts, will be followed as closely as practicable.[21] The residential choices selected by the families in each need-based category of refugees would then be weighted according to their place on the list or resolved in an order corresponding to the relevant category's degree of urgency.

The joint population commission will then collect applications containing each family's ranked list of preferred options and perform a matching service, facilitated by the use of a sophisticated computer program, which will generate for each family its highest ranked preference consistent with urgency of need and available positions, based on the target absorption figures for each residential choice.[22] (If there are too many applicants for any particular target setting, the commission may decide to make its final selections through a lottery.) Depending on the outcome, the refugees will then make application to one of two other bodies, the repatriation committee or the compensation tribunal. (See figure 4.1 for a graphical layout of the relationship among the joint population commission, the committee and its appeal tribunal, and the compensation tribunal.)

Those Palestinians who are selected by the commission to repatriate to Israel will then submit documentation of their qualifications under the agreed-upon repatriation eligibility criteria to an independent repatriation committee (composed of representatives of each of the signatories to the peace treaty; in contrast to the joint population commission, a majority of seats on this committee will be held by Israelis). An impartial repatriation tribunal (composed of a majority of arbitrators from non–Middle Eastern states) will hear appeals of denials by the repatri-

Figure 4.1   Decision-making Bodies

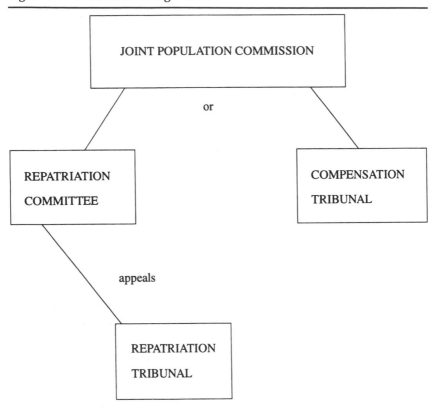

ation committee. Once a Palestinian family has been deemed eligible for repatriation, Israel would not restrict the actual place of residence within the country, except for a limited number of clearly demarcated security zones. Applications for repatriation will go through the committee and tribunal process until the target number (proposed here as 75,000) is achieved.

Because the overwhelming majority of original Palestinian properties either no longer exist as such or are occupied by second-, third-, or later-generation transferees, the repatriating refugees will need financial assistance in acquiring new homes and businesses. These funds would take the form of low-interest loans rather than grants, to distinguish them from payments of compensation to those who are not repatriating. Israelis will not be displaced from their own residences and properties by the returnees, except by consenting to a bona fide sale at contemporary market values. The same principle of nondisplacement except by bona fide sale will apply to Palestinians living in what before 1948 were Jewish-owned residences.

Those Palestinians who will not be repatriating will instead proceed to file for their compensation award from an impartial compensation tribunal (also composed of a majority of arbitrators from non–Middle Eastern states). Compensation awards will either be in the form of a cash "absorption" or "reintegration allowance"[23] or title to real property, as described in the next section. The experiences of the Iran–United States Claims Tribunal and the United Nations Compensation Commission, which resolves claims arising from Iraq's invasion of Kuwait, provide valuable lessons in areas such as valuation of property, dispute settlement procedures and mass claims processing techniques.[24]

Due to the success of these precedents, it is recommended that compensation tribunals be composed not only of representatives of the affected parties but also of impartial arbiters from uninvolved countries. In addition, in order to effectuate closure, and because the function of these proposed bodies is more in the nature of settlement than of adjudication, no other court or tribunal should have *de novo* or further appellate review of the final decisions of the repatriation and compensation tribunals.

Because immigration is traditionally considered a subject of domestic and not international jurisdiction, each state that will be absorbing refugees will naturally want to enact its own legislation to regulate the process. But as already noted, citizenship carries with it a package of rights, not the least of which is the right to equality. Those Arab states that have not heretofore been in the forefront of democratization trends will have the opportunity to demonstrate such a commitment in the case of their newly naturalized Palestinian citizens. Palestinians will themselves probably want to promulgate Laws of Return and of Nationality for the West Bank and Gaza that, perhaps ironically, may in many respects replicate Israel's own such legislation.[25] Just as Israel and Jordan promised, in their joint peace treaty, to repeal all their discriminatory legislation, the Palestinian Authority should avoid enacting laws that discriminate against non-Palestinians. (Chapter 5 elaborates on these nationality and human rights themes.)

Compensation and Funding Sources

As previously noted, claims for refugee compensation have rarely been sought because of the necessity of establishing causation. In a few instances of bilateral population transfers, such as the Greek-Bulgarian Agreement of 1919, the Lausanne Treaty of 1930 involving Greeks and Turks, and the New Delhi Accord of 1950 between Pakistan and India, mechanisms were established for valuation of and payment for evacuated properties, but without regard to fault.[26] None of the five major

Figure 4.2   Refugee Options: An Example

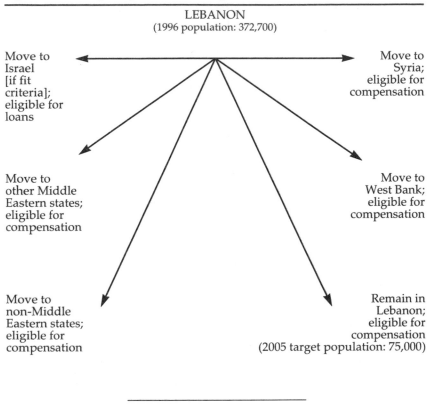

LEBANON
(1996 population: 372,700)

Move to
Israel
[if fit
criteria];
eligible for
loans

Move to
Syria;
eligible for
compensation

Move to
other Middle
Eastern states;
eligible for
compensation

Move to
West Bank;
eligible for
compensation

Move to
non-Middle
Eastern states;
eligible for
compensation

Remain in
Lebanon;
eligible for
compensation
(2005 target population: 75,000)

Non-options due to absorption limits:
Move to Gaza;
Move to Jordan

agreements that have been adopted to date pursuant to the Oslo process—the September 1993 Declaration of Principles (Oslo I), the May 1994 Gaza-Jericho Agreement, the August 1994 Early Empowerment Agreement, the October 1994 Israeli-Jordanian peace treaty, and the September 1995 Interim Self-Rule Agreement (Oslo II)—have even attempted to address the issue of causation in regard to refugee flows. A weak precedent for resolving the compensation question exists in the 1979 peace treaty between Egypt and Israel, which called for the establishment of a "claims commission for the mutual settlement of all financial claims." However, neither party has ever invoked this clause.[27]

Without giving up hope that they can be resolved, the political scientist and Middle East expert Don Peretz has delineated some of the more complex tasks concerning the issue of compensation:

1. Identify property that formerly belonged to Palestinian refugees.

2. Identify former owners.

3. Determine the relationship between current property values and those of 1948.

4. Determine which parties are responsible for payment.

5. Decide what the source of funding for compensation will be.

6. Decide what form compensation will take.

7. Establish who will be responsible for distribution of compensation payments.

8. Assess the status of Israeli counterclaims.

9. Determine to what extent resolution of the compensation issue will balance off other political, territorial, or moral claims.[28]

Other complications include the difficulty of distinguishing privately from communally held Palestinian property (the undivided village *musha*) and confiscated land from land that was duly purchased; the destruction of many if not most of the original land registration records; the problem of property in Israel that has had many subsequent owners or that no longer exists in its original form; and the existence of subcategories of refugees who have not heretofore been the beneficiaries of high-profile advocacy.[29] Unanswered political questions include whether previous distributions of development and rehabilitation sums, in the form of loans or payments to individuals and completed infrastructure projects, should be used to offset other compensation obligations.[30] Moreover, should the government of Jordan be reimbursed for its costs in long supporting Palestinians outside of the UNRWA system? Many of these issues may not realistically ever become resolvable, due to overly complicated fact patterns, politically charged negotiating positions, the unavailability of funding sources, or the lack of exact legal standards.[31]

Nevertheless, work is already being done to identify technical problems such as the location of land registration records and to articulate the specific legal basis for reacquiring private property in the wide variety of locales within Israel and the future Palestine.[32] Records from the Israeli Absentee Property office as well as UNRWA's family files should include some of the data relevant to compensation claims. The United Nations also holds the records used for property identification and evaluation by the Conciliation Commission, many of which came from the mandatory registry operated by the United Kingdom, as successor to the Ottoman land registry. The peace agreement must require that each of these relevant offices make its files available to potential claimants, who would be urged to act through a finite number of agents.[33]

Yet due to the difficulty in verifying literally hundreds of thousands of family claims, it is more realistic to offer a series of uniform payments that would be awarded to those claimants who fit into particular classifications, such as original owners of urban or rural property, perhaps subclassified by residential or commercial use, or by the amount of farmland originally owned.[34] Claimant families would then only have to prove their membership in the particular class to be eligible under the respective formula.

Because the estimated value of total compensation due might be in the range of tens of billions of 1990 U.S. dollars, it is much beyond the capability of any one country such as Israel to pay.[35] And that does not include the billions needed for new housing, infrastructural development, job production and training, and other forms of economic development and social rehabilitation.[36] Realistically, given the minimal likelihood of ever resolving the causation question, compensation must be paid out of a combined pool created as part of the final peace settlement and contributed to on an international basis by Arab states, Western industrialized governments, international institutions, private benefactors, and Israel. Contributions by Arab states could be inversely linked to their willingness to absorb refugees or to savings from ensuing reductions in military budgets due to regional peace. Israel's contribution to the compensation pool could, appropriately, come from the "rents" it collected in the late 1940s and early 1950s from the Jewish users of "absentee" Arab property.[37] Because it will be one of many contributors to a collective pool of funds, Israel will not be forced into admitting that its contribution constitutes "compensation" that it is under a legal obligation to pay.

In some cases, property exchanges can constitute a substitute for cash compensation. Just as many Israeli immigrants from Europe and Arab states were housed in Palestinian refugee homes in the late 1940s and early 1950s, newly resettling Palestinians can be housed in the homes of Jewish settlers who decide to leave the West Bank or Gaza to return to live in Israel—a number that could approach 100,000 persons.[38] Often overlooked is the fact that during the 1948 war there were Jews living in the West Bank and Gaza Strip who fled to within Israel's borders, leaving behind property that then became the homes of Palestinians. Similar de facto "property transfers" have occurred in other contexts, such as between India and Pakistan after 1947.[39] A final peace treaty between Israel and the Palestinians could transfer title to these evacuated settler homes to the joint population commission, which could then assign the titles to some of the resettling refugees, in lieu of cash compensation.

Although psychologically, the departing settlers may prefer to see their homes demolished, as was the practice when Israel withdrew from the Sinai, it is more sensible for the structures to be left intact so as to expedite the resettlement of Palestinians leaving refugee camps.[40] Already by the end of 1995, some settlers, concerned about losing their investment in a depressed housing market, had begun to leave the West Bank and Gaza. "The market goes ahead of the politicians," as a real estate appraiser has put it pragmatically.[41]

Finally, while most of this chapter has discussed compensation to individual families for expropriated property, another form of compensation may, in the long run, serve a more important function: communal compensation to the Palestinian communities that will be developing or redeveloping both inside and outside of Palestine. Moreover, those refugees who have suffered the most—that is, those still living in the camps and those without meaningful sources of current income—tended to come originally from the poorest sectors of Palestinian society. Concomitantly, the refugees who are likely to benefit most from reparations for loss of property are those who were better off to begin with, having the largest landholdings, and for the most part, who managed to rebuild their post-1948 lives in the diaspora. Thus, the refugees who suffered most will benefit least from a compensation system solely tied to prior property ownership.

Given that the peace negotiations are envisioned as a forward-looking process, the parties should acknowledge that the foundation of refugee rehabilitation is more than merely restitution for past injuries. It is primarily about building hope for the future. Therefore, it would be advisable to maintain a realistic ceiling on the payment of private compensation claims so that greater sums in the form of collective reparations can be awarded to community projects, whether of an infrastructural, educational, or communal nature, thereby benefiting the refugees most in need of support.[42]

Enforcement and Extinguishment of Claims

Although the Palestinian refugee crisis has endured for almost three generations, it must eventually come to an end. Closure is necessary not only for the refugees but also for the Israelis, who will need assurance that a Palestinian will not someday show up on their children's or grandchildren's doorstep demanding title to the property and/or with a multimillion-dollar compensation claim. Therefore, a window for compensation claims should be left open for a specified period of time—two years after the final status treaty, perhaps—and then be permanently shut, except in extraordinary circumstances.[43] Thereafter, all claims previously resolved by the compensation tribunal will be treated as *res judicata*, "settled by judgment." Although the analogy is not necessarily a propitious one, the U.S. Supreme Court has similarly applied the principle of extinguishment to the land claims of Native Americans.[44]

Lawyers, in their inherently irritating way, will naturally ask how compliance with all of these absorption targets, promises of citizenship, and other proposed procedures and guidelines can be enforced and guaranteed. After all, it is a fundamental principle of any legal system that rights without remedies for their deprivation are but illusory and meaningless.[45] The answer, most likely, is that they cannot be formally enforced, at least not in an adjudicatory forum. After all, issues of immigration and citizenship are normally a matter of sovereign discretion. The only real guarantee of compliance is the adequacy of incentives to participate in the settlement plan itself, through the advantages that will come with regional peace and stability. But as chapter 5 demonstrates, in other contexts, nonbinding regional agreements can sometimes be more successful than binding regimes that states do not take seriously.

One such model is the Conference on Security and Cooperation in Europe (described more fully in the next chapter), which in the midst of the Cold War proved to have a well-utilized system of "enforcement" through periodic review meetings.[46] Perhaps the final settlement agreement among Israel, the Palestinians, and their neighboring states should include a commitment to a similar series of periodic review meetings, during which compliance with absorption targets can be surveyed and, if necessary, numerically adjusted to fit economic and other conditions that will emerge over time. Amendments to the procedural elements of the settlement should be permitted, if they are found by mutual agreement to be necessary. Further sets of target populations may even need to be devised every five or more years. If the participants are assured that the plan is flexible and capable of adjusting to changing needs, while remaining fair, practical, and balanced, they will have the incentive to comply with it.

Chapter 5

Norms of
Implementation

"Large-scale movements of refugees and other forced migrants have become a defining characteristic of the contemporary world. At few times in recent history have such large numbers of people in so many parts of the globe been obliged to leave their own countries and communities to seek safety elsewhere."[1] So begins a 1995 study titled *The State of the World's Refugees,* which goes on to describe mass displacements of 10,000 or more persons in each of 70 separate countries around the world, for a total of 27.4 million people receiving protection and assistance by the United Nations High Commissioner for Refugees. These include 3.7 million who have been displaced by the war in the former Yugoslavia, close to three million Afghani refugees remaining in Iran and Pakistan, and 1.6 million in the Horn of Africa and Sudan, who are finally undergoing repatriation to Eritrea more than 30 years after the first refugees left that country.[2]

Yet despite the specter of persistent trouble spots such as the Balkans, the world has begun to appreciate that not all intercommunal conflicts need lead to refugee outflows and not all are permanent features of human history. Witness the tranquil borders between France and Germany, despite generations of mutual enmity, the relative quiescence of a federal state like Malaysia, composed of three major races, four language groups, and over six religions, or the miraculous process of national reconciliation that is taking place in the former apartheid state of South Africa.[3] In the last decade alone, dozens of countries have undergone radical transformations, throwing out totalitarian or authoritarian regimes and grappling with the problems of democratic governance.

The challenges that Palestinian refugees and their neighbors and supporters will face will be no less daunting than those facing South Africa or the new Balkans states. Fortunately, they will be able to benefit from the experiences of so many other national and regional transformations, both concurrent and antecedent, that can serve as either positive or negative models. With such a variety of examples from which to select, this chapter offers neither a comprehensive nor a definitive coverage of all such relevant instances, but merely a sampling of those that can provide valuable instruction for Palestinians, Israelis, and the Arab states, who will be implementing the refugee aspects of the peace settlement. Rather than focusing on the socioeconomic and technical aspects of refugee rehabilitation, which are no less compelling but are outside this author's expertise, this chapter concentrates on the legal and policy aspects of granting citizenship, allowing freedom of movement, and human rights issues related to the absorption of refugees and the treatment of minorities.[4]

Where chapter 4 centered on decision-making procedures and institutions, this chapter concentrates on substantive norms. Moreover, instead of expounding on the inevitable factual and contextual features that may either analogize or distinguish the Palestinian case from these others, the chapter highlights the policy recommendations and guidelines that governments and intergovernmental and nongovernmental organizations have developed to deal with specific problems of transformation. The language of these guidelines, which will be quoted liberally, may suggest adaptable provisions for the final status treaties and other agreements among Palestinians, Israel, and the neighboring Arab states that have yet to be written. The existence of similar experiences in other regions of the world can also serve as persuasive precedents for Middle East negotiators advocating the adoption of particular solutions to similar problems. In other cases, existing international law or practice may already provide the answer.

The Dynamics of Permanent Absorption

The process of administering a permanent regional absorption plan for Palestinians will be complex, multifaceted, and of considerable length. But it will not have been the first such effort to resolve a major refugee crisis. According to a 1983 report of refugee experts convened by the UNHCR:

> Refugee problems demand *durable* solutions. . . . A genuinely durable solution to a refugee problem means integration of the refugee into society: either reintegration in the country of origin after voluntary repatriation, or reintegration in the country of first asylum or [third] country of resettlement.[5]

As already noted, deliberately negotiated population transfers took place pursuant to the 1919 Peace of Neuilly-sur-Seine, the 1923 Lausanne Treaty, the 1945 Potsdam Agreement, and the 1950 New Delhi Accord, as well as in other bilateral agreements in Eastern Europe during the early years of the Cold War.[6] More recent examples include the return from exile of Namibian and South African dissidents upon the independence of the former and the end of apartheid in the latter,[7] the Comprehensive Plan of Action for Vietnamese and Laotian boat people,[8] the agreement for the voluntary return of refugees from Pakistan to Afghanistan,[9] and the work of the International Conference on Central American Refugees (CIREFCA) and related efforts in that region of the world.[10]

By contrast, the majority of Palestinian refugees have never, on a comprehensive basis, been given the opportunity to experience any three of these traditional durable solutions: either repatriation, local integration, or third-country resettlement. Instead, they have been subjected to a plethora of what has been called "interim assistance": "relief" (emergency rations, housing, and other services), "works" (labor projects, often temporary), and economic integration through longer-term development projects. According to refugee expert Howard Adelman:

> UNRWA provides a case study of an agency set up to provide a durable solution in the ordinary meaning of that term—to eliminate the Palestine refugee problem—which later became a durable solution in the ironic, second sense of the term [durable], where the solution applied continued on and on but the refugee situation was perpetuated.[11]

Adelman notes, however, that at least until now, the international community has preferred to use UNRWA as a conduit for its donations to assist the Palestinians, given the Palestinian Authority's lack of either experience or credibility in administering such funds. Nevertheless, "as long as UNRWA remains as a distinct enterprise for taking care of the health, welfare and educational needs of the Palestinian refugees, particularly in Gaza and the West Bank, there can never be a coherent policy in these areas equally applicable to all Palestinians in the territory."[12]

Regardless of whether the U.N. Relief and Works Administration was originally intended to do more than simply provide just that, relief and works, it is widely agreed that UNRWA is not suited to take the refugees to the next stage, the transition to permanent absorption and statehood. (In fact, it has recently been targeted for final phase-out around May 1999, the same time that the final status talks between Israel and the Palestinians are scheduled to be completed.)[13] Instead of UNRWA, Palestinians might look to the UNHCR, which in the last half-decade has directly overseen and itself often administered refugee repatriation movements in Afghanistan, Angola, Bosnia, Burundi, Cambodia, Croatia, Ethiopia/Eritrea, Guatemala, Laos, Liberia, Mozambique, Namibia, Rwanda, Serbia, Sierra Leone, Somalia, South Africa, Sudan, Western Sahara, Zaire, Zimbabwe, and elsewhere,[14] as well as regional resettlement and reconstruction efforts in Zaire, Burundi, Uganda and other parts of Africa.[15] It has also assisted in the global resettlement of refugees in Australia, Canada, Denmark, Finland, the Netherlands, Norway, New Zealand, Sweden, Switzerland, and the United States.[16]

Many of these efforts to administer solutions to refugee crises have generated a series of guidelines to ensure the voluntary, orderly, and humanitarian character of the absorption programs. For instance, the Executive Committee of the UNHCR has, among other requirements for repatriation, reaffirmed that:

> The repatriation of refugees should only take place at their freely expressed wish; the voluntary and individual character of repatriation of refugees and the need for it to be carried out under conditions of absolute safety, preferably to the place of residence of the refugee in his country of origin, should always be respected.[17]

The same body has also:

- Recognized the importance of refugees being provided with the necessary information regarding conditions in their country of origin in order to facilitate their decision to repatriate; recognized further that visits by individual refugees or refugee representatives to their country of origin to inform themselves of the situation there—without such visits automatically involving loss of refugee status—could also be of assistance in this regard.

- Called upon governments of countries of origin to provide formal guarantees for the safety of returning refugees and stressed the importance of such guarantees being fully respected and of returning refugees not being penalized for having left their country of origin for reasons giving rise to refugee situations. . . .

- Called upon the governments concerned to provide repatriating refugees with the necessary travel documents, visas, entry permits and transportation facilities and, if refugees have lost their nationality, to arrange for such nationality to be restored in accordance with national legislation.[18]

UNHCR has usually been involved in assessing the feasibility of repatriations as well as in the planning and implementation stages, and has additionally undertaken the task of monitoring the repatriation to ensure that the governmental guarantees are so provided. It encourages the formation of tripartite commissions consisting of representatives of the countries of origin and asylum and the UNHCR.[19]

The Refugee Project of the nongovernmental organization Lawyers Committee for Human Rights has issued a set of ten General Principles

Relating to the Promotion of Refugee Repatriation, along with useful commentaries on implementation of the principles:

1. Repatriation should not be promoted unless all countries involved in the repatriations can ensure the protection of and respect for the fundamental human rights of the refugees.

2. Refugees must not be returned to any country where they would face persecution.

3. Refugee repatriations must be voluntary.

4. Repatriation should be promoted only if it can be accomplished in a manner that ensures safety and dignity upon return.

5. The UNHCR should be involved in a meaningful way from the inception of the repatriation plan to its conclusion.

6. Nongovernmental organizations, in addition to the UNHCR, should have independent access to the refugees, both before and after their return.

7. Any repatriation plan should establish that the conflict has abated and its attendant risks eliminated before promoting return.

8. Repatriation should be promoted only if there is no longer a likelihood of recurrence of the human rights abuses that precipitated flight.

9. Particular emphasis must be placed on the unique protection needs of returning women and children, who are a high-risk group within an already vulnerable population; and

10. These principles and considerations may apply as well to unassisted repatriations.[20]

Many of these same guidelines would also apply to third-country resettlement.

Of course, the refugees whom the UNHCR has helped repatriate have not, in general, been in exile nearly as long as have the Palestinians; nor, with a few exceptions, have the reabsorption programs involved nearly as many people.[21] As chapter 2 demonstrated, the Palestinian diaspora currently consists of a vast patchwork of divergent political, legal, economic, and social statuses. That is why Shaml, the newly established, Ramallah-based Palestinian Diaspora and Refugee Centre, has concluded that a unified, regional effort is needed to study the existing legislation in Middle Eastern states on residency, citizenship, and freedom of movement. "Such steps would lead to breakthroughs for the region in its efforts to achieve peace, economic development and democracy. A collective regional cooperation would facilitate the achievement of such ambitious goals through a framework of comprehensive settlements."[22] Presumably, Shaml is referring not only to an exhaustive research project but to a collective endeavor to create—and implement—uniform standards for the region. Such an effort would require an unusual degree of consensus, because issues of citizenship, immigration, and the like are traditionally within the domain of sovereign discretion. Yet it need not be a futile venture.

A significant element of the absorption plan discussed in chapter 4 is the ability of Palestinians to acquire the full rights of citizenship in any of the states where they might permanently reside—including Israel, Lebanon, and even Kuwait—as well as dual citizenship or a Palestinian passport for those who do not initially return to the West Bank and Gaza. With citizenship will come equality, residency, freedom of movement across borders, and other entitlements that will bring stability to the region. But the prospect of citizenship also raises some problems, five of which include:

1. How will the other Middle Eastern states—Egypt and Syria, for instance, as well as Israel, where Palestinians may in the future reside—treat the former refugees? Will Palestinians be able to obtain citizenship in these states, whether they do or do not also acquire Palestinian citizenship and whether they have or have not previously resided there?

2. What are the implications of the Palestinian Authority (or a future Palestinian state) granting citizenship to all Palestinians, wherever they reside, including in neighboring Arab states? What will be their rights (for example, regarding voting) and obligations (say, for military service) vis-à-vis the Palestinian state or Authority?

3. Can a future Palestinian Authority or state that grants citizenship to any Palestinian who wants it also limit the number of Palestinians who can, at least in the short run, return to live in that state?

4. What, if any, restrictions can be placed on the transborder movement of Middle Eastern residents, Palestinian citizens, and others, who do not otherwise pose risks to national security, public health, or public order (the standard limitations accepted under international law)?

5. More broadly, how are the Palestinian, Israeli, and Arab national communities to be defined, both internally and in relation to each other, and in the context of a comprehensive commitment to human rights?

Two regions that have undergone recent shifts in nationality policy due to changes in sovereignty are the Baltic states (and, to a lesser extent, other former republics of the Soviet Union) and eastern and western Europe, as exemplified by Germany in the reunification of its eastern and western halves. Like the future Palestine and even Israel, Germany's democratic state-building has until recently suffered from a confusion concerning its territorial borders. The Baltic states, as well, have suffered an identity confusion of sorts, given the 50-year-long Soviet annexation. In the process of these transformations, some of the same issues facing Palestinians, such as dual citizenship and restrictions on movement and repatriation, have arisen. Many of the examples in the following sections will be taken from these two regions.

Entitlement to Citizenship

The first of these five issues, the future legal status of Palestinians in states other than Palestine, including the possibility of obtaining dual citizenship, is illuminated by the experiences of the former republics of the Soviet Union. Other than Russia, which now usually recognizes dual citizenship, particularly with constituent republics of the Soviet Union, many of the other former Soviet republics have rejected it. For instance, after heated debate, the new Constitution and Citizenship Laws of Kyrgyzstan prohibit dual citizenship. Armenia and Lithuania, among others, have followed suit. However, Kyrgyzstan law also requires that foreigners and stateless persons enjoy the same rights, privileges, and legal protections as Kyrgyzstan citizens, including the rights of permanent residence, work, and equal access to public schools, to divorce, and to freedom of religion, culture, and association.[23]

The dissolution of the Soviet Union has also resulted in massive discrimination against Russian nationals who had resided in the outer republics, often, like Palestinians, for more than two generations and usually not by choice but at the very forceful insistence of the Soviet government. Hundreds of thousands of ethnic Russians have feared they would be rendered either stateless and permanently disenfranchised or at least temporarily disenfranchised in important early elections by new citizenship laws such as those in Latvia and Estonia, which grant automatic citizenship only to those who resided in these two states (and their descendants) before 1940, when the Soviet Union occupied and annexed the Baltic region. Those who do not qualify as automatic citizens can become naturalized later, but only if they meet additional requirements, such as passing arduous Estonian or Latvian language tests. Of the three Baltic states, only Lithuania has decided to make naturalization automatic upon the request of any permanent resident. Similarly, in the wake of the breakup of Yugoslavia, Croatia has also been criticized for denying citizenship to non-Croatians who have lived, worked, and owned property in Croatia for most of their adult lives.[24]

Officials of the Russian government "have equated the restrictive citizenship laws with human rights violations against Russian minorities in the Baltics, even comparing the Estonian and Latvian strategy to 'ethnic cleansing' in the former Yugoslavia."[25] Especially in Latvia, where ethnic Russians constitute close to 50 percent of the population, they are analogizing it to apartheid. Unlike the Russians residing in the Baltics, Palestinians have not held privileged stations in the Arab host states and if they have been despised by their neighbors, it is not because they represent an oppressive, imperial power. In fact, if and when they achieve independent statehood, Palestinians may feel more like the Baltic peoples, who have overthrown an occupying power and consider their states to be "restored" rather than newly independent sovereignties. But a key to the analogy between the two groups of peoples may lie in the alienation, vulnerability, and abandonment that many ethnic Russians feel they have suffered as a result of the disintegration of the Soviet Union.[26] If the fate of Palestinians who will continue living outside of the West Bank and Gaza is not carefully protected, they may develop similar attitudes toward the Palestinian state and the rest of the international community.

In the context of these developments in the Baltic region of the former Soviet Union, the New York–based nongovernmental organization Human Rights Watch/Helsinki issued a policy statement on the citizenship legislation that was in the process of being adopted there. While the conditions giving rise to this particular declaration are vastly different from those that Palestinians have experienced, most of the basic principles and particular considerations are germane and adaptable to the other setting. Where the policy statement refers to Russian nationals or "former Soviet citizens continuing to reside in a former Soviet Republic," one could substitute "Palestinians who remain in Arab host countries."

For instance, Human Rights Watch states that "in no event should the establishment or reestablishment of independence serve as a pretext for cutting back on the rights to which former Soviet citizens are entitled under international human rights law." Similarly, the rights of individuals "to continue in their habitual residence should not be impaired because of political changes in the world around them," nor be contingent on "whether a person moved to the republic of his or her own free will or was forced to do so by the Soviet government."[27] The establishment of a Palestinian state (or some other form of final settlement between Israel and the Palestinians) would constitute an obvious parallel to the political changes in eastern Europe. It will be particularly important to prohibit states such as Libya, which may continue to oppose the peace settlement, to try again to expel its Palestinian residents or to otherwise use them as scapegoats for foreign policy motives. Similarly, in emphasizing the "Obligation to Ensure Protection of the Rights of All Persons Subject to Governmental Authority, Whether or Not They Are Formally 'Citizens,' " Human Rights Watch notes that "most aspects of international human rights law apply to 'everyone' or to 'all persons,' regardless of citizenship or nationality. A government's obligations do not end with ensuring the rights of only its citizens."

The organization also warns that "it is incumbent on the former republics to develop and implement their citizenship laws in a manner that avoids rendering individuals stateless. This is especially crucial for individuals who are of a nationality that has no corresponding territorial unit in the former U.S.S.R. [which is] empowered to extend citizenship."[28] This principle already applies to Palestinians now, but it should continue to apply in the event that a final peace settlement lacks a provision for extending Palestinian citizenship to those who remain outside the West Bank or Gaza. Moreover, citizenship laws that "mandate excessively long periods of residence or other restrictive conditions" would harm the vast numbers of Palestinians who were forced to undertake secondary and even tertiary migrations in search of work and ended up being expelled, only to move again.[29] In addition, Human Rights Watch would oppose "citizenship proposals that would have the effect of arbitrarily dividing a family into citizens and non-citizens," for instance, "by allocating citizenship entitlement to one but not both spouses, to a child and one parent but not to the other parent, or on other similarly arbitrary lines."[30] This might require a reversal of the Shariah-based patrilineal descent policies of many Muslim states—an unlikely but not inconceivable possibility.[31]

Some of the more specific considerations in the Human Rights Watch policy statement are equally pertinent to Palestinians. In particular, the nongovernmental organization states that the categorical exclusion from citizenship of persons:

> who worked for the U.S.S.R. Communist Party, KGB, or any other institution, on the grounds that they perpetrated grave abuses of human rights, collectively punishes individuals and violates the . . . freedom of association. Before such a person is denied citizenship, he or she should be individually proven culpable in a court of law for specific crimes that were outlawed at the time of the acts in question. The record of each citizenship applicant should be judged individually with the appropriate recourse to judicial institutions.[32]

Similar considerations would apply to members of Hamas, Islamic Jihad, or any radical Palestinian organization. An individual is entitled to a fair trial on specific charges of terrorism before being denied citizenship or residence.

Finally, "persons with a reasonable expectation of continued residence who do not elect or qualify for citizenship of that state should be allowed to remain in their habitual residence in any event, and to return there after temporary absences."[33] Those Palestinians who choose not to become citizens should be treated as permanent residents, without having to risk loss of their right to remain or to reenter the country. The rights of noncitizens should be governed by the standards in the U.N. Declaration on the Human Rights of Individuals Who Are Not Nationals of the Country in Which They Live, adopted without a vote by the General Assembly in 1985. Subject to lawful limitations, these norms include the rights to own property, to admission to a country to rejoin a spouse and minor children, to safe and healthy working conditions, and to a hearing and review before being expelled. The declaration also states: "Individual or collective expulsion of such aliens on grounds of race, colour, religion, culture, descent or national or ethnic origin is prohibited."[34] As demonstrated in chapter 2, many of the Middle Eastern states in which Palestinians currently reside have been in egregious violation of the norms articulated in the declaration.

Rights, Duties, and Limits on Citizenship

The next two issues, the rights and duties of Palestinian citizenship for those living outside the West Bank and Gaza, and the ability of a Palestinian state to limit the return of such citizens, can be addressed together, for both involve the relationship of Palestinians to the future Palestine. What might the rights and duties of such "diasporan Palestinian citizens" consist of? Again, some of the former Soviet republics offer themselves as precedents. For instance, Armenia has begun issuing a special passport to diaspora Armenians that does not convey either the right to vote or the duty to report for military service.[35] By contrast, some older citizenship schemes, such as those for Algerians and Poles, allow citizens living outside of Algeria or Poland to vote in national elections through a form of absentee ballot. This is somewhat analogous to the designation "British Overseas Citizen" created by the United Kingdom's Nationality Act of 1981, which conveys the right to vote in the United Kingdom but not, significantly, the automatic "right to abode" there. Only British citizens and citizens of independent British Commonwealth countries who were originally granted the right of abode under Britain's 1971 Immigration Act now possess the right of automatic abode in the United Kingdom. Residents of Hong Kong, for instance, do not have it; they can enter England as tourists but not as immigrants.[36] This limitation was created in order to prevent millions of what used to be called "British subjects" from rushing to England to escape Chinese control of Hong Kong after 1997.

Germany has also begun to restrict the number of ethnic Germans living outside Germany (called *Aussiedler*, "out-settlers," or *Auslandsdeutsche*, "Germans abroad") who can repatriate and obtain German citizenship. Somewhat analogously to Israel's own Law of Return, Article 116(1) of the German Basic Law and a 1953 West German implementing statute authorize repatriation for *Aussiedler* who have "acknowledged German nationality and can confirm it through characteristics like parentage, language, upbringing and culture," regardless of how many generations they have lived abroad. In 1949, about 3.5 million ethnic Germans remained outside Germany from the group of over 12 million who fled or were driven out in the immediate post–World War II period. About two million have repatriated, mostly from Poland, Romania, and the former Soviet Union, since the early 1970s, but another 3.5 million potential returnees of the original group and their descendants are believed to remain in various east European states. The number who returned in the year 1992, about 200,000, was twice as many as those who, for family reunification purposes, moved from East to West Germany that same year.[37]

With national reunification and its attendant economic burdens, Germany has attempted to staunch the flow of returning *Aussiedler*, both by expending billions of deutsche marks in eastern Europe to encourage them to stay put and, for the first time in German history, by setting quotas of between 180,000 and 220,000 returning ethnic Germans a year. While popular domestic support for the quotas may stem from the suspicion that many of their links were quite attenuated— merely "once owning a German Shepherd dog," for instance—reunification has also diminished the need to justify the repatriation program on the idealist image of "a divided Germany made whole once again."[38] While the German law of return, like the Israeli version, has been subjected to criticism for its chauvinistic if not racist nationalism—particularly in light of the exacting barriers posed to naturalization of nonethnic group members—perhaps Palestinians, too, in a similar vein of ideological adjustment tempered with economic pragmatism, will be able to justify realistic quotas on the number of future Palestinian passport holders who will be allowed to resettle permanently in the West Bank and Gaza. Both Germany and Palestine—and perhaps also Israel, in this same regard—will have "reached some viable territorial shape and a legitimate structure as a nation state."[39]

What about the duties of Palestinian citizens who are also citizens of another state? "Traditionally, the sacralization of citizenship has found its central and most poignant expression in the obligation to perform military service for the state, to fight for the state, and to die for it if need be."[40] How then to avoid accusations of dual loyalty and, worse, treason, when both states demand conscription? Conflicts in the military obligations of dual nationals can be resolved through the norms codified in the 1930 Protocol Relating to Military Obligations in Certain Cases of Double Nationality—which exempts nationals who habitually reside in other countries—or through bilateral treaties, such as the 1959 convention between Israel and France, which similarly uses a place-of-permanent-residence standard for reconciling conflicting duties.[41] The French-Algerian accord on military service for dual nationals allows such persons to choose in which national army they wish to serve—a solution that has, nevertheless, outraged French ultra-nationalists.[42]

Movement and Minorities

The final two citizenship-related issues, freedom of movement and the place of minorities within national and regional communities, must necessarily be addressed from a regional rather than a single-state perspective, as freedom of movement implies the crossing of borders and communities are defined as much by who is outside the group as by who is within. These issues relate not only to the rights of Palestinians who will live outside the West Bank and Gaza but also to non-Palestinians, such as Jews, Samaritans, or other religious or ethnic minorities, who might continue to remain within an independent or autonomous Palestinian territory.[43]

Both the Israeli 1948 Declaration of Independence and the 1988 Palestine National Council Declaration of Independence provide for protection of minorities within their respective midst. For instance, the Israeli declaration calls on "the Arab inhabitants of the State of Israel to preserve peace and participate in the upbuilding of the state on the basis of full and equal citizenship and due representation . . ." while the Palestinian counterpart refers to a democratic parliamentary system based on ". . . the heed of the majority for minority rights" as well as equality and nondiscrimination.[44] However, more explicit and detailed guidelines should be included in final treaties between all of the parties to the peace settlement.

As noted, an important precedent from the post–World War II period is the 1950 New Delhi Accord between India and Pakistan, which regulated the migration of Hindus and Muslims between the two newly independent, partitioned states.[45] Significantly, these events took place at virtually the identical time, and under similar circumstances—the withdrawal of Britain—as the plan for the partition of Palestine into two states. Although implementation of the accord was troubled by disorder and violence, Article A is worth quoting almost in full:

> The Governments of India and Pakistan solemnly agree that each shall ensure to the minorities throughout its territory complete equality of citizenship, irrespective of religion, a full sense of security in respect of life, culture, property, and personal honour, freedom of movement within each country and freedom of occupation, speech, and worship, subject to law and morality. Members of the minorities shall have equal opportunity with members of the majority community to participate in the public life of the country, to hold political or other office and to serve in their country's civil and armed forces. Both Governments declare these rights to be fundamental and undertake to enforce them effectively. It is the policy of both Governments that the enjoyment of these democratic rights shall be ensured to all their nationals without distinction.[46]

The foremost contemporary precedent on this issue is the achievement of the Conference on Security and Cooperation in Europe, or CSCE (now OSCE, for Organization), which in the 1970s and 1980s forged a common bond of humanitarian principles among the disparate political and economic systems of Eastern and Western Europe (plus Canada and the United States and, after the dissolution of the Soviet Union, the Central Asian states). Although not legally binding, the CSCE's various agreements, which were reached by the rule of consensus, have realized better than any formal set of treaties the establishment of "standards for the behavior of governments, creation of a diplomatic process and encouragement of social movements that continue to this day."[47]

For instance, in the area of national minority rights—probably the most contentious issue, outside of security, to engage the East/West divide—the member states of the CSCE have agreed on a series of general principles, including:

- Persons belonging to national minorities have the right to exercise fully and effectively their human rights and fundamental freedoms without any discrimination and in full equality before the law . . . with the other citizens. . . .

- Persons belonging to national minorities can exercise and enjoy their rights individually as well as in community with other members of their group. No disadvantage may arise for a person belonging to a national minority on account of the exercise or non-exercise of any such rights. . . .

- The participating States will respect the right of persons belonging to national minorities to effective participation in public affairs, including participation in the affairs relating to the protection and promotion of the identity of such minorities.[48]

Specifically enumerated rights include the right of national minorities:

- to establish and maintain their own educational, cultural and religious institutions, organizations or associations, which can seek voluntary financial and other contributions as well as public assistance, in conformity with national legislation; or

- to establish and maintain unimpeded contacts among themselves within their country as well as contacts across frontiers with citizens of other States with whom they share a common ethnic or national origin, cultural heritage or religious beliefs.[49]

A related right is the opportunity of minorities to run for political office.[50] Rights such as these are essential to Palestinians living outside Palestine who seek to sustain communal identities and political representation within their country of residence as well as ties to their fellow nationals in the homeland. In places such as Lebanon, where Palestinians have been the target of sectarian violence, another CSCE commitment is salient: "to take appropriate and proportionate measures to protect persons or groups who may be subject to threats or acts of discrimination, hostility or violence as a result of their racial, ethnic, cultural, linguistic or religious identity, and to protect their property."[51] Similar norms are outlined in the U.N. 1992 Declaration on the Rights of Persons Belonging to National or Ethnic, Religious and Linguistic Minorities,[52] which expounds on Article 27 of the International Covenant on Civil and Political Rights.[53]

In regard to freedom of movement, the CSCE-participating states have affirmed that "freer movement and contacts among their citizens are important in the context of the protection and promotion of human rights and fundamental freedoms."[54] Included among their specific commitments in this regard are the good faith and expeditious processing of visa applications and customs controls, the reduction of visa application fees, and the simplification of administrative procedures. They also have paid deliberate attention to the protection and promotion of the rights of migrant workers.[55] In all CSCE documents on "the human dimension," the problem of family reunification is given special emphasis. Each of these standards is equally important to Palestinians, many of whose families are split and scattered, often against their will, across many borders and who have endured repeated indignities while attempting to obtain travel documents for family, personal, or employment purposes.

In the recent negotiations between Israel and Jordan over the Treaty on Transportation, facilitating the free movement of people and vehicles on both states' territories, negotiators from both sides followed the basic guideline that the transportation sphere was the primary mechanism promoting "the wheels of peace" through which tourism and economic and trade relations will be created and which "will give rise to the feeling that peace is real and full of promise."[56] For instance, due to mutual recognition of each side's passports and travel documents, border crossings will now be expedited. The Israelis and Palestinians had previously agreed that returning Palestinian entrepreneurs could bring with them, tax free, household appliances and cars. "VIP" identity cards, valid for two years, have recently been issued to Palestinian businesspeople to facilitate their movement among Israel, Gaza, and the West Bank.[57]

Open borders are more than just a symbol of peace; they are a precondition of peace. As the frequent Israeli closures of the Gaza and West Bank borders have demonstrated:

> [C]losure has not prevented terrorist attacks or effected the terrorists. It has only caused suffering to the broader population: Arab laborers who lose their sources of income; merchants who find it difficult to buy and sell merchandise; ill people who seek to reach the medical institutions in eastern Jerusalem; students from Gaza studying in the West Bank; and thousands more cases of residents from the territories seeking to obtain visas from foreign consulates, travel abroad from Ben Gurion airport, or visit family members outside the West Bank and Gaza. The closure is directed against them and they are the ones being punished, not the terrorists.[58]

Any law-abiding resident of the region should have the right to pass freely across the region's borders on the way to work, to visit relatives, for tourism, or for other lawful reasons. For instance, as pointed out at the 1995 Amman Economic Conference, computer experts in Jordan and other Arab states with a skilled labor surplus may wish to work in Israel, which currently has a shortage of such workers, or Palestine, which will begin to develop high-tech industries.[59]

The free flow of people across borders naturally leads to the free flow of goods and ideas and the growth of regional tolerance and understanding.[60] But open borders among Jordan, Israel, and Palestine are not enough. It should be considered a normal feature of the region that nonnationals may live within another state's borders, including Palestinians and even Syrians or Jordanians within Israel, or Jordanians and Syrians as well as Jews within Palestine. Moreover, in order to avoid creeping movements toward irredentism, Israel must not attempt, other than through the recognition of dual citizenship, to exercise jurisdiction over Jews who choose to remain in the West Bank and Gaza; similarly, the Palestinian Authority should not attempt the same with regard to Palestinians living in Israel, Jordan, or elsewhere.[61] This restraint would contribute to an atmosphere of "postnationalism" that would provide an incentive to avoid future conflicts in the region. No longer would the nationhood of each country of the Middle East be grounded in ethnocultural obsessions. Each state could then get on with the task of state-building.

Human Rights, Democracy, and Peace

Mutual respect for human rights, including giving Palestinians the voice they have been denied for over three generations, will be central to the success of any final peace arrangements in the region. Yet among the treaties and agreements negotiated to date between Israel and the Palestinians, very little space has been devoted to the subject of human rights and democratization. For instance, the Agreement on the Gaza Strip and the Jericho Area, signed on May 4, 1994, merely states: "Israel and the Palestinian Authority shall exercise their powers and responsibilities pursuant to this Agreement with due regard to internationally accepted norms and principles of human rights and the rule of law."[62] The Israeli-Palestinian Interim Agreement on the West Bank and Gaza Strip (Oslo II), signed over 16 months later on September 28, 1995, states in full: "Israel and the [Palestinian] Council shall exercise their powers and responsibilities pursuant to this agreement with due regard to internationally-accepted norms and principles of human rights and the rule of law."[63] In other words, it virtually repeats the prior text, without advancing the parties to a more sophisticated level of commitment.

Given the checkered record of most Middle Eastern states when it comes to ratification of—let alone compliance with—existing human rights treaties, this does not bode well. See table 5.1 at the end of this chapter for a sampling of such spotty regional treaty participation by those states with significant Palestinian populations. At the very least, the final peace agreements should guarantee that Israel and the Palestinian Authority will ratify and duly enact legislation to implement all of these other multilateral treaties. It is hoped that, by the persuasion of example, other states in the region will eventually adhere, as well. A collective goal for the not-too-distant future should be the adoption of a Middle Eastern convention on human rights and a regional implementation system, including a human rights commission and court such as already exist in Europe and the Americas and, to a less-developed degree, in Africa.[64] In this context, "Middle Eastern" must include Israel and not merely the member states of the Arab League. The Arab states are not the only ones that must make the necessary psychological adjustments to accomplish this task. Israel, too, must demonstrate clearly "that it considers itself a Middle Eastern state and not a western state in the Middle East."[65]

A generation of Israeli occupation, plus the *intifada*, has created two communities—Israelis and Palestinians—that have given little regard to—if not outright defied—international human rights norms.[66] Accordingly, one of the most essential undertakings of the period leading up to and after the final peace settlement will be the development of a popular political culture that respects the rule of law.[67] This process has already begun. For instance, the PLO's Fateh wing, which won most of the seats in the January 1996 West Bank and Gaza elections, produced an election platform that included the objectives of "strengthening national unity and building a democratic civil society, a society of freedom, freedom of expression and pluralism, a society in which all potential may be realized, a society of justice and bounty. . . ."[68] Free and fair elections, of course, should not be considered the be-all and end-all of democracy, which is more than just a matter of majority rule. The separation of powers, the protection of minorities through an independent judiciary, popular and governmental respect for freedom and equality, and a tolerance for dissent and nonviolent opposition are equally as central.[69] Democratization requires hard work, particularly in the form of long-term adult and childhood education. Israel, too, must adapt its school curricula and training of its police, military, and governmental personnel, to include greater emphasis on human rights, democracy, and the rule of law. It received no starker message of the urgency of these changes than in the assassination of Prime Minister Yitzhak Rabin by, of all people, a law student, a young man supposedly studying how democratic institutions and legal process are civilization's substitutes for violence.[70]

The presence in the Middle East of two democratic states, Palestine and Israel, will have a salutary effect all around, perhaps even by lessening the growing ideological divide between Western leaders, who espouse the universality of human rights norms, and Eastern states, led by Iran and other Islamic regimes, that castigate the idea of human rights as the West's cultural imperialism.[71] It is true that many Muslim states have been guilty of egregious violations of human rights and, as stated by Islamic law scholar Ann Elizabeth Mayer, it has therefore been "in their political interest to find rationales for asserting the nonapplicability of international rights norms."[72] But these very rationales are articulated by political elites anxious to insulate their own abusive acts and perpetuate their own oppressive rule by invoking ostensibly authoritative religious doctrines. There is no reason to believe that the majority of average Muslims accepts the self-serving justifications of their nonelected political leaders. Or as King Hussein of Jordan himself noted in 1994, after terrorist attacks on Jewish and Israeli targets in London and Buenos Aires: "Nothing irritates me more or is more painful to me than to witness and see acts and attitudes attributable to Islam that have nothing to do with Islam, my faith and my religion."[73] Moreover, to assume that international human rights norms do not apply to Arabs or Muslims is to adopt a patronizing, racist stereotype that they are barbaric and inferior to Westerners.

Israel's treatment of its Arab citizens has also been unfairly subjected to stereotypes, such as in the 1975 "Zionism is Racism" U.N. General Assembly Resolution, since repealed, or by those authors who have compared it to apartheid regimes, to tsarist Russia's Pale of Settlement, or to the wartime internment of Japanese Americans in the United States.[74] A more appropriate comparison might be to the conditions of African Americans, especially in the American South before the 1960s, or to those of Native Americans, whose land was expropriated but who are no longer geographically confined. Like the Muslim terrorists who invoke Islam to justify their violence against others, Israel, too, has religious fanatics who distort Judaism's tenets in order to legitimize their own acts of terrorism. In a similar fashion, the distortions of an extremist minority should not be mischaracterized as representing a whole people.

The improved status of human rights under the Palestinian Authority will likewise affect human rights in Israel. Having a pluralistic democracy next door will make Israel more democratic and more pluralistic, too.[75] With peace, it will no longer be permissible to justify derogation from human rights norms on the grounds of "public emergency," or threat to the life and existence of the state, or through abuse of the doctrine of "national security."[76] In other words, regional peace, democracy, and human rights are inextricably linked.

Table 5.1 Human Rights Treaties: Year of Accession or Ratification

Treaty Subject	Egypt	Jordan	Kuwait	Iraq	Israel	Lebanon	Saudi Arabia	Syria
Civil/Political Rights	1982	1975	No	1971	1991	1972	No	1969
Economic Rights	1982	1975	No	1971	1991	1972	No	1969
Race Discrimination	1967	1974	1968	1970	1979	1971	No	1969
Genocide	1952	1950	No	1959	1950	1953	1950	1955
Torture	1986	1991	No	No	1991	No	No	No
Women, Discrimination	1981	1992	1994	1986	1991	No	No	No
Child, Rights of	1990	1991	1991	1994	1991	1991	No	1993
Refugees/Convention	1981	No	No	No	1954	No	No	No
Refugees/Protocol	1981	No	No	No	1968	No	No	No
Stateless/Status	No	No	No	No	1958	No	No	No
Stateless/Reduction	No	No	No	No	Signed only	No	No	No

SOURCE: *Multilateral Treaties Deposited with the Secretary-General*. Status as of December 31, 1994 (New York: United Nations, 1995).
Treaties covered: International Covenant on Civil and Political Rights (1966); International Covenant on Economic, Social and Cultural Rights (1966); International Convention on the Elimination of All Forms of Racial Discrimination (1966); Convention on the Prevention and Punishment of the Crime of Genocide (1948); Convention Against Torture and Other Cruel, Inhuman or Degrading Treatment (1984); Convention on the Elimination of All Forms of Discrimination Against Women (1979); Convention on the Right of the Child (1989); Convention Relating to the Status of Refugees (1951); Protocol on the Status of Refugees (1967); Convention Relating to the Status of Stateless Persons (1954); and Convention on the Reduction of Statelessness (1961).

Conclusion:
Accepting Reality

Over the decades, many have argued that the Palestinian refugee crisis—the longest standing in modern history—is unresolvable. This book has attempted to refute that assertion. True, the road to Middle East peace has had many detours, from long breaks in the negotiations to outright walkouts, not to mention assassinations, suicide bombings, and other senseless killings. But despite these setbacks, the process moves forward and, in its wake, changes the very nature of the region and its inhabitants. What has been altered most dramatically—and irreversibly—by the Madrid and Oslo peace negotiations is the realization that the two sides of the Middle East conflict are not Israeli and Palestinian or Jew and Arab but those who, on the one hand, recognize the reality that peace can come only through compromise and those who, on the other hand, refuse to accept the need for compromise: the moderates versus the rejectionists, the tolerant versus the intolerant. The election of Benjamin Netanyahu as prime minister of Israel does not change that.

A large plurality if not a majority of Palestinians have already accepted the reality that they will not achieve their two most sacred demands—all the land they consider Palestine, from the Jordan to the Mediterranean, and complete return of all Palestinians to that land. "Return," they realize, will be "primarily a return to the Palestinian state to be established, rather than to Israel proper."[1] This reluctant acceptance is conditioned on the provision of citizenship and the rights attendant to that status, on adequate compensation, and on the ability of individuals truly to exercise choice and to affect the course of their own lives, which has been called the most important criterion of a person's standard of living, that is, human dignity.[2]

Moreover, the possibility of obtaining a Palestinian passport would serve, for many of those who will return neither to their original homes nor to the Palestinian Authority, as a restoration of "community membership" in the Palestinian nation, as "an asylum, symbol of identity and protection" and of international recognition.[3] In other words, so long as the refugees can obtain a dignified, symbolic representation of each of their two original demands—independence in part of the land and return to the original homeland of a portion of their people—many Palestinians are willing to accept compromise.

By contrast, while much of the Israeli mainstream has, if only begrudgingly, come to accept the inevitable establishment of a Palestinian state next door, there still persists an almost universal Israeli rejection of the idea that even a single Palestinian refugee should be able to return home, if that home is within the boundaries of Israel.[4] And because the topic of refugees is so much of a taboo, there is very little dialogue about it among Israelis and even less between Israelis and Palestinians. Therefore, Israelis have had little chance to hear from Palestinians that no, they do not want to take their houses away from them, they do not hope to bankrupt them with inordinate compensation claims, they do not even all want to return.

Yet even without that vital dialogue, Israelis are gradually coming to realize that the concept of "peace," as envisioned by the Madrid and Oslo frameworks, and including a resolution of the refugee problem, does not have to be translated as "Israel's destruction." Terrorists are rarely recruited from communities of permanently absorbed citizens, whereas refugee camps remain a potential wellhead of violence. Moreover, the much-feared "demographic bomb" can be significantly altered if Palestinian refugees are finally given decent housing, job training, and other indicia of economic development, along with greater participation in public life for Palestinian women, all of which normally result in lower birthrates.[5] The number of family reunification cases this book has recommended for return within the Green Line of Israel is in fact so minimal that it is really but a red herring when considered within the complex of benefits that peace will bring. When matched with a similar figure of 75,000 Palestinians to be permanently absorbed in Lebanon, the mutual symbolism and goodwill that will inure to Israel should be considered invaluable.

"Normalcy," as proffered in the introduction to this book, is an essential principle of a peace settlement. Normalcy will be achieved when Israelis no longer feel threatened—either militarily or demographically—by Palestinians and when Palestinians no longer feel "unsettled," both literally and figuratively, by Israelis. Both peoples will then come to realize that not only are their respective roles in history so similar but their futures are alike, as well. Just as not all Jews live in Israel, not all Palestinians will live in Palestine. But for both peoples, statehood is an integral part of their collective identity.

It has taken great fortitude and maturation on the part of the parties to reach the agreements that have been signed to date; not so long ago even the rudimentary provisions of the Declaration of Principles seemed inconceivable, if not surreal. What Israelis and Palestinians need now is greater encouragement to further progress by the supporters of peace, both in the region and outside, to help build global constituencies for peace and regional constituencies for tolerance. While undoubtedly more setbacks will occur before the final status talks are concluded, the participants need to be assured that the compromises they make on behalf of peace will rebound to the mutual benefit of all.

Jordan has already recognized that peace is in its interest. The absorption plan proposed in this book should similarly be acceptable in the kingdom because it keeps steady the relative number of Palestinians there and eventually will result in decreasing costs of sustaining the refugees, as the camps are eliminated. Greater financial assistance (perhaps in the form of major debt forgiveness), which could be portrayed as "reimbursement" to Jordan for its prior willingness to pay for refugee absorption, would be an added incentive.

Similar financial incentives probably also will be needed to win the endorsement of other Arab states for a regional absorption plan, even though no country, not even Lebanon, will be "targeted" with a Palestinian population so large as to undermine its political or demographic stability. Rather, given the already high levels of Palestinian education, their permanent absorption as productive citizens of the neighboring states should greatly benefit national economies. It should also be widely appreciated that absorption of Palestinians in states throughout the region is necessary for the economic and political stability of the new Palestinian enterprise in the West Bank and Gaza. Perhaps even Iraq, which could benefit from the influx of immigrants to populate its sparsely settled rural areas, will come around to the wisdom of absorbing Palestinian refugees, such as the excess from Lebanon who will neither stay there nor be repatriated in the Galilee.

Moreover, Palestinian statehood, or some other viable and dignified form of sovereignty (such as confederation with Jordan), and a permanent solution to the refugee problem will help to neutralize the support for regional radicalism that has heretofore threatened the more conservative Arab states, particularly those in the Gulf.[6] It is therefore in the interest of Saudi Arabia and even Kuwait to help fund the compensation pool and other rehabilitation projects that will be integral to regional refugee absorption. The United States, the European Union, and Japan also know that Middle East peace promotes their interests, too, when peace can result in greater protection for oil resources, control over the drug trade in Lebanon, the eventual elimination of support for terrorism by Damascus, and the creation of a strong regional bloc against fundamentalist extremism.

Thus, if the parties receive the international support that they need and deserve, they will be able to deal with each other in good faith with the confidence that the refugee problem can be resolved. Even without the near-term achievement of the standard of international normalcy, peace is attainable. The future Palestinian-Israeli peace treaty would not be the first international agreement built around mutual mistrust. Indeed, the last stages of the Cold War were fought and, finally, concluded around the very theme of refugees and family reunification.[7]

As one realistic Palestinian recently explained to a receptive Israeli: "The hatred can never disappear, but [just as] the war with the Germans is over, the same will happen to us," the Palestinians and Israelis. "The war will end, we'll exchange diplomats and we'll live."[8] It will be so because the neighbors are not moving out of the neighborhood.

Notes

Introduction: Principles of Peace

1. Fawaz Turki, quoted in Baruch Kimmerling and Joel S. Migdal, *Palestinians: The Making of a People* (Cambridge, MA: Harvard University Press, 1994), p. xvii. Palestinian poet Mahmoud Darwish has similarly referred to Palestinians as "victims of the map" in his 1984 book of the same name (London: Saai Books, 1984). Israeli journalist Danny Rubinstein dubs them "people of nowhere" in his book by that title (New York: Times Books, 1991).

2. See Salim Tamari, "Fading Flags: The Crises of Palestinian Legitimacy," *Middle East Report* (May–June/July–Aug. 1995), pp. 10, 11, describing the assessment of historian Musa Budeiri that "Palestinian national identity was primarily forged in the camps and communities of the diaspora rather than in Palestine, and came into its present form only after the 1964 formation of the PLO under Arab League tutelage, reinforced by the alienation of Palestinians from the host Arab countries where they had sought refuge." That does not mean that Palestinians were not a distinct people before 1948 or 1964. See the "History/Origins" section of the bibliographical essay at the end of this book.

3. Louis Rapoport, *Stalin's War Against the Jews: The Doctors' Plot and the Soviet Solution* (New York: Free Press, 1990), pp. 141, 205, 158. See generally Michael Curtis, ed., *Antisemitism in the Contemporary World* (Boulder, CO: Westview Press, 1986); Robert S. Wistrich, ed., *Anti-Zionism and Antisemitism in the Contemporary World* (New York: New York University Press, 1990).

4. Ibrahim al-Shatti, the emir's *chef de cabinet*, quoted in Muhammad Faour, *The Arab World After Desert Storm* (Washington, DC: United States Institute of Peace Press, 1993), p. 22. Turki similarly describes how the Palestinian community of Lebanon in the 1950s was "held responsible for every ill in the country, from communist plots to unseasonable weather," which echoes Soviet and Nazi charges against the Jews. Fawaz Turki, *Exile's Return: The Making of a Palestinian American* (New York: Free Press, 1994), p. 54. See also Aziz Haidar, "The Different Levels of Palestinian Ethnicity," in Milton J. Esman and Itamar Rabinvich, eds., *Ethnicity, Pluralism and the State in the Middle East* (Ithaca, NY: Cornell University Press, 1988), pp. 95, 102.

5. As used in this book, the expressions "Arab-Israeli conflict" and "Palestinian-Israeli conflict" have slightly different meanings, the former referring to the broader confrontation involving virtually all the states of the Middle East and the latter referring to the clash between the two particular peoples, the Palestinians and Israelis, and their national representatives. The two conflicts are intimately interconnected. The Oslo Accord

and the Madrid peace process are both based on the assumption that resolution of the latter can lead to resolution of the former.

6. Ron Pundik, "Towards a New Chapter in the Israeli-Palestinian Negotiations?" *Palestine-Israel Journal* 2, no. 5 (Winter 1995), p. 6.

7. Serge Schmemann, "Negotiators, Arab and Israeli, Built Friendship From Mistrust," *New York Times*, Sept. 28, 1995, pp. A1, A10, quoting Palestinian chief negotiator Abu Alaa.

8. See Baruch Kimmerling, ed., *The Israeli State and Society: Boundaries and Frontiers* (Albany, NY: State University of New York Press, 1989).

9. Palestinian moderates have already made similar suggestions. See, for instance, Rashid Khalidi, "Toward a Solution," *Palestinian Refugees: Their Problem and Future* (Washington, DC: Center for Policy Analysis on Palestine, 1994), pp. 21–26; Abraham Rabinovich, "A Palestinian Trial Balloon on the 'Right of Return,' " *Jerusalem Post*, June 3, 1994, p. 3B (interview with Ziad Abu Zayyad); and Elia Zureik, "Palestinian Refugees and Peace," *Journal of Palestine Studies* 24, no. 1 (Autumn 1994), pp. 5–17.

10. T. H. Marshall and Tom Bottomore, *Citizenship and Social Class* (London: Pluto Press, 1992), p. 6. See Rogers Brubaker, ed., *Immigration and the Politics of Citizenship in Europe and North America* (New York: University Press of America, 1989), p. 3; Rogers Brubaker, *Citizenship and Nationhood in France and Germany* (Cambridge, MA: Harvard University Press, 1992), pp. 40–43.

11. Marshall and Bottomore, *Citizenship and Social Class*, pp. 8, 66.

12. Ibid., p. 34.

13. Alouph Hareven, "An End to the Era of Sacrifices," *Palestine-Israel Journal* 2, no. 3 (1995), pp. 81, 84.

14. Brubaker, *Citizenship and Nationhood*, p. 21.

15. Hareven, "An End to the Era of Sacrifices," p. 84.

16. 356 U.S. 44, 64 (1958) (Warren, C.J., dissenting). The full Court later adopted Warren's position in *Afrovim v. Rusk*, 387 U.S. 253 (1967).

17. Hareven, "An End to the Era of Sacrifices," p. 84.

18. Articles 25 and 27 of the International Covenant on Civil and Political Rights, 999 U.N.T.S. 171 (1966); Declaration on the Rights of Persons Belonging to National or Ethnic, Religious and Linguistic Minorities, G.A. Res. 47/135, U.N. Doc. A/RES/47/135, Feb. 3, 1993. See Patrick Thornberry, *International Law and the Rights of Minorities* (Oxford: Clarendon Press, 1991); Florence Benoit-Rohmer and Hilde Hardeman, "The Representation of Minorities in the Parliaments of Central and Eastern Europe," *International Journal on Group Rights* 2 (1994), pp. 91–111.

19. "Palestinians should strive to abolish Arab League statutes which prevent Arab citizens from holding dual Arab citizenship." Salim Tamari, "Return, Resettlement, Repatriation: The Future of Palestinian Refugees in the Peace Negotiations," unpublished paper for the Institute for Palestine Studies, Jerusalem (Feb. 1996), part X.3. One of the numerous "rec-

ommendations for action" concerning refugees reached at the Conference on Promoting Regional Cooperation in the Middle East, held in Vouliagmeni, Greece in Nov. 1994 was: "The merits and demerits of dual citizenship for Palestinians [and Jews] should be considered as one aspect of the solution which would allow the refugees to integrate in other countries without loss of their national and political identity." Report available at gopher://irpsserv26.ucsd.edu:70/OF-1%3A18800%3A WorkGroup-Refugees. See also Khadija Elmadmad, "Appropriate Solutions for the Palestinian Refugees," paper presented at same conference, available at same Internet site.

20. See Roger Fisher and William Ury, *Getting to Yes: Negotiating Agreement Without Giving In* (New York: Penguin Books, 1983) pp. 58–83; Richard D. Schwartz, "Arab-Jewish Dialogue in the United States: Toward Track II Tractability," in Louis Kriesberg, Terrell A. Northrup, and Stuart J. Thorson, eds., *Intractable Conflicts and Their Transformation* (Syracuse, NY: Syracuse University Press, 1989), pp. 180–209.

21. See Donna E. Arzt, "Negotiating the Last Taboo: Palestinian Refugees," *Jordan Times*, July 12, 1995, pp. 6–7, reprinted on <fofognet@ atvm1.mcgill.ca>, internet bulletin board from McGill University, Jan. 31, 1996; Daoud Kuttab, "Many Taboos Between Israelis and Palestinians Are Falling Away: An Interview with Faisal Husseini," *Palestine-Israel Journal*, no. 3 (Summer 1994), pp. 36–40.

22. Some of the more recent descriptions of the myriad proposals appear in "Roundtable: In Search of Solutions," *Palestine-Israel Journal* 2, no. 1 (1995), p. 87; Ann Mosely Lesch et al., *Transition to Palestinian Self-Government: Practical Steps Toward Peace* (Bloomington, IN; American Academy of Arts & Sciences, Indiana University Press, 1992), pp. 54–56; Letty Cottin Pogrebin, "Two Forevers and a Maybe," *Tikkun* 8, no. 6 (1994), p. 72; *Jerusalem: Perspectives Towards a Political Settlement* (Tel Aviv: New Outlook/United States Institute of Peace, 1993); Paul Goldberger, "Passions Set in Stone," *New York Times Magazine*, Sept. 10, 1995, p. 42; Isabel Kershner and Tom Sawicki, "The Battle for Jerusalem," *Jerusalem Report*, July 28, 1994, p. 11; and Yair Sheleg, "Jerusalem: One City—56 Solutions," *Kol Ha'ir*, Aug. 6, 1993 (trans. by Israel Government Press Office News Division).

23. For instance, the Palestinian Islamic Resistance Movement, known as Hamas, has repeatedly stated its "refusal to consider our entire people's right to return to their territory an issue that is subject to bargains or negotiations with the usurpers of this right." "Hamas Says Right to Repatriation Is Not 'Subject to Bargains,' " *British Broadcasting Corporation Summary of World Broadcasts*, Mar. 11, 1995, ME/2249/MED. The official Israeli position, even under the Labor government of Rabin, was stated by Deputy Defense Minister Mordechai Gur as: "In the worldview of the government, the right of return is unacceptable in this accord and we will not allow any clause permitting refugees to return and flood Israel." "Israel Rejects Palestinian Right of Return," *Reuters*, Sept. 3, 1993.

24. The latter two topics, although sometimes stated to be part of "the population issue" or "the refugee issue," are beyond the scope of this book. The
settler question is more naturally discussed in the context of permanent
borders and security. On the claims of Jewish refugees from Arab countries, see Joseph B. Schechtman, *On Wings of Eagles: The Plight, Exodus and
Homecoming of Oriental Jews* (New York: T. Yoseloff, 1961); Maurice M.
Roumanie, *The Case of the Jews from Arab Countries: A Neglected Issue* (Tel
Aviv: WOJAC 1977); Terence Prittie and Bernard Dineen, *The Double Exodus: A Study of Arab and Jewish Refugees in the Middle East* (London: Good-
hart Press, 1974); Ya'akov Meron, "Why Jews Fled the Arab Countries,"
Middle East Quarterly (Sept. 1995), pp. 47–55. A summary of the experi-
ences of Jewish communities in 12 Muslim countries appears in the Israel
Government Press Office document, "The Refugee Issue: A Background
Paper" (Oct. 1994), pp. 15–18. It is frequently noted that the number of
these Jewish refugees from Arab states, about 588,000, is coincidentally
close to the estimated number of Palestinians who fled Israel in 1948.

Palestinians have responded to the attempt to equate Jewish and Palestinian refugees by noting that the two movements are not parallel: most of
the Jews left voluntarily and not in the midst of war. Compensation for
Jewish property left behind is, accordingly, a topic for bilateral discussions
between Israel and the respective Arab states and does not concern the
Palestinians. Moreover, as stated by Ziad Abu Zayyad: "We, the Palestinians, did not force them to leave those countries. Therefore, the issue
should be negotiated directly with the Arab countries those refugees came
from." Abraham Rabinovich, "A Palestinian Trial Balloon on the 'Right of
Return,'" *Jerusalem Post*, June 3, 1994, p. 3B.

25. "Peres: Jerusalem Will Not Become Another Berlin," *Jerusalem Post*, July 1,
1994, p. 1. See generally Shimon Peres, *Battling for Peace: Memoirs* (London:
Weidenfeld & Nicolson, 1995). See also Schmemann, "Negotiators, Arab
and Israeli, Built Friendship From Mistrust," describing how the chief negotiators from each side furiously debated their respective origins "back
to Abraham" and then stopped. "At that point, we decided never again to
discuss the past, and only the future." In his speech before the U.S. Congress upon becoming prime minister after Rabin was assassinated, Peres
spoke implicitly to Syria's President Hafez al-Assad: "Without forgetting
the past, let us not look back. Let fingertips touch a new hope. Let each
party yield to the other, each giving consideration to the respective needs
of the other mutually. We stand ready to negotiate relentlessly until gaps
are bridged—if you are." Quoted by Jacob Stein, "Like No Two Other Sovereign Peoples: Americans and Israelis," *Jewish World*, Dec. 15–21, 1995,
pp. 8, 9.

26. "[G]overnments and humanitarian organizations have become increasingly aware of the fact that refugee problems are by definition transnational problems, and that they cannot be resolved by means of uncoordi-
nated activities in separate countries. Recent years have therefore
witnessed a growing interest in regional approaches to refugee questions,

combining the efforts of countries of origin and asylum, as well as other governments, international organizations and voluntary agencies." United Nations High Commissioner for Refugees, *The State of the World's Refugees, 1995: In Search of Solutions* (Oxford: Oxford University Press, 1995), p. 49.

27.   Nabil Elaraby, "The Peace Process: Some Implications," *Proceedings of the 89th Annual Meeting of the American Society of International Law* (1995), pp. 363, 364. Elaraby is the Egyptian ambassador to the United Nations. Rami Khouri suggested the broader articulation of this principle in an email letter to this author.

28.   Salim Tamari, "Return, Resettlement, Repatriation: The Future of Palestinian Refugees in the Peace Negotiations," part 7, quoting Vision Paper 2.2 of the Refugee Multilateral Working Group.

29.   "King Husayn's Remarks at Washington Summit," *BBC Summary of World Broadcasts*, July 27, 1994. Similarly, Saudi Foreign Minister Prince Saud al-Faisal al-Saud has stated to Jewish leaders in New York: "If there is peace in the region, I can say unequivocally that we will normalize relations with Israel." "Quote, Unquote," *Jerusalem Report*, Nov. 2, 1995, p. 13.

Chapter 1: The Historical Framework

1.   See the bibliographical essay at the end of this book for citations to some of these works.

2.   See the bibliographical essay for references to the new studies.

3.   G.A. Resolution 181(II), Nov. 29, 1947.

4.   Benny Morris, *The Birth of the Palestinian Refugee Problem* (Cambridge: Cambridge University Press, 1987), pp. 297–98. He describes the exodus as occurring in four clearly identifiable stages: December 1947–March 1948; April–June 1948; July 9–18, 1948; and October–November 1948.

5.   This 726,000 figure is used by both the United Nations Conciliation Commission for Palestine, Report of the U.N. Economic Survey Mission for the Middle East, U.N. Doc. A/AC.25/6, p. 18, and the United Nations Relief and Works Agency for Palestine Refugees, Annual Report of the Director General, U.N. Doc. 5224/5223, Nov. 25, 1952. The British government statistics are from PROFO371-754196 E2297/1821/31, cited in *Facts and Figures About the Palestinians* (Washington, DC: Center for Policy Analysis on Palestine, Apr. 1993), p. 13.

6.   Morris, *The Birth of the Palestinian Refugee Problem*; Simha Flapan, *The Birth of Israel: Myths and Realities* (New York: Pantheon, 1987), p. 83. See Baruch Kimmerling and Joel S. Migdal, *Palestinians: The Making of a People* (Cambridge, MA: Harvard University Press, 1994), pp. 146–56. According to Dr. Sharif Kana'ne of Bir-Zeit University, the number of Arab villages destroyed by Israel in 1948 is 450. Danny Rubinstein, *The People of Nowhere: The Palestinian Vision of Home* (New York: Times Books, 1991), p. 9; Kamel

Abdel Fatah, ed., *The Map of the Destroyed Villages, 1948–1950* (Ramallah: Bir-Zeit University, 1964). In his preface, Morris lists 369 destroyed villages.

7. See Mark Tessler, *A History of the Israeli-Palestinian Conflict* (Bloomington: Indiana University Press, 1994), p. 279; Israel Government Press Office, "The Refugee Issue: A Background Paper" (Oct. 1994).

8. For instance, are Bedouins (nomadic Arabs) considered Palestinians? Are Druze, who are Arabs with a secretive religion, derived from Islam? What about the Samaritans, a sect living on the West Bank that broke away from Judaism over 2,500 years ago? Or the Circassians, approximately 2,500 of whom live in Israel at present, a group of non-Arab Sunni Muslims whose ancestors fled to the Middle East in the 1860s when their original home in the Caucasus was faced with Russian invasion? See Michael Wolffsohn, *Israel: Polity, Society and Economy, 1882–1986: An Introductory Handbook* (Atlantic Highlands, NJ: Humanities Press International, 1987), p. 166. The definition of Palestinian in the 1968 Palestine National Charter would presumably include the Bedouin and the Druze: "[T]hose Arab nationals who, until 1947, normally resided in Palestine regardless of whether they were evicted from it or have stayed there. Anyone born, after that date, of a Palestinian father—whether inside Palestine or outside it—is also a Palestinian" (Article 5). Reprinted in John N. Moore, ed., *The Arab-Israeli Conflict*, vol. 3 (Washington, DC: American Society of International Law, 1974), p. 705.

9. Tessler, *A History of the Israeli-Palestinian Conflict*, p. 279. Others put the number remaining at 170,000. Don Peretz, *Israel and the Palestine Arabs* (Washington, DC: Middle East Institute, 1958), p. 95.

10. *Facts and Figures About the Palestinians*, p. 7; Wolffsohn, *Israel: Polity, Society and Economy*, pp. 119–21. The slight variations are due to differences in specific dates and in the boundaries used to demarcate the actual territory designated as Palestine and then Israel.

11. Equally significant, and almost equally subject to debate, are the estimates of how many reached the various destinations that would become the "temporary" shelters of the refugees for the next half century. These estimates are discussed in chapter 2. See map 2.1.

12. At the conclusion of the war, 63,000 were granted immediate Israeli citizenship, while the rest applied for citizenship under the 1950 Nationality Law. See Yoav Peled, "Ethnic Democracy and the Legal Construction of Citizenship: Arab Citizens of the Jewish State," *American Political Science Review* 86, no. 2 (June 1992), pp. 432, 435; David Kretzmer, *The Legal Status of the Arabs in Israel* (Boulder, CO: Westview Press, 1990), pp. 37–39.

13. *Facts and Figures About the Palestinians*, p. 12; Peretz, *Israel and the Palestine Arabs*, p. 95. With the Israeli Arab birthrate being what it is, even a starting figure of 25,000 could have evolved into about 150,000 today, meaning that about 18 percent of the current Israeli-Arab population of approximately 840,000 consists of "internal" refugee descendants. See chapter 2 for more on this population.

14. Tessler, *A History of the Israeli-Palestinian Conflict*, p. 281.

15. The Israeli embassy in Washington has stated the official Israeli version, that Palestinians voluntarily left their towns and villages "in order to make way for the Arab invasion of Israel in 1948." Carol Giacomo, "U.S. Clarifies View on Palestinian Right of Return," *Reuters*, May 13, 1992. See a more thorough statement of the official Israeli view in Israel GPO, "The Refugee Issue." The "new Israeli historiography" rejects this version as illogical: "The Arab armies, coming long distances and operating in or from the Arab areas of Palestine, needed the help of the local population for food, fuel, water, transport, manpower and information." Flapan, *The Birth of Israel*, p. 85. "The myth of voluntary exodus became Israel's major argument against accepting even partial responsibility for the refugee problem, not to mention consideration of the refugees' right to repatriation." Ibid., p. 118.

   The Palestine Information Center states that between December 27, 1947, and May 9, 1948—that is, before the date of Israeli independence and British evacuation—16 Arab villages, including 12 in the part of Palestine that was proposed by the United Nations as an Arab state, were attacked and occupied by Jewish armies with the goal "to extend the boundaries of the Jewish State beyond those called for by the U.N. Partition Plan of November [29], 1947." "Arab Villages Attacked by the Zionists Prior to May 14, 1948," Palestine Information Center (web site). The official Israeli position is that Palestinian violence against Jewish neighborhoods in Jerusalem, Haifa, and Jaffa as well as against Jews living elsewhere in the Middle East began at the beginning of December 1947—a few days after the U.N. Partition vote, which none of the Arab states supported. By March 1948, "there were nearly 7,000 Arab irregulars in the country. They launched assaults against urban Jewish quarters, attacked outlying kibbutzim and cut vital roads linking major cities and Jewish centers." Israel GPO, "The Refugee Issue," pp. 2–3.

   On the Deir Yassin episode, see Leonard J. Davis, *Myths and Facts 1989: A Concise Record of the Arab-Israeli Conflict* (Washington, DC: Near East Reports, 1990), pp. 27–28, 108–10, for an official Israeli explanation. See Flapan, *The Birth of Israel*, pp. 94–96, as well as Morris, *The Birth of the Palestinian Refugee Problem*, for alternative explanations.

16. "A minority certainly fled to join the Arab armies; the vast majority of civilians simply fled before an advancing army and the collapse of their own institutions; an even smaller minority were terrorised or driven out at gunpoint." Baruch Kimmerling, "Shaking the Foundations," *Index on Censorship* 24, no. 3 (1995), pp. 47, 50, paraphrasing Benny Morris.

17. Flapan, *The Birth of Israel*, p. 84.

18. Shlomo Gazit, "Solving the Refugee Problem: A Prerequisite for Peace," *Palestine-Israeli Journal* 2, no. 4 (Autumn 1995), p. 65. Put similarly: "If the plight of the refugees is not resolved—including, at least for some, resettlement in a Palestinian political entity—then there can be no stable and permanent solution to the conflict." Joseph Alpher, "Israel: The

Challenges of Peace," *Foreign Policy*, no. 101 (Winter 1995–96), pp. 130, 140. "[The refugee issue] is still at the heart of the Middle East problem, as it has been since 1948. If every effort is not made to deal with it fully in *all* its aspects, including the ones that now seem most intractable, it will gnaw away remorselessly at whatever agreements may be signed—and at all our hopes for long-term stability in the area." Marc Perron, talk at the Institute for Social and Economic Policy in the Middle East, Kennedy School of Government, Harvard University, Feb. 16, 1994, p. 12.

19. Rubinstein, *The People of Nowhere*, pp. 17, 13. "The Jew had a different order of priorities   The dominant components of his identity are sovereignty in the land of his forefathers, the Hebrew language, and collective historical memories, not an attachment to a specific house or address." Ibid., p. 17.

20. "The Israeli government destroyed most of the approximately 350 abandoned Arab villages and towns, and arguing that the concept of land ownership was meaningless in a total war, Ben-Gurion initiated the allocation of the refugees' land to Jews. Through the middle of 1949, Israeli leaders also established about 130 new Jewish settlements where Arab villages and towns had stood. . . ." Kimmerling and Migdal, *Palestinians: The Making of a People*, p. 155.

21. Newly declassified documents reveal that in September 1948, Prime Minister Ben-Gurion had proposed extending the war in order to expel 100,000 more Arabs from the Galilee. The cabinet voted down the idea. "14 Days: Ben-Gurion Plan," *Jerusalem Report*, Mar. 9, 1995, p. 11. A related question is when, if there was such an Israeli plan, it was first launched. Arab sources claim it began before the date of independence, May 14, 1948, and that many of the villages attacked were within the proposed Arab state under the U.N. partition plan. See Nur Masalha, *Expulsion of the Palestinians: The Concept of 'Transfer' in Zionist Political Thought 1882–1948* (Washington, DC: Institute for Palestinian Studies, 1992), pp. 175-99. Morris believes that an informal decision to bar a refugee return was made at an Israeli cabinet meeting on June 16, 1948, a month after indepencence, Benny Morris, "Falsifying the Record: A Fresh Look at Zionist Documentation of 1948," *Journal of Palestine Studies* 24, no. 3 (Spring 1995), pp. 44, 56–57.

22. On these laws, see Donna E. Arzt and Karen Zughaib, "Return to the Negotiated Lands: The Likelihood and Legality of a Population Transfer Between Israel and a Future Palestinian State," *New York University Journal of International Law and Politics* 24, No. 4 (1992), pp. 1399, 1423–25. There are other precedents, in India and Pakistan and in Cyprus, for using evacuated property to settle new immigrants. See Eyal Benvenisti and Eyal Zamir, "Private Claims to Property Rights in the Future Israeli-Palestinian Settlement," *American Journal of International Law* 89 (April 1995), pp. 295, 323–24.

The official Israeli estimate of expropriated land, 3,250 square kilometers, is reported in *Israel Government Yearbook 5715* (Jerusalem: Israeli Yearbook Publications, 1955), p. 74; the United Nations Conciliation Commission for Palestine estimate, 4,574 square kilometers, is reported in Progress Report of the United Nations Conciliation Commission for Palestine, U.N. GAOR, 6th Sess., Supp. No. 18, Ann. A, para. 8, U.N. Doc. A/1985 (1951).

23. See Don Peretz, "Early State Policy Toward the Arab Population, 1948–1955," in Laurence J. Silberstein, ed., *New Perspectives on Israeli History: The Early Years of the State* (New York: New York University Press, 1991), pp. 82, 95.

24. Paul R. Mendes-Flohr, ed., *A Land of Two Peoples: Martin Buber on Jews and Arabs* (Oxford: Oxford University Press, 1983), p. 262, quoting letter of Mar. 7, 1953. The daily newspaper *Haaretz* also protested. See Peretz in Silberstein, *New Perspectives on Israeli History*.

25. Wolffsohn, *Israel: Polity, Society and Economy*, p. 121.

26. Quoted by Bernard Avishai, *The Tragedy of Zionism: Revolution and Democracy in the Land of Israel* (New York: Farrar, Straus, Giroux, 1985), p. 215.

27. The number of refugees also included 15,000 from Algeria, 30,000 from Egypt, 25,000 from Iran, 3,000 from Lebanon, 37,000 from Libya, 7,000 from Syria, and 38,000 from Tunisia. Wolffsohn, *Israel: Polity, Society and Economy*, p. 131. While some Arab states prohibited Jews from emigrating, others used official laws and unofficial violence to force Jewish emigration. See Joseph B. Schechtman, *On Wings of Eagles: The Plight, Exodus and Homecoming of Oriental Jews* (New York: T. Yoseloff, 1961). See also introduction, note 24.

28. Don Peretz, *Palestinians, Refugees and the Middle East Peace Process* (Washington, DC: United States Institute of Peace Press, 1993), p. 13; *Facts and Figures About the Palestinians*, p. 14; Paul Lahor, "The Palestinians," in Dorothy Stannard, ed., *Jordan* (Boston: Houghton Mifflin, 1994), p. 101; Shlomo Gazit, "Misplaced Anxieties," *Jerusalem Post*, May 10, 1994, p. 6; and Shlomo Gazit, "Displaced Persons in Focus," *Jerusalem Post*, Mar. 10, 1995, p. 4. In 1968, acccording to Jordanian Foreign Ministry records, about 203,000 Palestinians registered in Jordan as "displaced persons" from the West Bank and Gaza. Ori Nir, "What is a Refugee? What is a Displaced Person?" *Ha'aretz*, Mar. 7, 1995 p. B3. According to UNRWA, 175,000 "registered refugees" (in other words, 1948 refugees) fled the West Bank for Jordan and another 38,500 fled the Gaza Strip, also for Jordan; the Jordanian government reported a total of 246,000 "non-refugee Palestinians" (first-time displaced) there after the war. See report of the Commissioner-General of UNRWA, 1 July 1967–30 June 1968, (U.N. General Assembly, *Official Records* (Twenty-third session, supp. No. 13, A/7213), p. 1. Sami Hadawi, *Bitter Harvest: A Modern History of Palestine* (London: New World Press, 1967) p. 146, gives a high figure of 416,000, which he claims does *not* include Syrians displaced from the Golan Heights and Egyptians displaced from Sinai.

A related category of displaced persons is those 18,000 or so who, subsequent to 1967, were outside of the West Bank and Gaza and whose exit permits expired. This topic is being discussed in the context of the "quadripartite committee." See the last section of this chapter.

29. Colbert C. Held, *Middle East Patterns: Places, People, and Politics* (Boulder, CO: Westview Press, 1994), p. 188, gives figures of 99,000 Druze and 35,000 Bedouins and Egyptians. But the 99,000 figure seems high. UNRWA reports that Syria received 17,500 displaced persons from the Syrian Golan Heights to Damascus and its vicinity. Report of the Commissioner-General, *Official Records* (1968), p. 4.

30. See sources cited in note 29.

31. See Areyeh Shalev, *Autonomy: Problems and Possible Solutions* (1979) (Hebrew), pp. 118–19, 164. Shalev states that few Israeli settlements have been established on the property "abandoned" in 1967. Ibid.

32. Hadawi, *Bitter Harvest*, pp. 146–47. See also chapter 3, note 2.

33. Martin Gilbert, *Atlas of the Arab-Israeli Conflict*, 6th ed., (New York: Oxford University Press, 1993), p. 3.

34. See the multivolume report prepared between December 1945 and January 1946 by the British Mandate Government of Palestine for the Anglo-American Committee of Inquiry, *A Survey of Palestine*, vol. 1 (1947). Reprinted in 1991 by the Institute for Palestine Studies, pp. 210–13.

35. Wolffsohn, *Israel: Polity, Society and Economy*, pp. 119, 121.

36. Ibid., p. 119.

37. See Chaim Simons, *International Proposals to Transfer Arabs from Palestine, 1895–1947: A Historical Survey* (Hoboken, NJ: Ktav Publication House, 1988); Nur Masalha, *Expulsion of the Palestinians: The Concept of "Transfer" in Zionist Political Thought 1882–1948* (Washington, DC: Institute for Palestine Studies, 1992).

38. Yossi Melman, *The New Israelis: An Intimate View of a Changing People* (New York: Carol Publishing Company, 1992), p. 53.

39. Simons, *International Proposals to Transfer Arabs*, p. 3.

40. Ibid., p. 4.

41. Tessler, *A History of the Israeli-Palestinian Conflict*, p. 167.

42. Ibid., p. 244.

43. Ben-Gurion has been quoted as stating in 1931: "[T]he Arab in Palestine has the right to self-determination. This right is not limited, and cannot be qualified by our own interests. . . . It is possible that the realization of the aspirations (of the Palestinian Arabs) will create serious difficulties for us but this is not a reason to deny their rights." Quoted by John A. Collins, "Self-Determination in International Law. The Palestinians," *Case Western Reserve Journal of International Law* 12 (1980), p. 137. See also Simons, *International Proposals to Transfer Arabs*, pp. 10–12.

On October 11, 1961, speaking as prime minister, Ben-Gurion stated: "Israel categorically rejects the insidious proposal for freedom of choice for the refugees, for she is convinced that this proposal is designed and calculated only to destroy Israel. There is only one practical and fair solution for the problem of the refugees: to resettle them among their own people in countries having plenty of good land and water and which are in need of additional manpower." Mendes-Flohr, *A Land of Two Peoples*, p. 294.

44. Simons, *International Proposals to Transfer Arabs*, pp. 88–89. Simons describes other transfer proposals by such non-Jews as Herbert Hoover, John Gunther, Edwyn Bevan, and Harry St. John Philby.

45. Ibid., pp. 123–24. See Tessler, *A History of the Israeli-Palestinian Conflict*, pp. 241–45.

46. Simons, *International Proposals to Transfer Arabs*, pp. 136–38.

47. Schectman is quoted in ibid., p. 127. See Joseph B. Schechtman, *Population Transfers in Asia* (New York: Hallsby Press, 1949), pp. 84–141. For Wedgwood's comments, see Simons, *International Proposals to Transfer Arabs*, p. 144.

48. Joel Brinkley, "Arab-Expulsion Party in Israel's Cabinet," *New York Times*, Feb. 4, 1991, p. A3. See generally Ehud Sprinzak, *The Ascendance of Israel's Radical Right* (New York: Oxford University Press, 1991); and David Kretzmer, "Racial Incitement in Israel," in Monroe H. Freedman and Eric M. Freedman, *Group Defamation and Freedom of Speech: The Relationship Between Language and Violence* (Westport, CT: Greenwood Press, 1995), p. 175.

49. For instance, Jewish immigration had risen from 1,806 in 1919 to over 8,220 in both 1920 and 1921, and from 45,267 in 1934 to 66,472 in 1935. The 1929 figure had gone up to 5,249 from 2,178 the year before, but was down from 34,386 in 1925. Tessler, *A History of the Israeli-Palestinian Conflict*, p. 170. Israeli journalist Yossi Melman considers the riots to have been a Palestinian nationalist outcry, which the Jews downplayed as mere "incidents" and "disturbances." Melman, *The New Israelis*, p. 54.

50. Articles 9 and 10. Reprinted in Moore, ed., *The Arab-Israeli Conflict*, vol. 3, pp. 705–11. Also available at http://www.teleport.com/~alquds/pnc.html. On the recent decision by the Palestine National Council to remove the offending provisions of the charter, see Serge Schmemann, "P.L.O. Ends Call for Destruction of Jewish State," *New York Times*, Apr. 25, 1996, p. A1. Both the September 1993 Declaration of Principles and the September 1995 Interim Agreement between Israel and the PLO had committed the PLO to revocation of these provisions. Asked in October 1995 about them, Yasser Arafat said that as far as he was concerned, they were null and void, using the old French term, *caduc*. "A Tactful Arafat Meets Jews," *New York Times*, Oct. 24, 1995, p. A11.

51. Article 6. The population figure is based on 1882 estimates. A later date, such as 1917, at the time of the Balfour Declaration, which pledged the British to help establish a Jewish national home, would cap the figure at about 56,000 (and, presumably, their descendants). Wolffsohn, *Israel: Polity, Society and Economy*, p. 121.

52. Speech at Helouan, Nov. 11, 1965, reprinted in *Al-Ahram*, Nov. 20, 1965. See also *Al-Masri* (Cairo), Oct. 11, 1949, quoting Egyptian Foreign Minister Muhammad Salah al-Din: "In demanding the return of the Palestinian refugees, the Arabs mean their return as masters, not slaves; or, to put it quite clearly—the intention is the termination of Israel." "The Refugee Question: A Background Paper" (Jerusalem: Israel GPO, Oct. 1994), p. 8.

53. David P. Forsythe, *United Nations Peacemaking: The Conciliation Commission for Palestine* (Baltimore: Johns Hopkins University Press, 1972), pp. 98–99. Of the Arab states' refusal to absorb the Palestinians, Malvina Halberstam has pointed out:

> Although there are twenty-one Arab states with a land mass of over 5,000,000 square miles, this large block of states has generally refused to absorb the Palestinian refugees and to allow them to assimilate into the local population. Israel, on the other hand, with a territory of less than 10,000 square miles, absorbed 1.3 million Jewish refugees, 600,000 from Europe and over 700,000 from Arab states [to which could be added over 500,000 from the former Soviet Union].
>
> Resettlement of the Arab refugees would not only have solved the refugee problem but would have benefited Iraq and Syria, who needed additional population.

Halberstam, "Self-Determination in the Arab-Israeli Conflict: Meaning, Myth and Politics," *New York University Journal of International Law and Politics* 21 (1989), pp. 465, 477 (citation omitted).

54. See Rubinstein, *People of Nowhere*, p. 37.

55. Beryl I. Cheal, "Refugees in the Gaza Strip, December 1948–May 1950," M.A. thesis, University of Washington, 1985, p. 39, quoted by Kimmerling and Migdal, *Palestinians: The Making of a People*, p. 202.

56. Progress Report of the United Nations Mediator on Palestine Submitted to the Secretary-General for Transmission to the Members of the United Nations, U.N. GAOR, 3rd Sess., Supp. No. 11, pp. 17–19, U.N. Doc. A/648, Sept. 16, 1948, excerpted in Moore, *The Arab-Israeli Conflict*, vol. 3, pp. 367–369. The other five subjects of the report were return to peace, the Jewish state, boundary determination, continuous frontiers, and Jerusalem.

57. Quoted by Kurt R. Radley, "The Palestinian Refugees: The Right to Return in International Law," *American Journal of International Law* 72 (1978), pp. 586, 599.

58. See Moore, *The Arab-Israeli Conflict*, vol. 3, p. 371.

59. G.A. Resolution 194(III), 186th plenary meeting, Dec. 11, 1948. This resolution, cited numerous times throughout this book, is reproduced in the documentary appendix. Because the language of paragraph 11 is so central to the legal issues surrounding resolution of the Palestinian refugee question, it is examined at greater length in chapter 3.

60. Ibid., par. 11. On other proposals for resolution of the Palestinian refugee problem through either repatriation or resettlement, see Tessler, *A History of the Israeli-Palestinian Conflict*, pp. 137–38, 242–44, 307–15, and 537–38; Peretz, *Palestinians, Refugees and the Middle East Peace Process*, pp. 95–98.

61. For instance, "Throughout its involvement in the Palestine question, the United States was primarily concerned with checking Soviet influence in the Middle East. Specific issues arising out of the Palestine question such as boundaries and refugees consistently took second place. . . ." Forsythe, *United Nations Peacemaking*, p. 25. Arab states were unhappy about the inclusion of two Western states and only one Muslim but non-Arab state. Israel was made nervous by the support of all three states for an internationalized Jerusalem. Ibid., p. 31.

62. An Israeli author has offered four explanations for the ineffectiveness of the Conciliation Commission: (a) it suffered from the inherent weaknesses of a three-member body, as opposed to a single mediator model, and from interference from the home governments of the three powers; (b) it failed to mobilize effective support from the three home governments; (c) the experience, personalities, and talents of the men chosen as commissioners were unsuited and unequal to the task; and (d) they committed several tactical errors, especially their unwillingness or inability to get Arab states to meet directly with the Israelis. Neil Caplan, *The Lausanne Conference, 1949: A Case Study in Middle East Peacemaking* (Tel Aviv: Moshe Dayan Center for Middle Eastern and African Studies, 1993), pp. 124–30. See also Pablo de Azcarate, *Mission in Palestine: 1948–1952* (Washington, DC: Middle East Institute, 1966).

63. At approximately the same time, March 1949, an official Israeli memorandum on the refugee problem is reported to have stated that: Israel denied all responsibility for the creation of the problem; it estimated the number of refugees to be lower than did both the United Nations and Arab authorities; and the Israeli government, in the context of general peace talks, would consider whether conditions were stable enough for a certain number to come back without creating a security problem, but considered that the main solution was not repatriation but resettlement elsewhere. S. G. Thicknesse, *Arab Refugees: A Survey of Resettlement Possibilities* (London: Chatham House, 1949), p. 22.

64. See Forsythe, *United Nations Peacemaking*, pp. 48–63; Tessler, *A History of the Israeli-Palestinian Conflict*, pp. 313–314; Caplan, *The Lausanne Conference*, pp. 92–95; Caplan describes internal criticism of the reluctant Israeli offer, which reflected: "(a) security fears of the reintroduction of a 'fifth column,' (b) fears that Israel would be forced beyond the 100,000 to allow the return of larger numbers, (c) distaste for the apparent surrender to U.S. pressure, and (d) a popular backlash against the return of any of the refugees." Ibid., p. 93.

65. Benny Morris cites then–Foreign Minister Moshe Sharett as explaining that the offer would really only amount to 65,000, as approximately 35,000 of the 1948 refugees had already found their way back over the border.

Morris, *The Birth of the Arab Refugee Problem*, pp. 280–83; Morris, *1948 and After*, pp. 26–27; Caplan, *The Lausanne Conference*, p. 93.

66. Progress Report of the Conciliation Commission for Palestine, U.N. Doc. A/1985, Nov. 19, 1951, p. 4.

67. Forsythe, *United Nations Peacemaking*, p. 91.

68. James C. Hathaway, *The Law of Refugee Status* (Toronto: Butterworths, 1991), p. 206, citing Statement of Mr. Azkoul of Lebanon, 5 UNGAOR, Nov. 27, 1950, p. 358, and Statement of Mr. Baroodi of Saudi Arabia, 5 UNGAOR, Nov. 27, 1950, p. 359.

69. UNRWA Public Information Office, "UNRWA 1950–1990: Serving Palestine Refugees" (Vienna: Apr. 1990), p. 6. UNRWA was created by G.A. Resolution 302(IV), Dec. 8, 1949, and began operations on May 1, 1950. Technically, its definition included 17,000 Jews and some non-Arab Christians who had also fled under these conditions. Israel took responsibility for the Jews, as well as Arabs who had fled to other parts of Israel. See Peretz, *Palestinians, Refugees and the Middle East Peace Process*, p. 12. See also Louis B. Sohn and Thomas Buergenthal, *The Movement of Persons Across Borders* (Washington, DC: American Society of International Law, Oct. 1992), p. 145.

70. "UNRWA 1950–1990: Serving Palestine Refugees," p. 6.

71. UNRWA Public Information Office, "A Guide to UNRWA," (Vienna: Apr. 1994), p. 2. Two-thirds of the staff posts are education-related. The other paid positions are in health, relief and social services, operational services (including engineering, supply, and transport) and administration. See "A Guide to UNRWA."

72. Milton Viorst, *Reaching for the Olive Branch: UNRWA and Peace in the Middle East* (Washington, DC: Middle East Institute, 1989), p. 197. See also Benjamin N. Schiff, *Refugees Unto the Third Generation: UN Aid to Palestinians* (Syracuse, NY: Syracuse University Press, 1995). On conflicts between UNRWA and the Conciliation Commission, see Forsythe, *United Nations Peacemaking*, pp. 78, 94.

73. Refugee Working Group VIII, "Spirit of Cooperation Marks Refugee Working Group Meeting," press release, Feb. 18, 1996. See also Schiff, *Refugees Unto the Third Generation*, pp. 281–85, on the current and future role of UNRWA in the peace process.

74. Text of Agreements Signed September 17, 1978, *International Legal Materials*, vol. 17 (1978), pp. 1466, 1468.

75. Treaty of Peace Signed March 26, 1979, and Annex III, Protocol Concerning Relations of the Parties, article 4(1), *International Legal Materials*, vol. 18 (1979), pp. 362, 374, 389. See Ann Mosely Lesch and Mark Tessler, *Israel, Egypt and the Palestinians: From Camp David to Intifada* (Bloomington: Indiana University Press, 1989).

76. G.A. Res. 3379, Nov. 10, 1975. The "Zionism is Racism" resolution was repealed by the General Assembly in December 1991. According to the

World Jewish Congress: "The 1975 resolution equating Zionism with racism was the outstanding expression of UN hostility toward Israel, and the organization's outright antisemitism. The action made a mockery of the UN pretention of representing an objective moral authority of the family of nations. . . . The repeal of that infamous resolution in December 1991—the first retraction of this kind in UN history—was an important milestone in the restoration of Israel's international status—and the good name of the international body itself." "Background: Repeal of 'Zionism-Racism,' " http://www.jer1.co.il/orgs/wjc/dis1back.htm.

77. See Harris Schoenberg, *A Mandate for Terror: The United Nations and the P.L.O.* (New York: Shapolsky Publishing, 1989); Sidney Liskofsy and Donna Arzt, "Incitement to National, Racial and Religious Hatred in United Nations Fora," *Israel Yearbook on Human Rights*, vol. 17 (1987), p. 41.

78. Sami Hadawi, *Bitter Harvest*, p. 134.

79. See, for instance, G.A. Resolution 2672/C (XXV), Dec. 8, 1970, proclaiming that the people of Palestine "are entitled to equal rights and self-determination." See also Resolutions 2792D (XXVI), Dec. 6, 1971; 3089D (XXVIII), Dec. 7, 1973; and 3236 (XXIX), Nov. 22, 1974. See Committee on the Exercise of the Inalienable Rights of the Palestinian People, *The Right of Self-Determination of the Palestinian People*, U.N. Doc. ST/SG/SER.F/3 (1979).

80. Rubinstein, *The People of Nowhere*, p. 93.

81. Other pre-1989 developments include Jordan's decision in 1988 to disengage administratively from the West Bank; the internecine PLO battles that followed the defeat of the PLO army in 1982; the *intifada*, which convinced Israel that the Palestinian masses, as opposed to the PLO army, were no pushovers; and the pervasive rise of Islamic fundamentalism.

82. Palestine National Council, Political Communiqué and Declaration of Independence, Algiers, Nov. 15, 1988, *International Legal Materials*, vol. 27 (1989), p. 1660. Like Israel's Declaration of Independence, this declaration did not give specific, identifiable borders. The Palestine National Council's previous declaration of independence, issued as a "Provisional Charter of the Government of All Palestine" on Oct. 1, 1948, had delineated its western border as the Mediterranean. See *Palestinian Yearbook of International Law*, vol. 4 (1987–88), p. 294.

83. Robert H. Pelletreau, Statement Before the Subcommittee on Europe and the Middle East of the House Foreign Affairs Committee, Oct. 4, 1994, in "A Review of Developments in the Middle East," *U.S. Department of State Dispatch* 5, no. 41 (Oct. 10, 1994). Marc Peron stated that as of that date Syria and Lebanon had not yet joined the multilaterals, pending progress in their respective bilateral negotiations with Israel. Perhaps not surprisingly, the Refugee Multilateral was a last-minute addition to the other four multilateral topics. Talk to the Institute for Social and Economic Policy in the Middle East, John F. Kennedy School of Government (unpublished notes, Feb. 16, 1994), p. 3.

84. Refugee Working Group VIII, "Spirit of Cooperation Marks Refugee Working Group Meeting," press release, Feb. 18, 1996.

85. Peron, talk, p. 6, quoting the Canadian government's "gavel summary" for the Refugee Multilateral.

86. See "Palestinian Refugees Granted $250 Million," *United Press International*, Apr. 14, 1994; Abdelaziz Barrouhi, "Progress Reported at Mideast Refugee Talks," *Reuters*, Oct. 14, 1993; "The Middle East Peace Process: An Overview" (Jerusalem: Information Division, Israel Ministry of Foreign Affairs, June 2, 1994), p. 11; Rex Bryner and Jill Tansley, "The Refugee Working Group in Advancing Peace Negotiations," *Palestine-Israel Journal* 2, no. 4 (Autumn 1995), p. 53.

87. "Palestinian Reunions," *Jerusalem Report*, Nov. 4, 1993, p. 5.

88. "According to [Israeli] pollster Kalman Geyer, public support for such risks began building during the Gulf War, when Iraq's use of scud missiles against Israel made Israelis realize that radical regimes such as Iraq could exploit the unresolved Palestinian issue as a rallying cry for their own regional hegemonic purposes." David Makovsky, *Making Peace with the PLO: The Rabin Government's Road to the Oslo Accord* (Boulder, CO: Westview Press, 1996), p. 133. On changes in the Arab perspective, see Muhammad Faour, *The Arab World After Desert Storm* (Washington, DC: United States Institute of Peace Press, 1993), pp. 110–111 and passim.

89. "Israel's Agenda for Peace," *Near East Report*, Oct. 19, 1992, p. 193.

90. Remarks by Dr. Yossi Beilin, Multilateral Working Group on Refugees, Tunis, Oct. 12, 1993, par. 14, 15.

91. Article 2(f). The English-language texts notably use the moralistic "should," not the mandatory "shall."

92. Clyde Haberman, "Now, the Touchy Issue: Palestinian Refugees," *New York Times*, Mar. 9, 1995, p. A3; "Amman Meeting on Refugees," *British Broadcasting Corporation Summary of World Broadcasts*, Mar. 9, 1995, ME/2247/MED; "Israel, Arabs Hold First Meeting on Displaced Palestinians," (*Agence France Presse*, Mar. 7, 1995); Deborah Horan, "Palestine-Politics: Building Boom Signals Arrival of Refugees," *Inter Press Service*, Mar. 10, 1995.

93. It is hard to imagine that this refusal was more than an initial negotiating stance, as Israel had already accepted the principle of family reunification in other contexts. See Shlomo Gazit, "Displaced Persons in Focus," *Jerusalem Post*, Mar. 10, 1995, p. 4.

94. "Palestinian Refugee Talks in Egypt Make Progress," *Reuters World Report*, Feb. 14, 1996.

95. Clovis Maksoud, "Peace Process or Puppet Show?" *Foreign Policy*, no. 100 (Fall 1995), pp. 117, 120. "It also escalated tensions with the peoples of the host countries. In Lebanon in particular, this lapse is more acute as social peace there remains fragile and the political balance among contending religious groups precarious." Ibid.

Chapter 2: The Sociodemographic Framework

1. "Reasonable statistics relating to, for example, health, housing conditions, labour force participation, the status of women or educational attainment, are limited. Statistics which attempt to relate across these dimensions, say, for instance housing density and psychological welfare, are almost nonexistent. . . . Lacking comprehensive information, [international organizations working with Palestinians] are unable to make priorities between development requirements or to identify the groups in Palestinian society who are most deprived." Marianne Heiberg and Geir Ovensen, *Palestinian Society in Gaza, West Bank and Arab Jerusalem: A Survey of Living Conditions* (Oslo: FAFO report 151, 1993), p. 15 [hereinafter "FAFO"].

2. "The Palestinians have raised a kind of ideological barrier around this issue that does not allow for any question about the desire of every last refugee to return. Dr. Sharif Kana'ne of Bir-Zeit University confirms the impression, culled from conversations with refugees, that those who continue to live in difficult conditions insist upon their right to return, rejecting any substitute." Danny Rubinstein, *The People of Nowhere: The Palestinian Vision of Home* (New York: Times Books, 1991), p. 130.

3. See Kevin F. McCarthy, "The Palestinian Refugee Issue: One Perspective," Rand Corporation Greater Middle East Studies Center (DRU-1358-GMESC, Mar. 1996). An earlier version of this paper was presented at a workshop at Haifa University, Nov. 14, 1995.

4. McCarthy, "The Palestinian Refugee Issue." See also Michael Humphrey, "Migrants, Workers and Refugees: The Political Economy of Population Movements in the Middle East," *Middle East Report* 23, no. 2 (Mar.–Apr. 1993), pp. 2–9; Seteny Shami, "The Social Implications of Population Displacement and Resettlement: An Overview with a Focus on the Arab Middle East," *International Migration Review* 27, no. 1 (1993), p. 4; and Miroslav Macura and David Coleman, eds., *International Migration: Regional Processes and Responses* (Geneva: United Nations Economic Commission for Europe, Economic Studies no. 7, 1994), pp. 163–81.

5. Aziz Haidar, "The Different Levels of Palestinian Ethnicity," in Milton J. Esman and Itamar Rabinovich, eds., *Ethnicity, Pluralism and the State in the Middle East* (Ithaca, NY: Cornell University Press, 1988), pp. 95, 96, citing Don Peretz, "Palestinian Social Stratification: The Political Implications," *Journal of Palestine Studies* 7, no. 1 (1977), pp. 48–74; Salim Tamari, "Factionalism and Class Formation in Recent Palestinian History," in Roger Owen, ed., *Studies in Economic and Social History of Palestine in the 19th and 20th Centuries* (London: Macmillan, 1982), pp. 177–202; and Elia Zureik, "Reflections on Twentieth-Century Palestinian Class Structure," in Khalil Nakhleh and Elia Zureik, eds., *The Sociology of the Palestinians* (New York: St. Martin's Press, 1980), pp. 47–63. Even today, marriages

between propertied middle-class Palestinians and refugee camp-dwellers rarely occur and are strongly disapproved of when they do. Isabel Kershner, "The People Behind the Politics," *Jerusalem Report*, May 5, 1994, pp. 22, 28.

6. Rubinstein, *The People of Nowhere*, p. 31.

7. Rosemary Sayigh, "The Palestinian Experience: Integration and Non-Integration in the Arab Ghourba," *Arab Studies Quarterly* 1, no. 2 (Spring 1979), p. 108. See also Fawaz Turki, *Exile's Return: The Making of a Palestinian American* (New York: Free Press, 1994), pp. 167–68 and passim.

8. Milton Viorst, *Sandcastles: The Arabs in Search of the Modern World* (New York: Alfred A. Knopf, 1994), pp. 201–2. "I doubt whether, in 1948, these [subcultural differences] were any more salient between Palestinians and, say, Jordanians, than they were between one Palestinian region and another. (In fact, Galileans and Southern Lebanese were probably closer than Galileans and West Bankers.)" Sayigh, "The Palestinian Experience," p. 100.

9. Laurie A. Brand, *Palestinians in the Arab World: Institution Building and the Search for State* (New York: Columbia University Press, 1988), p. 10.

10. Viorst, *Sandcastles*, p. 202.

11. Sayigh, "The Palestinian Experience," p. 99.

12. Ibid.

13. Ibid., pp. 99–100. See also Turki, *Exile's Return*, pp. 49–72.

14. "The Palestinians, having been wrenched from their agrarian roots in 1948, had turned increasingly to education as the safeguard of their future." Viorst, *Sandcastles*, p. 220.

15. Sayigh, "The Palestinian Experience," pp. 108, 109. See also Rosemary Sayigh, *Palestinians: From Peasants to Revolutionaries* (London: Zed Press, 1979).

16. Brand, *Palestinians in the Arab World*, p. 11. See also Benny Morris, "The Initial Absorption of the Palestinian Refugees in the Arab Host Countries, 1948–1949," in Anna C. Bramwell, ed., *Refugees in the Age of Total War* (London: Unwin Hyman, 1988), pp. 252–73. Palestinian political consciousness need not be marked as emerging only in 1948. Kimmerling and Migdal describe the 1936–1939 revolt, which was aimed at Britain as much as the Zionists. "The revolt was a distinct watershed, crystalizing Palestinian national identity as nothing before." Baruch Kimmerling and Joel S. Migdal, *Palestinians: The Making of a People*, (Cambridge, MA: Harvard University Press, 1994), p. 123.

17. The chart and number ranges are adapted from Mark Tessler, *A History of the Israeli-Palestinian Conflict* (Bloomington: Indiana University Press, 1994), p. 280; Martin Gilbert, *Atlas of the Arab-Israeli Conflict*, 6th ed. (New York: Oxford University Press, 1993), p. 47 (reprinted as map 2.1); and Benny Morris, *1948 and After: Israel and the Palestinians* (Oxford: Clarendon Press, 1994) p. 82. Rubinstein, *The People of Nowhere*, relies on research (in

Arabic) conducted by Bir-Zeit University's Center for Documentation and Research on destroyed Arab villages. The number ranges given here are themselves on the high end of the plethora of disputed estimates. The combined totals are 621,000 to 954,000. The large disparity in the West Bank figures is probably attributable to the date of estimation. Many Palestinians moved from the West Bank to the East Bank of the Jordan after 1950.

18. See Yossi Melman, *The New Israelis: An Intimate View of a Changing People* (New York: Carol Publishing Company, 1992), pp. 163–164; Rubinstein, *The People of Nowhere*, p. 15.

19. Brand, *Palestinians in the Arab World*, p. 7. The passage continues: ". . . and the intimidation and massacre of thousands by local Lebanese militias. Given such a history, Palestinians' feelings of insecurity and transcience are easily understood." Ibid.

20. On movements in the wake of the Persian Gulf War, see Gil Feiler, "Labour Migration in the Middle East Following the Iraqi Invasion of Kuwait," *Israel/Palestine: Issues in Conflict, Issues for Cooperation* 2, no. 7 (Israel/Palestine Center for Research and Information, Dec. 1993). On Libya, see "14 Days: No Entry," *Jerusalem Report*, Oct. 5, 1995, p. 2; "The Case of Palestinian Refugees in Libya," *Shaml Newsletter* (Ramallah: Palestinian Diaspora and Refugee Center, Dec. 1995), p. 2.

21. See Rubinstein, *The People of Nowhere*, p. 108–9. On secondary and tertiary migration during and after the 1967 war, see Ori Nir, "What is a Refugee? What is a Displaced Person?" *Ha'aretz*, Mar. 7, 1995, p. B3, summarizing the estimate of 88,000 returnees in a report written by Shlomo Gazit for the Jaffee Center for Strategic Studies, Tel Aviv University. In the first half year after the war, over 9,000 families were reunited. By 1976, over 44,000 people had rejoined their families on the West Bank. See Mitchell Bard, "Homeless in Gaza," *Policy Review*, no. 47 (Winter 1989), pp. 36, 40. However, UNRWA reports that by June 1995, only 14,170 refugees had returned. Report of the Commissioner-General, UNRWA, *Persons Displaced as a Result of the June 1967 and Subsequent Hostilities*, U.N. Doc. A/50/451 (Sept. 20, 1995).

22. For instance, where will an extended family want to relocate if its four second-generation children married children from four other places of origin and its 16 grandchildren married others from entirely different origins? According to master's research conducted by Adnan Abdul-Razzeq at the Hebrew University School of Social Work in 1977, for the first 30 years, most refugees continued to marry within their clans, maintaining family blood ties as well as geographical origins; even unique local dialects were kept alive. "Changes in the Family Life of the Arab Refugees in Refugee Camps," cited in Rubinstein, *The People of Nowhere*, p. 31 n. 2. But there may be more intermarriage in the last 20 years, among the third generation.

23. UNRWA General Information Sheet, Programme Planning and Evaluation Office, January 1996. UNRWA provides services in and out of refugee camps. The legal status of the camps varies, but all are under the jurisdiction of the host country or in the case of Gaza and parts of the West Bank, the Palestinian Authority. The camps are all on rented or government lands. UNRWA currently provides services in 10 camps in Jordan, 12 in Lebanon, 10 in Syria, 19 in the West Bank, and 8 in Gaza. Syria also has three "unofficial" camps.

24. *Guide to UNRWA*, pp. 2–5. See also Benjamin N. Schiff, *Refugees unto the Third Generation: UN Aid to Palestinians* (Syracuse, NY: Syracuse University Press, 1995), p. 25.

25. Fagbevegelsens senter for forskning, utredning og dokumentasjon (hereinafter FAFO), published in English as *Palestinian Society in Gaza, West Bank and Arab Jerusalem: A Survey of Living Conditions* (Oslo: FAFO report 151, 1993). The study used a representative sample of 2,500 persons, not a universal census of the three areas. Note that there are few if any Palestinians currently living in the Golan Heights. The non-Jews there consider themselves to be Syrian Druze. UNRWA reports that after the 1967 war, Syria received 17,500 displaced persons from the Syrian Golan Heights, without identifying their ethnicity. *Report of the Commissioner-General of UNRWA, 1 July 1967–30 June 1968*, UN General Assembly *Official Records.* Twenty-third Session, supp. no. 13 (A/7213), p. 4.

26. FAFO, pp. 19, 71, 387, Table A 7.1. See also Sarah M. Roy, "Gaza: New Dynamics of Civic Disintegration," *Journal of Palestine Studies* 22, no. 4 (Summer 1993), pp. 22, 28; and "The Palestinians: Who Are They?" *New York Times*, Sept. 12, 1993, p. E3, summarizing the FAFO report and other studies.

27. FAFO, p. 39, Table 2.1. A different figure for West Bankers living in their original villages, 61 percent, was reported by the Palestinian Health Development Information Project in 1994. Isabel Kershner, "The People Behind the Politics," pp. 22, 23. Data on fathers and not mothers are used because Palestinian families are patrilineal.

28. See *Developing the Occupied Territories: An Investment in Peace*, vol. 6, *Human Resources and Social Policy* (Washington, DC: The World Bank, Sept. 1993), p. 14.

29. FAFO, pp. 16, 188–94. FAFO's margin of sampling error is plus or minus 4 percent, so these figures are rough estimates. See also *Report of the Commissioner-General of UNRWA, 1 July 1944–30 June 1995, UN General Assembly, Official Records*, Fiftieth Session, Supp. no. 13 (A/50/13).

30. FAFO, pp. 41, 185–87. Eighty percent of Gazans live in urban areas compared to only 38 percent of West Bank Arabs. Ibid., p. 23. Table A2.2 on p. 360 reports the following percentages by refugee status:

	Combined Occupied Territories (%)	Gaza (%)	West Bank (%)
Nonrefugees	58	38	74
Refugees outside camps	24	32	17
Urban camps	14	25	5
Rural camps	4	5	4
Totals	100	100	100

31. See *Report to the UN Secretary General: Economic Mission to the Occupied Territories* (May 1995).

32. "The Palestinians: Who Are They?"; Kershner, "The People Behind the Politics," pp. 22, 24, 26.

33. FAFO, pp. 87–91. But see Kershner, "The People Behind the Politics," p. 24. For instance, two-thirds of the telephone system in the territories predates 1967.

34. "Palestinian Public Opinion Poll III," Center for Policy Analysis on Palestine, p. 5.

35. "New Regulations for Jordanian Passports," *Shaml Newsletter* (Dec. 1995), pp. 6–7. According to the new regulations, applicants for the new five-year passports cannot include their wives and children on the same passport.

36. Abbas F. Shiblak, "Residency Status and Civil Rights of Palestinian Refugees in Arab Countries," *Journal of Palestine Studies* 25 (Spring 1996), 36; Pinchas Inbari, "The Coalition as an Institution," *Al Hamishmar*, Feb. 17, 1995, Supp. pp. 7–8.

37. FAFO, Table A2.2, p. 360. See Viorst, *Sandcastles*, p. 202. According to a more recent estimate, fewer than 6,000 Christians remain in Jerusalem and fewer than 40,000 in all of Palestine (undefined). Heidi Shoup, "Father Emil Salayta: 'Palestinian Christians Face the Future,' " Center for Policy Analysis on Palestine, *Newsletter* 3, no. 5 (Fall 1995), p. 6. If true, that would lower the percentage of Christians in East Jerusalem to the same 4 percent in the West Bank as a whole. See also Serge Schmemann, "Palestinian Christians Feeling Like a Minority," *New York Times*, Dec. 31, 1995, p. E5, giving an estimate of 50,000 for the West Bank and noting that five of the 88 seats on the Palestinian Council have been set aside for Christians.

38. FAFO, pp. 135, 137.

39. Youssef M. Ibrahim, "Mayor Laments a Christian Exodus," *New York Times*, Aug. 2, 1995, p. A6.

40. Melman, *The New Israelis*, p. 190. Melman and others warn that Bethlehem might eventually become a kind of "Christian Disneyland or reserve to be visited by tourists."

41. FAFO, pp. 25, 41, 129, 242, 260.

42. See Ibrahim Matar, "To Whom Does Jerusalem Belong?" in *Jerusalem: A Special Report* (Washington, DC: Center for Policy Analysis on Palestine, 1993), pp. 7–14; FAFO, pp. 43, 360. See also B'Tselem, "A Policy of Discrimination: Land Expropriation, Planning and Building in East Jerusalem," May 14, 1995, excerpted in *Journal of Palestine Studies* 25, no. 1 (Autumn 1995), pp. 149–55. The 150,000 Jewish settlers in East Jerusalem are in addition to the approximately 130,000 in the rest of the West Bank. Institute for Palestine Studies, Jan. 1992 figures.

43. "Israeli Jerusalem Arabs," *Jerusalem Post*, Jan. 4, 1995, p. 6; Bill Hutman, "More J'lem Arabs Becoming Citizens," *Jerusalem Post*, Jan. 17, 1995, p. 1. To obtain Israeli citizenship, they must prove they have lived in the city for three of the past five years, have no serious security or criminal record, and pass a minimal Hebrew language test.

44. "Palestinian residents of Jerusalem who may not vote in the elections to the Knesset will be able to vote in the elections for the Palestinian Council." Israel Foreign Ministry Information Division, "The Participation of Palestinians of Jerusalem in the Elections For the Palestinian Council" (Dec. 1995). This document refers to "several hundred" Palestinians resident in Jerusalem who have received Israeli citizenship. The figures of 3,000 to 10,000, however, may only indicate applications for citizenship.

45. UNRWA reports the overall growth rate for registered Palestine refugees as averaging 3.8 to 4 percent per year since the *intifada* (which began in Dec. 1987), ranging from a low of 2.2 percent for the registered refugees in Lebanon to a high of 6.11 percent for the Gaza Strip. "If this trend continues, the refugee population will double in less than 20 years." UNRWA General Information Sheet (January 1996). See also Joseph Alpher, "Israel: The Challenges of Peace," *Foreign Policy*, no. 101 (Winter 1995–96), pp. 130, 140. The U.S. Bureau of the Census report, *World Population 1994* (Washington, DC: U.S. Government Printing Office, 1995), gives a 1994 fertility rate for Gaza of 7.4, the highest in the Near East, North Africa, and Asia (Table 7, p. A-23); and a rate of natural increase of 4.0, also the highest of those three regions plus Latin America and the Caribbean (Table 4, p. A-10). The comparable figures for the West Bank are 4.2 and 2.7, which are closer to the average for the Near East and North Africa. See also FAFO, p. 62.

46. FAFO, p. 23, Table 1.1; UNRWA *Planning Statistics Report* (Nov. 1991); *UNRWA in the Gaza Strip* (May 1992).

47. Unlike Jordan's incorporation of the West Bank, Egypt never annexed the Gaza Strip. On the relationship between Gaza and Egypt, see Brand, *Palestinians in the Arab World*, pp. 46–50.

48. See Isabel Kershner, "Half a Homeland," *Jerusalem Report*, Jan. 11, 1996, pp. 26–27.

49. FAFO, pp. 259, 360. See also Ziad Abu-Amr, *Islamic Fundamentalism in the West Bank and Gaza: Muslim Brotherhood and Islamic Jihad* (Bloomington: Indiana University Press, 1994).

50. See Sarah M. Roy, "Gaza: New Dynamics of Civic Disintegration," *Journal of Palestine Studies* 22, no. 4 (Summer 1993), pp. 20, 23.

51. Ibid., p. 29.

52. UNRWA General Information Sheet (Jan. 1996); "Fact Sheet: 'Palestinian Refugees: Their Problem and Their Future' " (Washington, DC: Center for Policy Analysis on Palestine, 1994), Table B, derived from U.S. Bureau of Census projections. A "non-Palestinian Jordanian" is defined as anyone who inhabited the East Bank of the Jordan when Jordan was created in 1921 and their descendants. Indigenous Jordanians originated as nomadic Bedouin tribes, quite distinct from Palestinian urban merchants and village-based farmers. Circassians and Syrians also make up part of Jordan's non-Palestinian population. See Naseer H. Aruri and Samih Farsoun, "Palestinian Communities and Arab Host Countries," in Nakhleh and Zureik, *The Sociology of the Palestinians*, pp. 112, 119–20. See also Lawrence Tal, "Is Jordan Doomed?" *Foreign Affairs* (Nov. 1993), p. 45; Colbert Held, *Middle East Patterns: Places, People and Politics*, 2nd ed., (Boulder, CO: Westview Press, 1994), pp. 242–43. Of course, in the current generation, there has been intermarriage between East and West Bankers, thereby blurring the distinctions.

53. See "Jordan Keeps Secret Population's Palestinian Rate," *Reuters World Report*, Jan. 27, 1996; "In Mideast, a Census Reveals Too Much . . ." Reuters World Report, Feb. 12, 1996.

54. According to Brand, the Palestinians were "made citizens to legitimize the annexation and to further the Hashemite claim to their economic and human capital." Brand, *Palestinians in the Arab World*, p. 16. Moreover, due to a property ownership requirement, "camp dwellers were effectively disenfranchised until the passage of the 1986 Election Law." Ibid., p. 12. As in other Arab states, the wife of a citizen can obtain Jordanian citizenship but not the husband of a citizen.

55. Shiblak, "Residency Status and Civil Rights," pp. 39–41.

56. Feiler, "Labour Migration in the Middle East," p. 19.

57. Paul Lalor, "The Palestinians," in Dorothy Stannard, ed., *Jordan* (Boston: Houghton Mifflin, 1994), p. 101. On "Black September," see Tal, "Is Jordan Doomed?"

58. Viorst, *Sandcastles*, pp. 211–12. See also Ali Jarbawi, "The Triangle of Conflict," *Foreign Policy*, no. 100 (Fall 1995), pp. 92, 96–97. Many of the wealthier Palestinians live in million dinar mansions in western Amman, with perhaps an additional home in, for instance, Jerusalem. See Neal Sandler and Kirk Albrecht, "Building Palestine, Share by Share," *Business Week* (International Edition), Oct. 30, 1995, p. 26.

59. Laurie A. Brand, "Palestinians and Jordanians: A Crisis of Identity," *Journal of Palestine Studies* 24, no. 4 (Summer 1995), pp. 46, 48–50. For individual expressions of identity and future residential intent, see Isabel Kershner, "Home Away from Home," *Jerusalem Report*, Jan. 13, 1994, pp. 28–29; Sarah Helm, "Election in Jordan Focuses on Palestine: Will Palestinians

Remain or Move to New West Bank State?" *The Independent*, Oct. 29, 1993, p. 15; and Walter Ruby, "Passport to a Royal Welcome," *Long Island Jewish World*, Nov. 4–10, 1994, pp. 23, 26.

60. According to a 29-year-old Palestinian accountant in Amman: "Only those who have nothing here, no land and no money, want to go back." Kershner, "Home Away from Home."

61. *Guide to UNRWA*, p. 7; Rosemary Sayigh, "Palestinians in Lebanon: Harsh Present, Uncertain Reality," *Journal of Palestine Studies* 25, no. 1 (Autumn 1995), pp. 37–53 (hereafter "Harsh Present, Uncertain Reality"). Very few of the Palestinians in Lebanon are displaced persons from the 1967 war.

62. See Cheryl A. Rubenberg, "Palestinians in Lebanon: A Question of Human and Civil Rights," *Arab Studies Quarterly* 6 (Summer 1984), pp. 194, 202–209.

63. See Ihsan A. Hijazi, "Palestinians Exit Lebanon in Droves," *New York Times*, Jan. 3, 1993, p. 3.

64. A typical family situation: eight people living on one son's salary of $6 per day as an apprentice carpenter, supplemented by handouts from nongovernmental organizations of approximately $16 per month for each of four younger children, where the poverty line for a family of five is estimated by the United Nations at $618 per month. Muhammad Ali Khalidi, "Palestinian Refugees in Lebanon," *Middle East Report* (Nov./Dec. 1995), p. 28. "These gaps are more dramatic considering that only in Lebanon are the refugees excluded from public services as well as from most kinds of unemployment." Sayigh, "Harsh Present, Uncertain Reality," p. 38.

65. Decree no. 17561 of 1964. Palestinians were officially designated as "Third Category foreigners" pursuant to the August 2, 1962 Lebanon Ministry of the Interior Decision no. 319. The category refers to "foreigners who do not carry documents from their country of origin and who reside in Lebanon by virtue of residency cards issued by the Directorate of the Sureté Générale or identification cards issued in Lebanon." See Issam el-Kaisy, *Lebanon's Labour Law* (Beirut: Institute of Palestine Studies, 1983), pp. 80, 87.

66. Khalidi, "Palestinian Refugees in Lebanon," p. 28; According to official figures, only 7,362 Palestinians out of 300,000 have been granted work permits. Ibid., p. 29. In 1994, the total was 100. See Sayigh, "Harsh Reality, Uncertain Future," pp. 44, 49, 50. Moreover, "An increasing number of young children are being hit by serious sicknesses, due doubtless to poverty, lower nutritional levels, poor habitat and drinking water, and accumulated war stress." Ibid., p. 48. See also Rosemary Sayigh, "Palestinians in Lebanon: Status Ambiguity, Insecurity and Flux," *Race & Class* 30, no. 1 (1988), pp. 13–32; Rosemary Sayigh, "Palestinian Refugees in Lebanon," (unpublished paper, June 1996, available at http://www.facl.mcgill.ca/MEPP/PRRN/prfront.html).

67. See "Palestinians Raise Black Flags in Mourning Over Taba Accord," *Agence France Presse* (Sept. 28, 1995); Khalidi, "Palestinian Refugees in Lebanon," Sayigh, "Harsh Reality, Uncertain Future," p. 44. See also Hilal Khashan, "The Despairing Palestinians," *Journal of South Asian and Middle Eastern Studies* 16, no. 1 (Fall 1992), pp. 2–17; Rubenberg, "Palestinians in Lebanon: A Question of Human and Civil Rights," pp. 194–221.

68. Sayigh, "Harsh Present, Uncertain Reality," p. 53, n. 25; Nawaf A. Salam, "Between Repatriation and Resettlement: Palestinian Refugees in Lebanon," *Journal of Palestine Studies* 24, no. 1 (Autumn 1994), pp. 18, 19.

69. Sayigh, "Harsh Present, Uncertain Future," p. 37. In April 1994, Foreign Minister Faris Buwayz strongly implied that all Palestinians should eventually be removed from Lebanon and explicitly stated that naturalization was out of the question. See interview in *Al-Safir*, Apr. 18, 1994, excerpted in *Journal of Palestine Studies* 24, no. 1 (Autumn 1994), pp. 130–31; and "Al-Hariri on Palestinians, Disarming Resistance," *Middle East Intelligence Report*, Oct. 27, 1993.

The October 22, 1989 Ta'if Accord led to major amendments to the Lebanon Constitution. The new preamble, paragraph H, reflects the agreement in calling for the abolition of political sectarianism. See Gisbert H. Flanz, "Republic of Lebanon," in Gisbert H. Flanz, ed., *Constitutions of the Countries of the World* (Dobbs Ferry, NY: Oceana Publication, 1996), p. xxiii.

70. Sayigh, "Harsh Present, Uncertain Future," pp. 42–43.

71. Khalidi, "Palestinian Refugees in Lebanon." Also quoted in "Human Garbage," *Shaml Newsletter* (Dec. 1995), p. 6. "One of the few common denominators among Lebanese politicians is a general contempt for Palestinians, whom many like to blame for the 12 year civil war." Khalidi, "Palestinian Refugees in Lebanon."

72. Turki, *Exile's Return*, p. 132.

73. Sayigh, "Harsh Present, Uncertain Future," p. 41, citing survey reported by Hussein Sha'ban in *Al-Safir*, June 2, 1994.

74. Law no. 260 (July 10, 1956).

75. Estimate by Abbas Shiblak, conversation with author, November 1995. Note that the 3,500 figure includes registered refugees who had "another non-Palestinian nationality," which must mean persons married to Palestinians.

76. See Pinchas Inbari, "The Coalition as an Institution," *Al Hamishmar*, Feb. 17, 1995, pp. 7–8.

77. Khaled Abu Toameh, "Syria Urged to Free Hundreds of Palestinians," *Jerusalem Report*, Oct. 5, 1995, p. 12; U.S. Department of State, "Syria," *1991 Human Rights Report* (Feb. 1992). See also Middle East Watch, "Throwing Away the Key: Indefinite Political Detention in Syria" (New York: Middle East Watch, 1992); Human Rights Watch, *Syria Unmasked: The Suppression of Human Rights by the Assad Regime* (New Haven, CT: Yale University Press, 1991).

78. See U.S. Department of State, "Syria," *1993 Human Rights Reports* (Feb. 1994).

79. Haidar, "The Different Levels of Palestinian Ethnicity," p. 100.

80. Clyde Haberman, "Israeli Arabs Say P.L.O. Pact is a Path to First-Class Status," *New York Times*, Nov. 24, 1993, p. A1. Opposition to the Israel-PLO accords is probably also strongest among some Palestinian factions in Lebanon. See "Tension Heightened in Lebanon's Refugee Camp," *Xinhua General Overseas News Service*, Oct. 15, 1993, describing reactions to the previous month's Declaration of Principles. It seems natural that reaction to the declaration reflects the level of the refugees' own living conditions.

81. Israel Government Press Office, "Economic Survey," Nov. 14, 1995 (Israel Information Service Gopher). Because the Golan Heights and East Jerusalem were annexed by Israel, the non-Jewish populations there are included within the Israeli total, along with the Jewish settlers in all the occupied territories.

82. Jobs in the defense industry, which is Israel's largest economic sector, are closed to Arabs. See Ruth Gavison, "Minority Rights in Israel: The Case of Army Veterans Provisions," in *Relations Between Ethnic Majority and Minority: A Symposium* (Tel Aviv: International Center for Peace in the Middle East, March 1987), p. 18; David Kretzmer, *The Legal Status of the Arabs in Israel* (Boulder, CO: Westview Press, 1990), pp. 98–107. The Security Services Act (Consolidated Version) (1959) does not explicitly exclude Arabs, but they were released from serving in 1948. However, "[recent studies show that a majority of Israel's Arabs would willingly do three years of national service in return for full and equal rights, and some would even be prepared to join the armed forces." Isabel Kershner, "Faithful Citizens or Fifth Column?" *Jerusalem Report*, Sept. 21, 1995, pp. 14, 18. The Druze community petitioned for full and equal military service in 1957.

83. See Wolffsohn, *Israel: Polity, Society and Economy*, p. 121. See also Avraham Burg, "The Arabs of Israel: A Statistical Portrait, in Aloúph Hareven, ed., *Every Sixth Israeli: Relations Between The Jewish Majority and the Arab Minority in Israel* (Jerusalem: Van Leer Institute, 1983).
    In 1992 the Jewish birthrate was an average of 2.6 children per woman, down from earlier figures due to the early 1990s influx of 400,000 Russian Jews, who have a birthrate of 1.5 per woman. By contrast, the Muslim birthrate was 4.7 per woman, itself about half the figure of 30 years ago. Clyde Haberman, "Israel Study Finds Birth Rate at Lowest Level Since 1948," *New York Times*, Nov. 8, 1992, p. 20. Put another way, the average Jewish Israeli household has 3.43 persons, while the average non-Jewish Israeli household has 5.53 persons. Haberman, "Israeli Arabs Say P.L.O. Pact is a Path to First-Class Status." The dire predictions of the "biological time bomb" supposedly threatening Jewish hegemony make two questionable assumptions: that the occupied territories will become annexed, which would, indeed, create a Palestinian majority by the year

2000; and that Muslim women will continue to bear more children, even as their lives become more modernized. Both fly in the face of political and cultural trends. See Alon Ben-Meir, "Israelis and Palestinians: Harsh Demographic Reality and Peace," *Middle East Policy* 2, no. 2 (1993), pp. 74–86; and Arnon Soffer, "Demography and the Shaping of Israel's Borders," *Contemporary Jewry* 10 (1989) pp. 91, 98.

84. See George Kossaifi, "Demographic Characteristics of the Arab Palestinian People," in Nakhleh and Zureik, *The Sociology of the Palestinians*, pp. 39–40. Kossaifi points out that even though the Palestinians of Israel suffer from racism and discrimination, their living conditions are better than their co-nationals endure elsewhere, another factor disfavoring emigration.

85. Arnon Soffer, "Demography in Eretz-Israel: 1988 and the year 2000," *The Jerusalem Quarterly* (Summer 1989), pp. 115–144.

86. Some of the villages of the "Little Triangle," such as Barta'ah and Baka al-Garbiyah, are so close to the border with the West Bank that it has been suggested they merge with it. See Kershner, "Faithful Citizens or Fifth Column?" pp. 14, 15.

87. Most of the "unrecognized villages" lack municipal services and water or utility hookups. Their residents live under constant threat of demolition orders. See Sabine Goodwin, "Unrecognised in Israel," *Index on Censorship* 23 (May/June 1994), pp. 171–75; "Life Under Threat," in ibid., pp. 176–81.

88. For instance, while 30.4 percent of Jewish Israelis go to school for more than 12 years, only 8.9 percent of non-Jewish Israelis do. Haberman, "Israeli Arabs Say P.L.O. Pact is a Path to First-Class Status." As reported in 1991, 70 percent of Arab pupils failed a national test of reading and math skills, while the Jewish failure rate was between 20 and 30 percent. Avigdor Feldman and Hussein Abu Hussein, American-Israeli Civil Liberties Coalition, "*Report to Membership, Coalition Litigation for Equality of Education*" (1991). In the mid-1980s, only 20 percent of Arab students studied technological subjects such as computers, compared to 60 percent of Jewish students. David Rudge, "School Gap for Arabs Called 'Wide as Ever,' " *Jerusalem Post*, Sept. 2, 1986, p. 4.

89. Balfour Declaration, Nov. 2, 1917, reprinted in Moore, ed., *The Arab-Israeli Conflict*, vol. 3, pp. 31–32. See also Mandate for Palestine (1922), reprinted in ibid., p. 74. The U.N. Partition Resolution, G.A. Res. 181, Nov. 29, 1947, also required that elections to Israel's (and the Arab state's) legislative body be conducted on the basis of "universal suffrage" and that the state guarantee "all persons equal and nondiscriminatory rights in civil, political, economic and religious matters and the enjoyment of human rights and fundamental freedoms." Part I.B.10.a and b. Arabs first voted in Israel's national elections of 1949. Yoav Peled, "Ethnic Democracy and the Legal Construction of Citizenship: Arab Citizens of the Jewish State," *American Political Science Review* 86, no. 2 (June 1992), pp. 432, 436.

90. Israel's Declaration of Independence has been widely reprinted. The formal citation is Declaration on the Establishment of the State of Israel, *Laws of the State of Israel*, vol. 1 (1948), p. 3.

91. In the view of Salem Jubran, director of the Jewish-Arab Center for Peace at the Givat Havivah Institute in Israel: "Anyway, the Law of Return isn't discrimination against me, it's affirmative action for the Jews. It's not a disaster." Kershner, "Faithful Citizens or Fifth Column?" p. 15. See Arthur Hertzberg, "The Left-Liberal Case for Zionism: Affirmative Action for the Jews," *Israel Horizons* (Summer/Autumn 1992), p. 7. Amnon Rubinstein, *The Constitutional Law of the State of Israel* (Tel Aviv: Schocken, 1980), pp. 180–81, argues that by granting one group, the Jews, a privilege not available to other groups, the Law of Return does not discriminate *against* anyone. See Kretzmer, *The Legal Status of the Arabs in Israel*, pp. 36–40. For a view that is highly critical of the Law of Return, see John Quigley, *Palestine and Israel: A Challenge to Justice* (Durham, NC: Duke University Press, 1990), pp. 116–30. See also Mandatory Defense (Emergency) Regulations (1945), kept in effect by the Law and Administration Ordinance, sections 9 and 11 (1948).

92. "There shall be no violation of the property of a person." Basic Law: Human Dignity and Liberty, Article 3, *Sefer HaChukkim* No. 1391, Mar. 25, 1992. "Every Israel national or resident has the right to engage in any occupation, profession or trade; there shall be no limitation on this right except by a Law enacted for a proper purpose and on grounds of the general welfare." Basic Law: Freedom of Occupation, Article 1, *Sefer HaChukkim* No. 1387, Mar. 12, 1992. See Leslie Susser, "We the People," *Jerusalem Report*, Nov. 5, 1992, p. 14.

93. Melman, *The New Israelis*, pp. 166–67.

94. Peter Grose, *A Changing Israel* (New York: Vintage Books, 1985), p. 76.

95. For instance, in the late 1970s, Israeli Arabs had a life expectancy of 63 years (71.5 for women), compared to 56 in Syria and Jordan, 55 in Egypt, and 45 in Saudi Arabia. Hareven, *Every Sixth Israeli*, pp. 24, 172.

96. Yosef Goell, "Bridging the Gap," *Jerusalem Post Magazine*, Dec. 27, 1985, p. 12.

97. See Kershner, "Faithful Citizens or Fifth Column?" See also Jerrold Kessel, "Israel Seeks Compromise on Refugee Land Dispute," CNN Transcript #63-3, Jan. 1, 1996, on the northern Galilee village of Ikrit, whose residents may be able to rebuild their homes though not regain their farmland.

98. For instance, the Knesset approved the Oslo II agreement by a vote of 61–59. See Haberman, "Israeli Arabs Say P.L.O. Pact is a Path to First-Class Status"; N. Tarnopolsky, "Knesset Triggers Debate Over Role of Arabs in Israel's Democracy," *Forward*, Nov. 3, 1995, p. 3.

99. See also Tarnopolsky, "Knesset Triggers Debate"; Kershner, "Faithful Citizens or Fifth Column?" p. 16, quoting Israeli writer and publisher Muhammad Ghanaim: "There is no Palestinian democracy. It was just a dream."

100. While as many as 50 percent have voted for Zionist parties (as alterna-
      tives to joint Arab-Jewish communist or all-Arab parties) in recent na-
      tional elections, an opinion survey in the mid-1980s reported that about
      75 percent of the Palestinians in Israel chose a self-identifying label that
      had no word "Israeli" in it. See Kershner, "Faithful Citizens or Fifth Col-
      umn?", p. 18; Murad A'si, *Israeli and Palestinian Public Opinion* (Washing-
      ton, DC: International Center for Research and Public Policy, 1986), pp.
      13–17. However, Palestinian citizens have not sought to register as
      "Palestinian" rather than "Arab" under the 1965 Population Registry
      Law. See Kretzmer, *The Legal Status of the Arabs in Israel*, p. 43. See also
      Sammy Smooha, *The Orientation and Politicization of the Arab Minority in
      Israel* (Haifa: Institute of Middle Eastern Studies, 1984); Sammy Smooha,
      Arabs and Jews in Israel: Conflicting and Shared Attitudes in a Divided Society
      (Boulder, CO: Westview Press, 1989); Sammy Smooha, *Arabs and Jews in
      Israel: Change and Continuity in Mutual Tolerance* (Boulder, CO: Westview
      Press, 1991).
         Since 1965, Rakah, the joint Arab-Jewish Communist party, had "a
      primarily non-nationalistic ideology [and] provided an opportunity for
      legitimate identification with the Arab cause, within the framework of
      the law. It produced the magic formula Israeli Arabs sought: how to be
      [a] Palestinian patriot and loyal Israeli citizen." Leslie Susser, "The Lost
      Garden," *Jerusalem Report*, Mar. 10, 1994, pp. 46–48. See Jacob M. Landau,
      The Arab Minority in Israel, 1967–1991 (Oxford: Clarendon Press, 1994).

101. Quoted by Thomas Friedman, "I Too Am Israeli, One Arab Declares (in
      Hebrew)," *New York Times*, Jan. 21, 1987, p. 3. See also Anton Shammas,
      "A Stone's Throw," *New York Review of Books*, Mar. 31, 1988, p. 9; Joel
      Brinkley, "Many Arabs Working in Israel Voice Mixed Views on Unrest,"
      New York Times, May 2, 1988, pp. A1, A6; Eleanor Gawne, "Bedouin in
      the Negev: 'It's Just a Matter of Time,' " *New Outlook* (July 1988), pp. 27,
      28; Farhat Igbaria, "Israeli Arabs Dissent, but Remain Loyal," *New York
      Times*, July 9, 1990, p. A16; Rubinstein, *The People of Nowhere*, p. 89.

102. Kershner, "Faithful Citizens or Fifth Column?," pp. 15–16. A July 1989
      poll of both Israeli Jews and Israeli Arabs revealed that greater numbers
      of the latter believed in the possibility of Jewish-Arab coexistence within
      the pre-1967 borders of Israel; only 29 percent of Israeli Arabs believed
      that many of their community would be interested in belonging to a
      Palestinian state. Yitzhak Reiter, "Forming Their Identity," *Israeli Democ-
      racy* (Fall 1989), pp. 31, 34. However, Leslie Susser warns: "Continued
      failure by the Jewish majority to give the Arab minority a sense of full
      equality in politics, work and social services, along with an increase in
      nationalist and fundamentalist activism, could exacerbate breakaway, ir-
      redentist tendencies," such as a move for autonomy in the Galilee region,
      where Israeli Arabs are becoming a majority. Susser, "The Lost Garden,"
      p. 48. See also Smooha, *Arabs and Jews in Israel*, p. 93.

103. U.S. Bureau of the Census, Center for International Research, *Palestinian
      Projections for 16 Countries/Areas of the World 1990 to 2010* (Washington,

DC: March 1991), mimeograph cited by Peretz, *Palestinians, Refugees, and the Middle East Peace Process* (Washington, DC: United States Institute of Peace Press, 1993), pp. 16–17. Smaller communities of Palestinians are also said to be in Yemen and the Sudan.

104. Held, *Middle East Patterns*, pp. 188–89; Muhammad Faour, *The Arab World After Desert Storm* (Washington, DC: United States Institute of Peace Press, 1993), p. 22; *Facts and Figures About the Palestinians*, p. 15.

105. *Facts and Figures About the Palestinians*, p. 15, and Feiler, "Labour Migration in the Middle East Following the Iraqi Invasion of Kuwait," p. 10. About 20,000 entered Gaza and the West Bank. Khaled Abu Toameh, "The Palestinian Aliyah," *Jerusalem Report*, Oct. 17, 1991, p. 43.

106. Humphrey, "Migrants, Workers and Refugees," pp. 6–7.

107. Brand, *Palestinians in the Arab World*, p. 12.

108. Kuwait, whose total population at the time was 1.13 million, rarely grants citizenship except to those adult males who have been inhabitants continuously since 1920 and their male offspring. Only about 50 people a year become nationalized citizens. Held, *Middle East Patterns*, p. 318. No foreigners can own real property in Kuwait or establish their own industries. A host of economic benefits are reserved exclusively for citizens. And no women, even citizens, can vote. See Naseer H. Aruri and Samih Farsoun, "Palestinian Communities and Arab Host Countries," in Nakhleh and Zureik, *The Sociology of the Palestinians*, pp. 112, 136–37; Brand, *Palestinians in the Arab World*, pp. 112–15; and *The Bedoons of Kuwait: "Citizens without Citizenship"* (New York: Human Rights Watch / Middle East, 1995).

109. Aruri and Farsoun, "Palestinian Communities and Arab Host Countries," pp. 135–36. See also Brand, *Palestinians in the Arab World*, pp. 115–17; and Ann M. Lesch, "Palestinians in Kuwait," *Journal of Palestine Studies* (Summer 1991), pp. 42–43. On Arafat's days in Kuwait, see Baruch Kimmerling and Joel Migdal, *Palestinians: The Making of a People* (Cambridge, MA: Harvard University Press, 1994) pp. 213–214.

110. The situation is similar in the United Arab Emirates, where 80 percent of the population is composed of foreign workers, including Palestinians, but where even permanent residents cannot own businesses or real estate. Aruri and Farsoun, "Palestinian Communities and Arab Host Countries," pp. 136–38; Brand, *Palestinians in the Arab World*, p. 121; Viorst, *Sandcastles*, pp. 245–46.

111. Brand, *Palestinians in the Arab World*, pp. 124–25. PLO schools, where children saluted the Palestinian flag and participated in Palestinian cultural and social activities, operated between 1967 and 1976. This relative autonomy came to an end when the Kuwaiti government feared it would turn into another Lebanon. See Kimmerling and Migdal, *Palestinians: The Making of a People*, pp. 228–29.

112. Faour, *The Arab World After Desert Storm*, p. 22. "It was hard to make the case to Kuwaitis that Palestinians were reacting not against Kuwait but

against America's long-standing preference for Israel over their own cause. Furthermore, Kuwaitis had never sensed the resentment that Palestinians felt toward the condescension and want of generosity they had so long experienced in Kuwait." Viorst, *Sandcastles*, p. 259. Palestinians were, of course, also reacting positively to Saddam Hussein's accusation that the United States practiced a double standard when it came to foreign occupations in the Middle East. See ibid., p. 265, on how the expulsions were effectuated.

113. See Feiler, "Labour Migration in the Middle East," pp. 9–10.

114. "The Palestinians in Kuwait," *Palestine Yearbook of International Law*, vol. 5 (1990/91), pp. 87–110 (reprinting Middle East Watch report). See also Middle East Watch, *A Victory Turned Sour: Human Rights in Kuwait Since Liberation* (Sept. 1991). Kuwait is not the only country to have expelled Palestinians. Iraq, Saudi Arabia, and Libya also, expelled striking Palestinian workers in the mid-1950s; in 1959, politically active Palestinian students were also expelled from Iraq. Brand, *Palestinians in the Arab World*, pp. 70, 126. See chapter 3's section on expulsion for other examples.

115. "Kuwait Dismisses Mass Return of Jordanians," *Reuters World Report*, Mar. 3, 1996.

116. Brand, *Palestinians in the Arab World*, pp. 8, 100, 126, 260 n.11. Throughout the Middle East and North Africa, about 48,000 Palestinians were working as teachers in the early 1970s. Ibid., p. 260, n. 11.

117. Held, *Middle East Patterns*, p. 299; Brand, *Palestinians in the Arab World*, pp. 126–27. By contrast, Kuwait had not required visas for Palestinians and Jordanians since the late 1950s. Faour, *The Arab World After Desert Storm*, p. 22.

118. Brand, *Palestinians in the Arab World*, pp. 41–46, 53.

119. "Expelled Palestinians Stranded," *Christian Science Monitor*, Sept. 15, 1995. Jordan agreed to admit 188. By contrast, Lebanon imposed entry visa restrictions on Palestinians expelled by Libya, including those with Lebanese travel documents. About one-third of Libya's 30,000 Palestinians have Lebanese travel documents. "Jordan Slams Libya's Expulsion of Palestinians," *Agence France Presse*, Sept. 12, 1995.

120. Brand, *Palestinians in the Arab World*, pp. 52–53.

121. Ibid., p. 61.

122. Sayigh, "Harsh Present, Uncertain Future," p. 41.

123. "The Case of Palestinian Refugees in Libya," *Shaml Newsletter* (Dec. 1995), pp. 2–4. Egypt will not let any of the Palestinians cross the border if they lack at least a one-year residence permit in another country. Khaled Dawoud, "Forgotten in Exile," *Associated Press*, Jan. 17, 1996.

124. For instance, in a recent book titled *Muslim Communities in North America*, edited by Yvonne Yazbeck Haddad and Jane Idleman Smith (Albany: State University of New York Press, 1994), not a single entry in the 11-page index mentions Palestinians.

125.   See John Zogby, *Arab America Today: A Demographic Profile of Arab Americans* (Washington, DC: Arab American Institute, 1990), pp. 31, 39. A small number of immigrants from Arab states might also be Jews and other non-Arabs. See ibid., p. 42 n.6. The Washington, DC, office of the United Nations High Commissioner for Refugees at one time attempted to compile a study of Palestinians who had applied for asylum in the United States, but the information was too incomplete to report. UNHCR correspondence with author.

126.   See table 1, "The Palestinian Diaspora," *New York University Journal of International Law and Politics* 24 (1992), p. 1512, which was compiled from estimates and projections by the Institute for Palestine Studies, the U.S. Committee for Refugees, the Dayan Center of Tel Aviv University, and the U.S. Bureau of the Census (Sept. 1990–March 1991). Also reporting the 150,000 U.S. figure is Held, *Middle East Patterns*, p. 189, citing the Institute of Palestine Studies.

127.   *Facts and Figures About the Palestinians*, p. 4. Any figure as specific as the PLO number is suspect on the ground that it could only have been derived from broad estimates.

128.   See Turki, *Exile's Return*, pp. 127–46.

129.   In November 1995, while traveling from Amman to Jerusalem, this author met a Palestinian from Chicago whose sister had lived in Brazil for a generation. He estimated that there are "dozens" of towns or cities in Brazil with 100 or more Palestinians.

130.   Zogby, *Arab America Today*, pp. v, viii, 33. The first wave, at the turn of the century, was predominantly from present-day Syria and Lebanon and 90 percent Christian. Ibid., p. vii.

131.   Ibid., pp. 8–16; Kimmerling and Migdal, *Palestinians: The Making of a People*, p. 206. On the stereotyping of Arab Americans as "terrorists," see, for example, Jonathan Broder, "Arabs in America: On the Defensive," *Jerusalem Report*, Aug. 26, 1993, p. 28; Peter Applebome, "Arab-Americans Fear a Land War's Backlash," *New York Times*, Feb. 16, 1991, p. A1; Yossi Shain, "Arab-Americans at a Crossroads," *Journal of Palestine Studies* 25 (Spring 1996), p. 46.

132.   Zogby, *Arab America Today*, pp. 1, 39. The 1980 Census was the first one in which ancestry could be voluntarily declared on the "long form," which itself is sent only to a 17 percent sample of households. Because of the likelihood of underreporting, the study concentrates on percentages and not absolute numbers.

133.   At any rate, the largest concentration of Palestinians is in the western United States (4.2 percent of the total Arab Americans live there) and the smallest (2.3 percent) in the Northeast. Ibid., p. 3. Particular areas with significant Palestinian communities include Paterson, New Jersey; Brooklyn, Westchester County, and Syracuse, New York; Michigan; Texas; California; and Virginia and Illinois, where Palestinians constitute 7.4 and 6.7 percent, respectively, of all Arab Americans. Ibid., pp. 20–30.

134.   Turki, *Exile's Return*, pp. 83–84, 85.

Chapter 3: The International Law Framework

1. On these questions, see, for instance, Eyal Benvenisti, *The International Law of Occupation* (Princeton, NJ: Princeton University Press, 1993); Raja Shehadeh, *Occupier's Law: Israel and the West Bank* (Washington, DC: Institute for Palestine Studies, 1988); Meir Shamgar, ed., *Military Government in the Territories Administered by Israel 1967–1980* (Jerusalem: Hebrew University, 1982); Esther R. Cohen, *Human Rights in the Israeli-Occupied Territories 1967–1982* (Manchester, U.K.: Manchester University Press, 1985); Ilan Peleg, *Human Rights in the West Bank and Gaza: Legacy and Politics* (Syracuse, NY: Syracuse University Press, 1995); Emma Playfair, ed., *International Law and the Administration of Occupied Territories: Two Decades of Israeli Occupation* (Oxford: Oxford University Press, 1992); Adam Roberts, "Prolonged Military Occupation: The Territories Since 1967," *American Journal of International Law* 84 (1990), pp. 44; and Behnam Dayanim, "The Israeli Supreme Court and the Deportation of Palestinians: The Interaction of Law and Legitimacy," *Stanford Journal of International Law* 30 (1994), p. 115.

2. "Even if the dispossession of the former owners violated international law, the fact that the local law created expectations in the individuals involved should be taken into consideration, especially when a long time has elapsed since the dispossession." Eyal Benvenisti and Eyal Zamir, "Private Claims to Property Rights in the Future Israeli-Palestinian Settlement," *American Journal of International Law* 89 (April 1995), pp. 295, 328, citing international judicial decisions in support of this proposition.

    Compensation for West Bank or Gaza homes demolished by Israeli military order, if such demolition is illegal under international law, would be a separate legal issue from compensation owed to refugees for property left behind. See Cheryl V. Reicin, "Preventive Detention, Curfews, Demolition of Houses and Deportations: An Analysis of Measures Employed by Israel in the Occupied Territories," *Cardozo Law Review* 8 (1987), p. 515.

3. This analysis is based on the generally accepted position that "foreign domination," along with colonialism and racism, is one of the three legal justifications for self-determination. See Antonio Cassese, *Self-Determination of Peoples: A Legal Reappraisal* (Cambridge: Cambridge University Press, 1995), pp. 238–40.

4. Robbie Sabel, "Remarks," in American Society of International Law, *Proceedings of the 89th Annual Meeting* (Washington, DC: American Society of International Law, 1995), p. 366.

5. "One of the most important sources of 'soft law' is the myriad of guidelines, resolutions and decisions that parties take to implement an international agreement. . . . In the course of [which], parties essentially act as an informal legislature." Edith Brown Weiss, "President's Message," *American Society of International Law Newsletter* (Sept.–Oct. 1995), pp. 1, 6.

6. Article 13(2), Universal Declaration of Human Rights, G.A. Res. 217(III), adopted Dec. 10, 1948. See Analysis of the Current Trends and Develop-

ments Regarding the Right to Leave Any Country Including One's Own and to Return to One's Own Country, and Some Other Rights or Considerations Arising Therefrom, Final Report by Special Rapporteur C.L.C. Mubanga-Chipoya, to the Sub-Commission on Prevention of Discrimination and Protection of Minorities, Fortieth Session, Item 5(e) of the Provisional Agenda, U.N. Doc. E/CN.4/Sub.2/1988/35, June 20, 1988, pp. 19–20.

7. Article 12(4), International Covenant on Civil and Political Rights, 999 U.N.T.S. 171, 6 *International Legal Materials* 368 (1967), adopted Dec. 16, 1966, by the General Assembly.

8. See Louis B. Sohn and Thomas Buergenthal, eds., *The Movement of Persons Across Borders* (Washington, DC: American Society of International Law, Oct. 1992), p. 7; Hurst Hannum, *The Right to Leave and Return in International Law and Practice* (Dordrecht, the Netherlands: Martinus Nijhoff, 1987), p. 45, citing Study of the Right of Everyone to Be Free From Arbitrary Arrest, Detention and Exile, U.N. Doc. E/CN.4/826/Rev.1 (1964), p. 7. Hannum explicitly states his opinion that Article 12 of the International Covenant is inapplicable "to the resolution of situations such as that of the Palestinians under Israeli occupation." Ibid., p. 108. Stig Jagerskjold, "The Freedom of Movement," in Louis Henkin, ed., *The International Bill of Rights* (New York: Columbia University Press, 1981), pp. 166, 180, agrees with Hannum that Article 12 does not apply to the Palestinians. But Hannum also concedes that "*ex post facto* or unilateral grants of citizenship by, e.g., a newly independent state, might create a right to enter for large numbers of previously stateless persons or even those who held another nationality at one time." Ibid., p. 60. This might apply to Palestinians returning to a newly independent Palestine, but not necessarily to Israel.

9. See Analysis of the Current Trends, pp. 19–20, describing the "Middle East approach" to this question. See also the rather indeterminate construction of nationality by the International Court of Justice in the *Nottebohm* case (Liechtenstein v. Guatemala), 1955 I.C.J. Reports 4, 23. "Nationality is a legal bond having as its basis a social fact of attachment, a genuine connection of existence, interests and sentiments, together with the existence of reciprocal rights and duties." However, in that case, Nottebohm's physical presence during a visit was considered insufficient to entitle Liechtenstein to claim him as a national.

10. *Laws of the State of Israel (LSI)*, vol. 4, p. 14 (1950), as amended by *LSI*, vol. 8, p. 144 (1954), as amended by *LSI*, vol. 24, p. 28 (1970). See Many Erez, "The Law of Return: Refuge or Racism?" *New Outlook* (May–June 1986), p. 53. For discussion of a similar provision in German law, see chapter 5.

11. African Charter on Human and Peoples' Rights, *International Legal Materials*, vol. 21 (1981), p. 59, article 12(2). The right to return is "subject to restrictions, provided for by law for the protection of national security, law and order, public health or morality." Ibid. See Donna E. Arzt and Karen Zughaib, "Return to the Negotiated Lands: The Likelihood and Legality of a Population Transfer Between Israel and a Future Palestinian State," *New*

York University Journal of International Law and Politics 24, no. 4 (1992), p. 1442. Note that in Article 12 of the International Covenant on Civil and Political Rights, the provision on the right to "enter" appears after the paragraph in which "the above mentioned rights" of freedom of movement are subjected to specified limitations, which may mean the drafters considered it an absolute right.

12. Resolution 194(III) of Dec. 11, 1948, is reprinted in full in the documentary appendix.

13. Paragraph 11 was later construed by Secretary-General Dag Hammarskjold to include integration of the refugees in Arab countries. Proposals of the Secretary-General on the Palestinian Refugees, U.N. Doc. A/4121, June 15, 1959, par. 14.

14. G.A. Res. 242, Nov. 22, 1967, par. 2(b).

15. See, for instance, Ruth Lapidoth, "The Right of Return in International Law, with Special Reference to the Palestinian Refugees," *Israel Yearbook on Human Rights*, vol. 16 (1986), pp. 103–25; Julius Stone, *Israel and Palestine: Assault on the Law of Nations* (Baltimore: Johns Hopkins University Press, 1981).

16. See, for instance, Henry Cattan, *Palestine and International Law* (London: Longman, 1973); Henry Cattan, *The Palestine Question* (New York: Croom Helm, 1988); and George J. Tomeh, "Legal Status of Arab Refugees," in John N. Moore, ed., *The Arab-Israeli Conflict*, vol. 1 (Washington, DC: American Society of International Law, 1974). See also John Quigley, "Family Reunion and the Right to Return to Occupied Territory," *Georgetown Immigration Law Journal* 6 (1992), p. 223.

17. See, for instance, Rashid Khalidi, "Observations on the Right of Return," *Journal of Palestine Studies* (Winter 1992), p. 29; Ziad Abu Zayyad, "The Palestinian Right of Return: A Realistic Approach," *Palestine-Israel Journal*, no. 2, (Spring 1994), pp. 74–78; Abraham Rabinovich, "A Palestinian Trial Balloon on the 'Right of Return,' " *Jerusalem Post*, June 3, 1994, p. 3B. See also the Fall 1995 issue of *Palestine-Israel Journal*, devoted to refugees and return.

     For interpretations of the 1988 Palestinian Declaration of Statehood and the accompanying Palestine National Council Communiqué that reflect these moderations, see Anis M. Al-Qasem, "Declaration of the State of Palestine: Background and Considerations," *Palestinian Yearbook of International Law*, vol. 4 (1987–88), p. 314; "Recent Developments: The International Legal Implications of the November 1988 Palestinian Declaration of Statehood," *Stanford Journal of International Law* 25 (1989), p. 681; and Muhammad Muslih, *Toward Coexistence: An Analysis of the Resolutions of the Palestine National Council* (Washington, DC: Institute for Palestine Studies, 1990).

18. See Kurt Rene Radley, "The Palestinian Refugees: The Right to Return in International Law," *American Journal of International Law* 72 (1978), pp. 586, 600–3. See also the discussion of the 1949 Lausanne Conference in chapter 1 of this book. Israel rejected other provisions of Resolution 194 that recommended the internationalization of Jerusalem.

19. See for instance, G.A. Res. 3236, Nov. 22, 1974; G.A. Res. 40/168, Jan. 14, 1986. See U.N. Committee on the Exercise of the Inalienable Rights of the Palestinian People, The Right of Self-Determination of the Palestinian People, U.N. Doc. ST/SG/SER.F/3 (1979). The tone of U.N. resolutions on this and related issues has changed over time, in part depending on the size of the anti-Israel majority in the General Assembly. It has notably moderated since the Madrid and Oslo peace processes were initiated. A recent example that refers to original Resolution 194, demonstrating its ongoing viability, is Resolution 48/158D of Dec. 20, 1993.

    On the U.S. view of Palestinian return, see the compilation edited by Norbert Scholz, *U.S. Official Statements: The Palestinian Refugees* (Washington, DC: Institute for Palestine Studies, 1994); Donald Neff, *Fallen Pillars: U.S. Policy Towards Palestine and Israel Since 1945* (Washington, DC: Institute for Palestine Studies, 1995), pp. 55–82. On the uproarious reaction to a surprise U.S. State Department reference to Resolution 194, see Clyde Haberman, "U.S. Comment on Old Issue Inflames Israelis," *New York Times*, May 15, 1992, p. A13; and Thomas Friedman, "U.S. Softens on '48 Palestinian Issue," *New York Times*, May 19, 1992, p. A3.

20. International Covenant on Civil and Political Rights, articles 12–13. See Sohn and Buergenthal, *The Movement of Persons Across Borders*, pp. 89–97.

21. Charter of the International Military Tribunal, 82 U.N.T.S. 279, signed Aug. 8, 1945; Geneva Convention III, 6 U.S.T. 3516, 75 U.N.T.S. 287, signed Aug. 12, 1949.

22. European Convention on Human Rights, Fourth Protocol, article 4 (1963); African Charter on Human and People's Rights, article 12(5)(1981). See Alfred M. de Zayas, "International Law and Mass Population Transfers," *Harvard International Law Journal* 16, (1975), p. 207; Jean-Marie Henckaerts, *Mass Expulsion in Modern International Law and Practice* (The Hague, Netherlands: Boston: Martinus Nijhoff Publishers, 1995); Christopher M. Goebel, "A Unified Concept of Population Transfer (Revised)," *Denver Journal of International Law and Policy* 22 (1993), pp. 1–27. Articles 32 and 33 of the 1951 Convention Relating to the Status of Refugees, 189 U.N.T.S. 137, prohibit the expulsion of de jure refugees except on grounds of national security or public order, in accordance with due process of law, and not to places where their life or freedom would be threatened. Of all the Arab countries in which Palestinians reside, only Egypt has ratified the Refugee Convention. See also Declaration of Principles of International Law on Mass Expulsion, International Law Association, 62nd Conference (Seoul, 1986), reprinted in Henckaerts, *Mass Expulsion in Modern International Law and Practice*, p. 223.

23. Quoted by Khaled Abu Toameh, "The Palestinian Aliyah," *Jerusalem Report*, Oct. 17, 1991, p. 43.

24. See de Zayas, "International Law and Mass Population Transfers"; Alfred M. de Zayas, "A Historical Survey of Twentieth Century Expulsions," in Anna C. Bramwell, ed., *Refugees in the Age of Total War* (London: Unwin Hyman, 1988), pp. 14–36; and Arzt and Zughaib, "Return to the Negotiated Lands," pp. 1451–62.

25. See, for instance, "Dumping the Palestinian Refugees," *Middle East Mirror*, Apr. 20, 1994.

26. Miral Fahmy, "Libya Expels Hundreds of Palestinian-Travellers," *Reuters*, Sept. 8, 1995; Douglas Jehl, "Libyan Refugee Camp Stirs Concern on Ouster of Palestinians," *New York Times*, Sept. 28, 1995.

27. The feminine gender is used here to make a political point. Worldwide, an estimated 80 percent all refugees are women and children. Susan Forbes Martin, *Refugee Women* (London: Zed Books, 1992), pp. 5, 13–14. The percentage of refugees who are adult women and girl children, in the 16 asylum countries that report by gender, include figures as high as 55, 58, and 63 percent in Benin, Kenya, and Algeria, respectively. United Nations High Commissioner for Refugees, *The State of the World's Refugees: In Search of Solutions* (New York: Oxford University Press, 1995), p. 251 (Table 6). Moreover, in the words of Sadako Ogata, U.N. High Commissioner for Refugees, "Refugee women and children bear a disproportionate share of the suffering." Ruth Marshall, "Refugees, Feminine Plural," *Refugees*, no. 100 (II-1995), pp. 3, 4. In Rwanda, for instance, during the genocide of 1994, "virtually every adult woman or girl past puberty who was spared from massacre by the militias had been raped." Ibid., p. 5. In some refugee situations, more than 30 percent of all households are headed by women. UNHCR, *The State of the World's Refugees*, p. 60.

28. See Guy Goodwin-Gill, *The Refugee in International Law* (Oxford: Clarendon Press, 1990), p. 13, summarizing the definition established by the 1950 Statute of the Office of the United Nations High Commissioner for Refugees, the 1951 Convention Relating to the Status of Refugees, and the 1967 Protocol Relating to the Status of Refugees. See generally United Nations High Commissioner for Refugees, *Handbook on Procedures and Criteria for Determining Refugee Status* (Geneva: United Nations, 1992), U.N. Doc. HCR/1P/4/Eng/REV.2.

29. Gil Loescher, *Beyond Charity: International Cooperation and the Global Refugee Crisis* (New York: Oxford University Press, 1993), p. 6. Persecution of refugees can also be by private actors and will give rise to claims for protection and asylum if it can be shown that the government knew about the private persecution and failed to stop it. See James Hathaway, *The Law of Refugee Status* (Toronto: Butterworths, 1991), pp. 125–133.

30. Hathaway, *The Law of Refugee Status*, p. 185 (emphasis in original).

31. In Africa and Latin America, regional agreements provide for broader definitions. See ibid., pp. 16–21.

32. Kurt R. Radley, "The Palestinian Refugees: The Right to Return in International Law," *American Journal of International Law* 72 (1978), pp. 609–10.

33. UNRWA's Consolidated Eligibility Instructions, quoted in *UNRWA 1950–1990: Serving Palestine Refugees* (Vienna: UNRWA Public Information Office, April 1990), p. 6. Note that the 1951 Convention on Refugees and the 1950 UNHCR Statute explicitly exclude from their coverage any persons who "are at present receiving from organs or agencies of the United

Nations other than the United Nations High Commissioner for Refugees protection or assistance." This reference was to UNRWA.

34. Convention, Article 1(F). See Hathaway, *The Law of Refugee Status*, pp. 214–29.

35. See Goodwin-Gill, *The Refugee in International Law*, pp. 11, 58–65.

36. See 1951 convention, articles 33 and 13–24.

37. See Goodwin-Gill, *The Refugee in International Law*, pp. 154–58. The "Convention Travel Document" does not carry with it diplomatic protection by the issuing state.

38. See United Nations, *Multilateral Treaties On Deposit with the Secretary General as of December 31, 1994* (New York: United Nations Press, 1995). See also table 5.1 in chapter 5.

39. "[R]eparation must, as far as possible, wipe out all the consequences of the illegal act and reestablish the situation which would, in all probability, have existed if that act had not been committed." *Chorzow Factory* case, 1928 P.C.I.J. (Ser. A), no. 17 (Judgment of Sept. 13, 1928)(Germany v. Poland). See generally Clyde Eagleton, *The Responsibility of States in International Law* (New York, NY: New York University Press, 1928); International Law Commission, Draft Articles on State Responsibility, *Yearbook of the International Law Commission*, vol. 2 (New York, NY: New York University Press, 1980), U.N. Doc. A/CN.4/SER.A 1980/Add.1; Eyal Benvenisti and Eyal Zamir, "Private Claims to Property Rights in the Future Israeli-Palestinian Settlement," pp. 295, 329–31.

40. See Declaration of Principles of International Law on Compensation to Refugees (with commentary), The International Law Association, 65th Conference, Cairo (April 1992); Luke T. Lee, "The Right to Compensation: Refugees and Countries of Asylum," *American Journal of International Law* 80 (1986), pp. 532–67. Lee, the leading authority on refugee compensation, considers whether refugees have the right to compensation for injuries other than to property suffered "in consequence of being made a refugee," for instance, for personal injuries, indignities, and mental anguish. Although international law has concentrated on compensation only for property, Lee cites the precedent of West Germany's reparations to Jewish Holocaust survivors for loss of liberty and dignity as well as property. Ibid., pp. 546, 537. See also Nicholas Balabkins, *West German Reparations to Israel* (New Brunswick, NJ: Rutgers University Press, 1971); Nana Sagi, *German Reparations* (New York: St. Martin's Press; Jerusalem: Magnes Press, Hebrew University, 1980); Agreement Between the Federal Republic of Germany and Israel, 162 U.N.T.S. 205, Sept. 10, 1952. A plan to provide reparations for war crimes committed by the Vichy government, in the form of pensions to French Jewish survivors, has recently been proposed. See "Klarsfeld Eyes Pension for War Orphans," *The Forward*, Oct. 20, 1995, p. 1.

41. The Conciliation Commission for Palestine interpreted the word "and" in this portion of paragraph 11 to mean that even those refugees who chose

to repatriate would be compensated for property damaged or lost. U.N. Doc. A/AC.25/W.81 Rev. 2, pp. 20–21.

42. For instance, in Resolution 36/148 of Dec. 16, 1981, the General Assembly "[e]mphasize[d] the right of refugees to return to their homes in their homelands and reaffirm[ed] the right, as contained in its previous resolutions, of those who do not wish to return to receive adequate compensation." Paragraph 3.

43. In 1973, the Knesset enacted the Absentees' Property (Compensation) Law, *Laws of the State of Israel*, vol. 7, p. 176, which granted Palestinian "absentees" living in Israel and East Jerusalem whose property was "vested"—otherwise known as expropriated—in the Custodian of Absentees' Property the right to compensation. Few accepted the offered sums, as acceptance would have been considered tantamount to relinquishment of the claim to self-determination. See Benvenisti and Zamir, "Private Claims to Property Rights in the Future Israeli-Palestinian Settlement," p. 301; Danny Rubinstein, *The People of Nowhere* (New York: Times Books, 1991), pp. 121–22; Mark Tessler, *A History of the Israeli-Palestinian Conflict* (Bloomington: Indiana University Press, 1994), p. 308. See also Don Peretz, "Early State Policy Towards the Arab Population, 1948–1955," in Laurence J. Silberstein, ed., *New Perspectives on Israeli History: The Early Years of the State* (New York: New York University Press, 1991), pp. 82, 95, on Knesset attempts to compensate Arab citizens of Israel for their former land.

44. See David Forsythe, *United Nations Peacemaking: The Conciliation Commission for Palestine* (Baltimore: Johns Hopkins University Press, 1972), pp. 115–19. The Conciliation Commission had identified property owned by Arabs as of May 15, 1948 (Israeli independence) and evaluated it on the basis of market rates prevailing on November 29, 1947 (U.N. partition resolution). The aggregate came to some 240 million U.S. dollars. When it conducted a further study in the mid-1960s, it decided not to release its new base figure, for fear of generating further controversy. Forsythe reports that it was rumored to be twice the earlier figure, or $480 million, and after adjustments for changing land and currency values and income earned from use, about $1.5 billion. Ibid., pp. 117–18. Arab-sponsored studies gave estimates from twice to seven times the commission's adjusted amount. See Sami Hadawi, *Palestine: Loss of a Heritage* (San Antonio, TX: Naylor Co., 1963).

45. Don Peretz, "The Question of Compensation," in *Palestinian Refugees: Their Problem and Future* (Washington, DC: Center for Policy Analysis on Palestine, Oct. 1994), p. 16, citing data compiled from reports of the Israel Custodian of Absentee Property. Israeli acknowledgment of the duty to pay compensation is evidenced by the Statement of then Foreign Minister Golda Meir to the U.N. General Assembly's Special Political Committee, Dec. 15, 1961.

46. Peretz, "The Question of Compensation," pp. 16–17. On the laws promulgated by Israel to "institutionalize the blockage of Palestinian return" and legitimize the confiscation of abandoned Arab property, see Arzt

and Zughaib, "Return to the Negotiated Lands," pp. 1423–24; and Benvenisti and Zamir, "Private Claims to Property Rights in the Future Israeli-Palestinian Settlement," pp. 300–1, 307–8.

47. Principle 1, Draft Declaration on Principles of International Law on Compensation to Refugees (emphasis added).

48. Elfan Rees, "The Refugees in the Middle East," *Christian News From Israel* 8, no. 2 (1957), pp. 36–41.

49. See generally Ruth Donner, *The Regulation of Nationality in International Law*, 2nd ed. (Irving on Hudson, NY: Transnational Publishers, 1994), pp. 183–246. See the U.S. Supreme Court decision *Kennedy v. Mendoza-Martinez*, 377 U.S. 144, 161 (1963), discussing Article 15 of the Universal Declaration of Human Rights. See also the 1930 Hague Convention on Certain Questions Relating to the Conflict of Nationality Laws, 179 U.N.T.S. 89, Article 1; and the 1961 Convention on the Reduction of Statelessness, 360 U.N.T.S. 117, Article 9.

50. See Rogers Brubaker, *Citizenship and Nationhood in France and Germany* (Cambridge, MA: Harvard University Press, 1992), p. 81; P. Weiss, *Nationality and Statelessness in International Law*, 2nd ed. (Westport, CT: Hyperion Press, 1979), p. 95; Stephen Hall, *Nationality, Migration Rights and Citizenship of the Union* (Dordrecht, the Netherlands: Martinus Nijhoff, 1995), p. 75, n. 5; and Lutz Reuter, "The Rights of National, Ethnic and Cultural Minorities in West Germany," paper presented at the annual meeting of the Law and Society Association, 1990. Other "combination" countries include Belgium, Greece, Ireland, Portugal, Spain, and Italy. Other sole *jus sanguinis* countries include Austria, Denmark, Luxembourg, Norway, and the Netherlands.

51. Laurie A. Brand, *The Bedoons of Kuwait: "Citizens without Citizenship"* (New York: Human Rights Watch / Middle East, 1995), p. 90. See the examples in chapter 2 of this book.

52. 1995 I.C.J. Reports 4. See Donner, *The Regulation of Nationality in International Law*, pp. 31–120.

53. "A Muslim *ipso facto* becomes the citizen of an Islamic state as soon as he sets his foot on its territory with the intent to live there and thus enjoys equal rights of citizenship along with those who acquire its citizenship by birth. Citizenship has therefore to be common among all the Islamic states that (may) exist in the world and a Muslim will not need any passport for entry to or exit from any of them." Abul A'la Mawdudi, *Human Rights in Islam* (London: The Islamic Foundation, 1976), p. 10.

54. Although Israel annexed both the Golan Heights and East Jerusalem, it did not confer automatic citizenship on the Druze and Arab populations living there.

55. Donner, *The Regulation of Nationality in International Law*, pp. 18–19.

56. See, for instance, the reasoning in the U.S. Supreme Court decision *Rogers v. Bellei*, 401 U.S. 815 (1971). See also the Council of Europe's 1963 Convention on the Reduction of Cases of Multiple Nationality, 634 U.N.T.S. 221, and its 1977 Protocols.

57. In the United States, someone can automatically become a citizen by birth on U.S. soil to parents who are nationals of a country that bases its citizenship on parentage. An American also can become a dual citizen by naturalization, if at the time of naturalization in the second state she makes explicit statements of intent not to relinquish U.S. citizenship and continues to meet the obligations of U.S. citizenship. See I.N.S. *Interpreter Releases* 67, Oct. 1, 1990, p. 1092. For more than 40 years, the U.S. Supreme Court has considered dual nationality as "a status long recognized in the law." *Kawakita v. U.S.*, 343 U.S. 717 (1952). See *Afroyim v. Rusk*, 387 U.S. 253 (1967) (naturalized American citizen who lived in Israel for 10 years and voted in a political election there cannot be stripped of U.S. citizenship without the citizen's intent to renounce it).

See generally Thomas Aleinikoff and David Martin, *Immigration: Process and Policy* (St. Paul, MN: West Publishing Co., 1991), pp. 1026–46.

58. Case of *Inouye Kanao v. the King*, Ann. Dig. 103, 106 (No. 39) (appellate jurisdiction, Hong Kong, 1947). See Donner, *The Regulation of Nationality in International Law*, pp. 204–7; Rogers Brubaker, *Citizenship and Nationhood in France and Germany*, p. 144; Jeff Chin and Lise A. Truex, "The Question of Citizenship in the Baltics," *Journal of Democracy* 7, no. 1 (Jan. 1996), pp. 139–43. In France and England, the second nationality is often of a former colony, such as Algeria.

59. See Annex VII to the Report of the U.N. Secretary-General on the International Conference on the Former Yugoslavia, *International Legal Materials*, vol. 31 (1992), pp. 1549, 1584, 1590–91. On Armenia, see Armen M. Khachaturian and Van Z. Krikorian, "New Armenian Constitution Strengthens Civil Society," *Survey of East European Law* 6, no. 9 (Sept. 1995), pp. 1, 7.

60. "Transfer of sovereignty may bring about the acquisition of dual nationality by residents of the transferred territory who obtain the nationality of their new sovereign while retaining the nationality of the State within whose territorial jurisdiction they were prior to transfer." Nissim Bar-Yaacov, *Dual Nationality* (New York: Frederick A. Praeger, 1961), p. 4.

61. Article 10. Article 5 of the Turkish law of January 19, 1869, provided that the naturalization of an Ottoman subject without the previous authorization of the Imperial Government was considered void. See Bar-Yaacov, *Dual Nationality*, pp. 208, 133–34, 213–14, 150–51, 153. In the 1931–32 Egyptian case of George Salem, an International Arbitral Tribunal found that Salem was in fact a Persian and not an Egyptian national.

62. See Don Peretz, *Palestinians, Refugees and the Middle East Peace Process* (Washington, DC: United States Institute of Peace Press, 1993) p. 103.

63. *The Bedoons of Kuwait*, p. 90. See also Donner, *The Regulation of Nationality in International Law*, pp. 193–96.

64. G.A. Res. 44.25, adopted Nov. 20, 1989.

65. ECOSOC Res. 319B III, U.N. Doc. E/1849 (1950).

66. Articles 31, 16, 17, 20–24. Note that statelessness and refugee status are neither synonymous nor mutually exclusive categories. Most

refugees may be legally (as well as practically) stateless, but not all stateless persons are refugees. It is even theoretically possible that a Palestinian could be stateless but not a refugee. "[A] person may possess a nationality or be stateless at the time when he becomes a refugee, and a refugee of the former category may retain or lose his nationality without his quality of refugee being in the least affected." Atle Grahl-Madsen, *The Status of Refugees in International Law*, vol. 1 (Leyden: A. W. Sijthoff, 1966), p. 77.

67. See Daniel C. Turack, *The Passport in International Law* (Lexington, MA: Lexington Books, 1972), pp. 215–216, 328–329; Warren Freedman, *The International Right to Travel, Trade and Commerce* (Buffalo, NY: William S. Hein & Co., 1993).

68. Laurie A. Brand, *Palestinians in the Arab World: Institution Building and the Search for State* (New York: Columbia University Press, 1988) p. 24.

69. Ibid., p. 26. See also Turack, *The Passport in International Law*, pp. 49–50, 180.

70. See Brand, *Palestinians in the Arab World*, pp. 25–26, 52, 242 n. 10; Suhayl al-Natour, "The Legal Status of Palestinians in Lebanon," (unpublished Arabic paper, Beirut, 1994), p. 41.

71. See Abbas F. Shiblak, "Residency Status and Civil Rights of Palestinian Refugees in Arab Countries," *Journal of Palestine Studies* 25 (Spring 1996) p. 36.

72. "News," *Shaml Newsletter* (Dec. 1995), pp. 7, 8. By November 17, 1995, over 40,000 had been printed. It was recently reported that even Lebanon had decided to recognize the Palestinian Authority's passports, although it would not allow to enter bearers whose documents contained Israeli stamps. "Lebanon Recognizes Palestinian Passports," Reuters World Report, Feb. 13, 1996. See Turack, *The Passport in International Law*, pp. 207–14, on the status of passports issued by nonstate entities.

73. Antonio Cassese, *Self-Determination of Peoples*, p. 242.

Chapter 4: From Refugees to Citizens

1. The Multilateral Working Group on Refugees is identified in article 8(2) (b) of the Israel Jordan Peace Treaty, Oct. 26, 1994, reprinted in 34 *International Legal Materials* 43 (1995), as the framework for seeking to resolve the problems of the 1948 refugees, in conjunction with bilateral or other negotiations and through United Nations and other international refugee assistance programs. The problems of the 1967 displaced persons are to be resolved in a quadripartite committee composed of representatives from Israel, Jordan, Egypt and the Palestinians. Ibid., article 8(2) (a). See Rex Brynen and Jill Tansley, "The Refugee Working Group of the Middle East Multilateral Peace Negotiations," *Palestine-Israel Journal* 2, no. 4 (Autumn 1995), pp. 53–58.

2. See Elia Zureik, "Palestinian Refugees and Peace," *Journal of Palestine Studies* 24, no. 1 (Autumn 1994), pp. 5, 15–16, on the differences between the liberal-individualist and the communitarian models of refugee rights.

3. See Gil Loescher, *Beyond Charity: International Cooperation and the Global Refugee Crisis* (New York: Oxford University Press, 1993), pp. 148–50.

4. See James C. Hathaway, *The Law of Refugee Status* (Toronto: Butterworths, 1991), p. 206, citing 1950 U.N. General Assembly discussion on why Palestinian refugees should be kept detached from the jurisdiction of the United Nations High Commissioner for Refugees.

5. G.A. Res. 393, U.N. GAOR, 5th Sess., Supp. No. 20, pp. 22, 23, U.N. Doc. A/1775 (1950) (emphasis added). The Conciliation Commission was also well aware that repatriation alone was not a feasible solution. Progress Report of the U.N. Conciliation Commission for Palestine, U.N. GAOR, 6th Sess., Supp. No. 18, Ann. A, par. 8, U.N. Doc. A/1985 (1951). By 1966, however, the General Assembly was noting "with deep regret" that "no substantial progress has been made . . . [in] the reintegration of refugees either by repatriation or resettlement." G.A. Res. 2154 (XXI), Dec. 2, 1966.

6. In a 1959 report on the question of integration of the Palestinian refugees into the region as beneficiaries of large-scale regional development, U.N. Secretary-General Hammarskjold wrote: "[T]he unemployed population represented by the Palestinian refugees should be regarded not as a liability but, more justly, as an asset for the future; it is a reservoir of manpower which in the desirable general economic development will assist in the creation of higher standards for the whole population of the area." Proposals of the Secretary-General on the Palestinian Refugees, U.N. Doc. A/4121, June 15, 1959, par. 11.

7. Absorption of entire families, rather than just working-age single adults, is more likely to result in permanence and is consistent with the important international principle of family reunification.

8. An example of the kind of critique that will no longer be acceptable is Manuel Hassassian, "The Emigration of Soviet Jews to Palestine and Israel," *Palestine-Israel Journal*, no. 2 (1994), p. 86.

9. See Alfred M. de Zayas, "Population, Expulsion and Transfer," *Encyclopedia of Public International Law*, vol. 8 (1985), pp. 438, 442; Donna E. Arzt and Karen Zughaib, "Return to the Negotiated Lands: The Likelihood and Legality of a Population Transfer Between Israel and a Future Palestinian State," *New York University Journal of International Law and Politics*, 24, no. 4, (1992), pp. 1451–53.

10. Dag Hammarskjold, 1959 proposal, par. 17.

11. Palestine National Council: Political Communiqué and Declaration of Independence, 27 *International Legal Materials* 1660, 1670 (1988). This language is conceptually similar to the references in Israel's 1948 Declaration of Independence that the establishment of the Jewish State would "confer upon the Jewish people the status of a fully-privileged member of the comity of nations." *Israel Official Gazette*, no. 1, May 14, 1948.

12. Gidon Gottlieb, "Israel and the Palestinians," *Foreign Affairs* 68, no. 4 (Fall 1989), p. 116. See Danny Rubinstein, *The People of Nowhere* (New York: Times Books, 1991), p. 93: "Some see this as an attempt to soften the original Palestinian demand for return to a specific village or house. . . . The

focus would no longer be on the specific house that was lost to him and his family."

13. They would, of course, be free to reject citizenship in the absorption state and still remain as permanent residents. Those Palestinians who have long had Jordanian citizenship should also be allowed to give up their Jordanian citizenship, if they so choose. See Ali Jarbawi, "The Triangle of Conflict," *Foreign Policy*, no. 100 (Fall 1995), pp. 92, 106–07.

14. Don Peretz, *Palestinians, Refugees and the Middle East Peace Process* (Washington, DC: United States Institute of Peace Press, 1993), p. 16, citing U.S. Bureau of the Census, Center for International Research, Palestinian Projections for 16 Countries/Areas of the World 1990 to 2010 (Washington, DC: March 1991, mimeo.). The figure of 8,265,000 is rounded off from the actual projection of 8,264,590.

15. The 1996 figures used in this chapter are taken from the sources cited in chapter 2. See table 2.1.

16. See Alan Nichols and Paul White, *Refugee Dilemmas: Reviewing the Comprehensive Plan of Action for Vietnamese Asylum Seekers* (Manila, Philippines: LAWASIA Human Rights Committee, 1993); Ruth Marshall, "Final Act: Closing Down the CPA," *Refugees*, no. 99 (1995), pp. 9–14; special issue focusing on resettlement, *Refugees*, no. 94 (Dec. 1993). See also Appeal by the U.N. Secretary-General to all Member States, United Nations Pledging Conference for the International Support and Verification Commission, SG/CONF.5/1, April 18, 1990, for a similar plan for Central America.

17. Another demographic comparison is to that of the approximately 130,000 Jewish settlers in the West Bank and Gaza. Only about 20 to 25 percent of them are considered "ideologically motivated" by the concept of a Greater Israel and therefore are unlikely to depart willingly. That still leaves close to 100,000 who can be persuaded to return to Israel, with the right mix of economic incentives. That would provide a number that is more than adequate, from the perspective of those who may need this kind of persuasion, to "offset" the addition of 75,000 Palestinians. Israel will probably want to encourage the returning settlers to move to the Galilee, where the Arab population currently outnumbers Jews. See Ehud Sprinzak, *The Ascendance of Israel's Radical Right* (New York: Oxford University Press, 1991), p. 312.

18. A precedent for this Israeli veto is Oslo II's veto by Israel over the appointment of every Palestinian policeman designated to serve on the West Bank and Gaza. But in the case of repatriation, there will be an appeal process. Although Israel in 1948 and 1949 was unwilling to rely on individual refugee declarations under the Resolution 194 safeguard language, "live at peace with their neighbors," that was due to the concomitant refusal of the Arab states to themselves make peace, a condition no longer true. See Mark Tessler, *A History of the Israeli-Palestinian Conflict* (Bloomington: Indiana University Press, 1994), p. 312.

19. Ziad Abu Zayyad, "The Palestinian Right of Return: A Realistic Approach," *Palestine-Israel Journal*, no. 2 (Spring 1994), pp. 74, 77.

20. See Arzt and Zughaib, "Return to the Negotiated Lands," pp. 1454–62.
21. See ibid., pp. 1472–74, on methods used to poll Namibian exiles. Also relevant would be guidelines patterned after those proposed in 1962 by Joseph E. Johnson, Special Representative for the U.N. Conciliation Commission for Palestine, including:

> 1) The wishes of the refugees were to be ascertained confidentially by the United Nations. 2) The refugees were to be shielded by the United Nations from external influences as they made their decisions. 3) The refugees were to be told what choices were available to them, that their first choice might not be granted, and that their first choice was not necessarily the final option that they could exercise. The refugees were to be given the right of choosing any country they wished for their future domicile. 4) The refugees were to be told as exactly as possible what their choice would entail for their future, particularly with regard to their return to a Jewish state.

David Forsythe, *United Nations Peacemaking: The Conciliation Commission for Palestine* (Baltimore: Johns Hopkins University Press, 1972), p. 134. See also Tessler, *A History of the Israeli-Palestinian Conflict*, p. 312, on early Israeli concerns about the refugees making informed and independent decisions about repatriation; and Human Rights Watch/Middle East, "Keeping It Secret: The United Nations Operation in the Western Sahara" (Oct. 1995), for a discussion of problems associated with the process of identifying participants in the U.N.-sponsored referendum.

22. The computer program would be similar to the one in which American medical students are assigned to a hospital internship program every year on "Match Day." See Lynne Amis, "The View From Valhalla: The Day that Makes the Difference for Med School Grads," *New York Times*, Mar. 28, 1993, p. WC2; "13,044 Medical Seniors Learn Their Futures on Match Day," *New York Times*, Mar. 18, 1982, p. B6. In the refugee context, there would be many more "students" but many fewer "hospital placements" to match them with.

23. See Louise Holborn, "The Palestine Arab Refugee Problem," in John Norton Moore, ed., *The Arab-Israeli Conflict*, vol. 1 (Washington, DC: American Society of International Law, 1974), p. 675.

24. See Allahyar Mouri, *The International Law of Expropriation as Reflected in the Work of the Iran-U.S. Claims Tribunal* (Dordrecht, the Netherlands: Martinus Nijhoff, 1994); Richard B. Lillich, ed., *The United Nations Compensation Commission* (Irvington, NY: Transnational Publishers, 1995); David J. Bederman, "The United Nations Compensation Commission and the Tradition of International Claims Settlement," *New York University Journal of International Law and Politics* 27 (1994), p. 1. See also Richard B. Lillich, ed., *The Valuation of Nationalized Property in International Law*, vol. 3 (Charlottesville, VA: University Press of Virginia, 1972) on valuation methods; and "Uruguay: Decree Establishing the National Commission for Repatriation," in Neil J. Kritz, ed., *Transitional Justice: How Emerging Democracies Reckon with Former Regimes*, vol. 3 (Washington, DC: United States Institute of Peace Press, 1995), p. 817, for sample language on the creation of a repatriation agency.

25. Law of Return, *Laws of the State of Israel*, *[LSI]*, vol. 4 (1950), p. 114, as amended by *LSI*, vol. 8 (1954), p. 144, as amended by *LSI*, vol. 24 (1970), p. 28; and Nationality Law, LSI, vol. 6 (1952), p. 50, as amended by LSI, vol. 34 (1980), p. 254. See David Kretzmer, *The Legal Status of the Arabs in Israel*, (Boulder, CO: Westview Press, 1990), pp. 35–48. Together, the two laws guarantee all Jews a virtually automatic right to emigrate to Israel and to become Israeli citizens. They have been subject to criticism, however, for denying this same right to others. (Palestinians can become citizens if they or their parents resided in Israel in 1952, but Israel does not allow them to become citizens simply upon emigration.) For an argument that the legislation is justified as a form of affirmative action for centuries of persecution of Jews, see Arthur Hertzberg, "The Liberal-Left Case for Zionism: 'Affirmative Action' for the Jews," *Israel Horizons* (Summer/Autumn 1992), p. 7.

26. See Arzt and Zughaib, "Return to the Negotiated Lands," pp. 1454–62.

27. Article VIII.

28. Don Peretz, "The Question of Compensation," in *Palestinian Refugees: Their Problem and Future* (Washington, DC: Center for Policy Analysis on Palestine, Oct. 1994), pp. 15, 17. See also Don Peretz, *Palestinian Refugee Compensation* (Washington, DC: Center for Policy Analysis on Palestine, May 1995). See his earlier studies, "Problems of Arab Refugee Compensation," *Middle East Journal* (Autumn 1954), and "Arab Blocked Bank Accounts in Israel," *Jewish Social Studies* (Jan. 1956).

29. For instance, approximately 32,000 Palestinians are believed to have fled in 1948 from one part of Israel to another. They have not been living in their original ancestral homes but have been citizens of Israel. See "Facts and Figures About the Palestinians" (Washington, DC: Center for Policy Analysis on Palestine, Apr. 1993), p. 12. Their situation has rarely if ever been discussed in the relevant negotiation sessions nor championed by the PLO. Should they also receive compensation for property losses, if they cannot recover their original property?

30. See Peretz, "The Question of Compensation," p. 20.

31. One controversial negotiating issue is likely to be the question of setoffs for Israel's absorption of Jewish refugees from Arab lands early in the state's history. See Julius Stone, *Israel and Palestine: Assault on the Law of Nations* (Baltimore: Johns Hopkins University Press, 1981), pp. 25–26; Valerie Yorke, "A Two-State Solution: Security, Stability and the Superpowers," in Michael C. Hudson, ed., *The Palestinians: New Directions* (Washington, DC: Center for Contemporary Arab Studies, Georgetown University, 1990), pp. 165, 175.

Regarding lack of exact legal standards, while there are standards (themselves quite controversial) on compensation for nationalized multinational corporate property, "in the context of refugees' property, there is too little practice to support any conclusion as to the lawful standard of compensation." Eyal Benvenisti and Eyal Zamir, "Private Claims to Property Rights in the Future Israeli-Palestinian Settlement," *American Journal of International Law* 89 (April 1995), p. 330. See p. 331 on possible meanings of the legal term "adequate compensation."

32. See Peretz, "The Question of Compensation," p. 19; and Benvenisti and Zamir, "Private Claims to Property Rights," passim.

33. Palestinian geographer Khalil Tufakji, operating out of Orient House in East Jerusalem, is already helping Palestinians check the registration of their land in the old Tabu (Ottoman) registry. Others who are familiar with the records include Jordan's ambassador to Israel, Marwan Muasher. See Isabel Kershner, "The West Jerusalem File," *Jerusalem Report*, Nov. 2, 1995, pp. 24–27. Currently, the files of the Israeli Custodian for Absentee Property are released only by court order. Ibid., p. 25.

34. See Benvenisti and Zamir, "Private Claims to Property Rights," pp. 331–40, on the advantage of lump sum payments. The U.N. Compensation Commission, established by the Security Council to administer the payment of reparation claims arising out of the Persian Gulf War, allows for expedited consideration of claims and automatic standardized benefits upon simplified proof. See Charles N. Brower, "U.N. Claims Process Off to a Good Start," *Middle East Executive Report* (Oct. 1991), p. 9.

35. "[E]stimates range as high as ten times the annual economic and military aid Israel receives from the United States; the amount is larger than the GNP or annual governmental expenditures of several Middle Eastern states." Peretz, "The Question of Compensation," p. 17.

36. In January 1996, donor countries (primarily the United States, the European Union, Japan, and Saudi Arabia) agreed to grant $1.2 billion to the Palestinian Authority for its 1996 budget, joint projects with the World Bank, and payment of previous pledges. Israel also agreed to transfer taxes placed on goods for the Palestinian Authority. Israel Foreign Ministry, Economic Survey, Jan. 16, 1996. See Rex Brynen, "International Aid to the West Bank and Gaza: A Primer," *Journal of Palestine Studies* 25, no. 2 (Winter 1996), p. 46.

37. See Kershner, "The West Jerusalem File"; and Laurence J. Silberstein, ed., *New Perspectives on Israeli History: The Early Years of the State* (New York: New York University Press, 1991), pp. 94–96.

38. It has been estimated that 75 to 80 percent of all the Jewish settlers, or close to 100,000, living in approximately 20,000 housing units, are nonideological and therefore will be willing to return to within Green Line Israel. See Sprinzak, *The Ascendance of Israel's Radical Right* p. 312; Ian S. Lustick, *For the Land and the Lord: Jewish Fundamentalism in Israel* (New York: Council on Foreign Relations, 1988), pp. 153–60.

39. See Benvenisti and Zamir, "Private Claims to Property Rights," pp. 328–29, 323.

40. See Angus Deming, "Israel: A Civil War in the Sinai?" *Newsweek*, Feb. 8, 1982, p. 54; "Israeli Army Seals Off Sinai from Protesters," *Washington Post*, Feb. 27, 1982, p. A25; Yossi Klein Halevi, "The Bitter Legacy of Withdrawal," *Jerusalem Report*, Apr. 14, 1982, p. 8.

41. Margo Lipshitz Sugarman, "A Year of Waiting," *Jerusalem Report*, Nov. 16, 1995, p. 36.

42. The author is indebted to Salim Tamari for suggesting such communal reparations, for pointing out the economic injustice of private compensation alone, and for the analogy of German reparations to the State of Israel as representative of the Jewish people as a whole, made in addition to individual reparations to Holocaust survivors.

43. An unnamed Jordanian official has suggested an even shorter deadline of six months for Palestinians to choose whether to repatriate to their former homes. "Very few would exercise the option, but it would certainly help the stability of Jordan. At least those who remain would be Jordanian by choice." Isabel Kershner, "Home Away From Home," *Jerusalem Report*, Jan. 13, 1994, pp. 28, 29.

44. *United States v. Dann*, 470 U.S. 39 (1985). See also *United States v. Southern Ute Tribe or Band*, 402 U.S. 159 (1971); Charles F. Wilkinson, *American Indians, Time and the Law: Native Societies in a Modern Constitutional Democracy* (New Haven, CT: Yale University Press, 1987). But see *County of Oneida, New York v. Oneida Indian Nation of New York State*, 470 U.S. 226 (1985); George C. Shattuck, *The Oneida Land Claims: A Legal History* (Syracuse, NY: Syracuse University Press, 1991).

45. See Carey T. Oliver, "Legal Remedies and Sanction," in Richard Lillich, ed., *International Law of State Responsibility for Injury to Aliens* (Charlottesville: University Press of Virginia, 1983), p. 61; Clyde Eagleton, *The Responsibility of States in International Law* (New York: New York University Press, 1928), pp. 22-23.

46. See, for instance, Arie Bloed, ed., *The Conference on Security and Cooperation in Europe: Analysis and Basic Documents* (Boston: Kluwer Academic Publishing, 1993); Vojtech Mastny, *The Helsinki Process and the Reintegration of Europe: 1986–1991* (New York: New York University Press, 1992); Igor Kavass et al., eds., *Human Rights, European Politics and the Helsinki Accord* (Buffalo, NY: W. S. Hein, 1981).

Chapter 5: Norms of Implementation

1. United Nations High Commissioner for Refugees, *The State of the World's Refugees, 1995: In Search of Solutions* (Oxford: Oxford University Press, 1995), p. 11.

2. Ibid., pp. 12–13, 19–20.

3. For Malaysia, see Visu Sinnadurai, "Unity and Diversity: The Constitution of Malaysia," in Robert A. Goldwin et al., eds., *Forging Unity Out of Diversity: The Approaches of Eight Nations* (Washington, DC: American Enterprise Institute, 1989), p. 327; Patrick Brogan, *The Fighting Never Stopped: A Comprehensive Guide to World Conflict Since 1945* (New York: Vintage Books, 1990), p. 204. See generally Louis Kriesberg, "Preventive Conflict Resolution of Inter-Communal Conflicts," PARC Working Paper 29, Syracuse University (Sept. 1993).

On the example that the South African transitional government has displayed as a virtual model of moderation, accommodation, and consensus in redressing past wrongs and addressing the entire population's present and future needs, see Stephen Ellmann, "The New South African Constitution and Ethnic Division," *Columbia Human Rights Law Review* 26 (1994), p. 5; Lourens du Plessis and Hugh Corder, *Understanding South Africa's Transitional Bill of Rights* (Holmes Beach, FL: Juta & Co., 1994); and Peter Levenberg, "South Africa's New Constitution: Will it Last?" *International Lawyer* 29, no. 3 (Fall 1995), p. 633; and Simcha Bahiri, "South African Parallels to the Palestinian-Israeli Talks," *Palestine-Israel Journal* 2, no. 4 (Autumn 1995), p. 110.

4. See *Annotated Bibliography on Themes Identified at the Middle East Peace Negotiations, Working Group on Refugees* (Toronto: Center for Refugee Studies, York University, Mar. 1993).

5. UNHCR meeting of August 29–31, 1983, Mont Pelerin, Switzerland, quoted by Howard Adelman, "Palestine Refugees, Economic Integration and Durable Solutions," in Anna C. Bramwell, ed., *Refugees in the Age of Total War* (London: Unwin Hyman, 1988), p. 295.

6. See Donna E. Arzt and Karen Zughaib, "Return to the Negotiated Lands: The Likelihood and Legality of a Population Transfer Between Israel and a Future Palestinian State," *New York University Journal of International Law and Politics* 24, no. 4 (Summer 1992), pp. 1399, 1454–62, for descriptions and citations.

7. Ibid., pp. 1472–74. See also Jeff Crisp and Kolude Doherty, "Countdown to Freedom," *Refugees*, no. 75 (May 1990), pp. 9–11, and other articles in this special issue on Namibia; Charles P. Gasarasi, "U.N. Resolution 435 and the Repatriation of Namibian Exiles," *Journal of Refugee Studies* 3, no. 4 (1990), pp. 340–364; Security Council Resolution 435, U.N. SCOR, 33rd Sess., 2087th mtg. at 13, U.N. Doc. S/RES/435 (1978), reprinted in 28 *International Legal Materials* 950 (1989); and Memorandum of Understanding on the Voluntary Repatriation and Reintegration of South African Returnees, Sept. 4, 1991, South Africa-UNHCR, 31 *International Legal Materials* 522 (1992).

8. See Leonard Davis, *Hong Kong and the Asylum-Seekers from Vietnam* (New York: St. Martin's Press, 1991); Alan Nichols and Paul White, *Refugee Dilemmas: Reviewing the Comprehensive Plan of Action for Vietnamese Asylum Seekers* (Manila, Philippines: LAWASIA Human Rights Committee, 1993); Josh Briggs, "Sur Place Refugee Status in the Context of Vietnamese Asylum Seekers in Hong Kong," *American University Law Review* 42 (1993), p. 433; and Ruth Marshall, "Final Act: Closing Down the CPA," *Refugees*, no. 99 (1995), pp. 9–14.

9. See Statement Regarding the Settlement of the Situation Relating to Afghanistan and Declaration of Guarantees, Apr. 14, 1988, U.S. State Dept. no. 88–163, kav. no. 1777, 1988 Westlaw 416548 (Treaty); and "Afghanistan: Operation Salam, Programme for 1992" (United Nations: UNOCA, Nov. 1991).

10. See Ron Redmond, "The Human Side of CIREFCA," *Refugees*, no. 99 (1995), pp. 15–21; Tanya Basok, "Repatriation of Nicaraguan Refugees from Honduras and Costa Rica," *Journal of Refugee Studies* 3, no. 4 (1990).

11. Adelman, "Palestine Refugees, Economic Integration and Durable Solutions," p. 296. UNRWA, which recently moved its headquarters from Vienna to Gaza, has also recently undergone a change in leadership. Peter Hansen, a former Danish professor of international relations and U.N. undersecretary for humanitarian affairs, has replaced Ilter Turkmen of Turkey as commissioner-general. "While still head of UNRWA, Turkmen ran unsuccessfully for parliament [in Turkey in 1995] as a candidate for the ultra-rightwing Nationalist Action Party." "New Head Appointed for Palestinian Relief Group," *Reuters*, Jan. 12, 1996. See also Ruth Marshall, "How Long Is Temporary?" *Refugees*, no. 99 (1995), pp. 23–24.

12. Howard Adelman, "Overview of the Refugee Problem: The Working Group on Refugees," paper presented at the Institute on Global Conflict and Cooperation, Vouliagmeni, Greece (Nov. 1994), p. 6, available at: gopher://irpsserv26.ucsd.edu:70/OF-1%3A18800%3AAdelman-Refugees.

13. See Shmuel Segev, "On the U.N. Map," *Davar Rishon*, Feb. 15, 1996, p. 7.

14. See "Going Home," *Refugees*, no. 88 (Jan. 1992), pp. 6–11; Jean-Victor Nkolo, "Journey's End," *Refugees*, no. 94 (Dec. 1993), pp. 34–35; "The Preferred Solution," *Refugees*, no. 96 (II-1994), p. 24; John Battersby, "UN, Mozambique, Begin Massive Repatriation," *Christian Science Monitor*, Aug. 11, 1993, p. 3; John Battersby, "Going Home in Southern Africa," *Christian Science Monitor*, Mar. 11, 1994, p. 6; Sylvie Girard, "Afghanistan: The Will But Not the Means," *Refugees*, no. 90 (July 1992), pp. 20–23.

15. See T. F. Betts, "Evolution and Promotion of the Integrated Rural Development Approach to Refugee Policy in Africa," *Africa Today* 31 (1984), pp. 7–24; Art Hansen, "Managing Refugees: Zambia's Response to Angolan Refugees, 1966–1977," *Disasters* 3 (1979), pp. 375–80. "As a general rule, the more racial, linguistic, religious or cultural characteristics incoming refugees have in common with the native population, the easier integration will be. . . . The generally celebrated receptivity of African countries to refugees from neighboring countries has been commonly credited to hospitality within related groups of people who straddle borders." Gil Loescher, *Beyond Charity: International Cooperation and the Global Refugee Crisis* (New York: Oxford University Press, 1993), p. 25. Examples of successful integration include Afghans in Pakistan and Iran, Bulgarian Turks in Turkey, Burmese Muslims in Bangladesh, Ethiopians in the Sudan, Ogadeni Ethiopians in Somalia, Southern Sudanese in Uganda, and Mozambicans in Malawi. Ibid.

16. Rupert Colville, "Resettlement: Still Vital After All These Years," *Refugees*, no. 94 (Dec. 1993), pp. 4–8; "Resettlement Criteria in a Changing World," *Refugees*, no. 94 (Dec. 1993), pp. 18–21. Additional source materials on these and other refugee absorption experiences are provided in the bibliographical essay.

17. UNHCR Executive Committee, "Voluntary Repatriation," no. 40 (XXXVI) (1985), para. b.

18. UNHCR Executive Committee, "Voluntary Repatriation," no. 18 (XXXI) (1980), para. e, f, and i.

19. No. 40 (XXXVI), para. g and j. On the effort by Denmark and other states to get the United Nations to adopt a Declaration on International Procedures for the Protection of Refugees, see U.N. Doc. A/C.3/41/L.51, Nov. 12, 1986.

20. Lawyers Committee for Human Rights, Refugee Project, "General Principles Relating to the Promotion of Refugee Repatriation," (New York, May 1992). The guidelines, with commentary, also appear in Arthur C. Helton, "Repatriation or Refoulement," *Refugees*, no. 90 (July 1992), pp. 38–40.

21. An estimated 10 million Bangladeshis returned in the 1970s. Gil Loescher, *Beyond Charity: International Cooperation and the Global Refugee Crisis* (New York: Oxford University Press, 1993), p. 82. Between 2.1 million and 2.25 million Afghanis returned in 1990–92, mainly from Pakistan. The next largest repatriation was the 1991 return of 1.3 million refugees to Iraq. After that, the numbers are between 100,000 and 400,000 per country (Ethiopia, 1991; Sudan, 1991; Cambodia, 1992; Somalia, 1991–92; Uganda, 1987–88; and Liberia, 1991–92), and smaller units. Compilation from "World Refugee Survey, 1988–1993," by Alan Dowty. The return of Muslims and Croats to Bosnia may compete with the Afghan repatriation in terms of size. For the study of a repatriation movement involving close to 1 million people who had been outside their country of origin for over 130 years, see Rosemary Manes, "The 'Pied-Noirs': A Case Study of the Persistence of Subcultural Distinctiveness," Ph.D. diss., Syracuse University, 1991.

22. "The Case of Palestinian Refugees in Libya," *Shaml Newsletter* (Dec. 1995), pp. 2, 5.

23. Laura Krupitsky, "Kyrgyzstan Defines Rights of Foreigners and Noncitizens," *Survey of East European Law* 5, no. 5 (June 1994), pp. 9–11; "Parliament Adopts Law Prohibiting Dual Citizenship," *British Broadcasting Corporation Summary of World Broadcasts*, Oct. 12, 1995 (on Armenia); George Ginsburgs, "Lithuanian Citizenship Issues: The Temptations of 'Purity,' " *Survey of East European Law* 2, no. 9 (Nov./Dec. 1991), pp. 9–10.

24. See *Civil and Political Rights in Croatia* (New York: Human Rights Watch, Oct. 1995), pp. 8–15.

25. Jeff Chin and Lise A. Truex, "The Question of Citizenship in the Baltics," *Journal of Democracy* 7, no. 1 (Jan. 1996), pp. 133–34. See also Bart Driessen, "Slav Non-Citizens in the Baltics," *International Journal on Group Rights* 2 (1994), pp. 113–37; Bill Bowring, "Whose Rights, What People, Which Community? The Rule of Law as an Instrument of Oppression in the New Latvia," in Peter Fitzpatrick, ed., *Nationalism, Racism and the Rule of Law* (Aldershot, England: Dartmouth Publishing, 1995), p. 117; "New Citizenship Laws in the Republics of the Former USSR," *Helsinki Watch* 4, no. 7 (Apr. 1992); "Violations by the Latvian Department of Citizenship and Im-

migration," *Helsinki Watch* 5, no. 19 (Oct. 1993); and Thomas L. Friedman, "Russia Appeals to U.N. to Safeguard Minorities," *New York Times*, Sept. 23, 1992.

Chin and Truex properly note that the Latvian and Estonian naturalization requirements are not as strict as those in, for instance, Switzerland and Germany. "The Question of Citizenship in the Baltics," pp. 143–46. See also Kay Hailbronner, "Citizenship and Nationhood in Germany," in Rogers Brubaker, ed., *Immigration and the Politics of Citizenship in Europe and North America* (Lanham, MD: University Press of America, 1989), pp. 67, 68; Gerald L. Neuman, "Immigration and Judicial Review in the Federal Republic of Germany," *New York University Journal of International Law and Politics* 23 (1990), p. 35.

26. See Claire Messina, "Russians Outside Russia: Hostages of the Empire," *Refugees* 4 (1994), p. 13.

27. The "Helsinki Watch Policy Statement on Citizenship Legislation Adopted or Under Consideration in Former Soviet Republics" appears as an appendix to a number of the Human Rights Watch/Helsinki Reports. See, for instance, "Integrating Estonia's Non-Citizen Minority" vol. 5, no. 20 (Oct. 1993). See General Consideration 2, ibid., p. 37, and Specific Consideration 1, pp. 38–39. The latter statement continues: "This principle applies regardless of . . . whether one views the Soviet presence in the former republic as an illegal occupation." In other words, a state's foreign policy should not dictate its immigration policy. But of course, it often does.

28. Ibid., General Considerations 3 and 4.

29. Ibid., Special Consideration 1, p. 39.

30. Ibid.

31. It is not inconceivable that the patrilineal descent policies could be reversed, given the family law reforms in, for instance, Tunisia and Morocco. See J. N. D. Anderson, "Modern Trends in Islam: Legal Reform and Modernisation in the Middle East," *International and Comparative Law Quarterly* 20 (1971), pp. 1, 5.

In Botswana, a woman successfully sued to overturn legislation that prevented women married to foreigners from passing their nationality on to their children. *Botswana Attorney General v. Unity Dow*, Ct. of App. #4/91, 1992, reported in 15 *Human Rights Quarterly* 243 (1993). This issue has also been raised in the Sudan. See Valerie Oosterveld, "UN Fourth World Conference on Women," American Society of International Law Newsletter (Nov./Dec. 1995), pp. 18, 20.

32. Helsinki Watch Policy Statement, Special Consideration 3(c), p. 40.

33. Ibid.

34. G.A. Res. 40/144, Dec. 13, 1985, article 7. The principal draft of the declaration was submitted by Morocco.

35. Armen M. Khachaturian and Van Z. Krikorian, "New Armenian Constitution Strengthens Civil Society," *Survey of East European Law* 6, no. 9 (Sept. 1995), pp. 1, 7.

36. Edward A. Gargan, "Britain Says It Will Monitor China's Rule of Hong Kong," *New York Times*, Mar. 5, 1996, p. A3. See Chin and Truex, "The Question of Citizenship in the Baltics," pp. 141–43. See also Brubaker, *Citizenship and Nationhood in France and Germany* (Cambridge, MA: Harvard University Press, 1992), on Algerians in France.

37. Daniel Kanstroom, "Wer Sind Wir Wieder? Laws of Asylum, Immigration, and Citizenship in the Struggle for the Soul of Germany," *Yale Journal of International Law* 18 (1993), pp. 155, 164–67; Michael W. Devine, "German Asylum Law Reform and the European Community: Crisis in Europe," *Georgetown Immigration Law Journal* 7 (1993), p. 795; Anna C. Bramwell, "The Resettlement of Ethnic Germans, 1939–1941," in Bramwell, *Refugees in the Age of Total War*, p. 102.

38. Kanstroom, "Wer Sind Wir Wieder?" pp. 166–67. Since 1990, out-settlers have had to apply first for repatriation permits from German consulates. The quotas were imposed in 1992, along with restrictions on asylum. See "Germany to Shut Door on Hundreds of Thousands in Immigration Clampdown," *Agence France Presse*, Dec. 7, 1992.

39. Jost Halfmann, "Immigration in Germany: Challenges to the Concept of Citizenship," unpublished manuscript, p. 2.

40. Brubaker, *Citizenship and Nationhood in France and Germany*, p. 145.

41. See 178 U.N.T.S. 229; Israel-France Convention Concerning the Military Service of Persons with Dual Nationality, 448 U.N.T.S. 107, 145, June 30, 1959; Ruth Donner, *The Regulation of Nationality in International Law*, 2nd ed. (Irving-on-Hudson, New York: Transnational Press, 1994) pp. 106–12.

42. See Brubaker, *Citizenship and Nationhood in France and Germany*, pp. 145, 229 n. 41–43. See ibid., p. 115, on the fulfillment of military obligations by *Auslandsdeutsche*.

43. See Alan Sipress, "Samaritans Fear Peace Will Mean an Irrevocable Split," *Philadelphia Inquirer*, Oct. 29, 1995, p. A7. The Samaritans, a tiny minority of 594 people, live in two settlements on either side of the Green Line. They seek papers guaranteeing them unrestricted access across any future border between Israel and Palestine. Yossi Klein Halevi, "The Anxious Samaritans," *Jerusalem Report*, Sept. 21, 1995, pp. 30, 32. On the treatment of religious minorities in Muslim states, see Donna E. Arzt, "The Treatment of Religious Dissidents Under Classical and Contemporary Islamic Law," in John Witte, Jr. and Johan van der Vyver, eds., *Religious Human Rights in Global Perspective: Religious Perspectives* (The Hague: Martinus Nijhoff, 1996), p. 387.

44. See "Comparative Extract of the Israeli and Palestinian Declarations of Independence," Annex 6 to Paul J. I. M. de Waart, *Dynamics of Self-Determination in Palestine: Protection of Peoples as a Human Right* (Leiden: E.J. Brill, 1994). On other relevant Palestinian Declaration provisions, see Arzt and Zughaib, "Return to the Negotiated Lands," pp. 1434–35. Other relevant language from the Israeli Declaration is quoted in chapter 2.

45. Agreement Between Pakistan and India, April 8, 1950, 131 U.N.T.S. 3. See Arzt and Zughaib, "Return to the Negotiated Lands," pp. 1459–62; Wayne A. Wilcox, *Pakistan: The Consolidation of a Nation* (New York: Columbia University Press, 1963), p. 54; Mohammad Waseem, *Politics and the State in Pakistan* (Lahore, Pakistan: Progress Publishers, 1989), pp. 111–16.

46. 131 U.N.T.S. at 4. Reprinted in Patrick Thornberry, *International Law and the Rights of Minorities* (Oxford: Clarendon Press, 1991), p. 403. See also Article 7 of the State Treaty of May 15, 1955 for the Re-establishment of an Independent and Democratic Austria, reprinted in ibid., p. 404.

47. Dennis DeConcini and Steny Hoyer, Letter of Transmittal (Feb. 24, 1992), in *The Conference on Security and Cooperation in Europe: An Overview of the CSCE Process, Recent Meetings and Institutional Development* (Washington, DC: Commission on Security and Cooperation in Europe, Feb. 1992), p. iii. See also the symposium issue on national minorities in the CSCE, *International Journal on Group Rights* 2, no. 1 (1994). A newer European agreement on national minorities, which may eventually prove as influential as that of the CSCE, is the Council of Europe's Framework Convention for the Protection of National Minorities, adopted at Strasbourg, Nov. 8, 1994, reprinted, along with an explanatory report and commentary, in *International Human Rights Reports* 2, no. 1 (Jan. 1995), pp. 217–40.

48. Document of the Copenhagen Meeting of the Conference on the Human Dimension of the CSCE, June 29, 1990, *International Legal Materials* 29 (1990), p. 1305, Principles 31, 32 and 35 (hereafter Copenhagen Document).

49. Ibid., Principles 32.2 and 32.4.

50. See, for instance, Florence Benoit-Rohmer and Hilde Hardeman, "The Representation of Minorities in the Parliaments of Central and Eastern Europe," *International Journal on Group Rights* 2 (1994), pp. 91–111.

51. Copenhagen Document, Principle 40.2.

52. G.A. Res. 47/135 (Dec. 18, 1992). See Natan Lerner, "The 1992 UN Declaration on Minorities," *Israel Yearbook on Human Rights* 23 (1994), pp. 111–28.

53. 999 U.N.T.S. 171, 179.

54. Copenhagen Document, Principle 19.

55. Ibid., Principles 19.1–19.3, 22–22.4.

56. See Israeli Transportation Ministry, Summary of Israel-Jordan Transportation Treaty, Jerusalem, Jan. 16, 1996. On tourism in particular, see Robin Twite and Gershon Baskin, eds., *The Conversion of Dreams: The Development of Tourism in the Middle East* (Jerusalem: Israel/Palestine Center for Research and Information, Nov. 1994); "December Set as Target Date for Joint Tourism Projects with Jordan, Mainly from the U.S.," *Mideast Mirror* 8, no. 158 (Aug. 17, 1994); and the special issue of *Middle East Report* 25, no. 5 (Sept./Oct. 1995) on tourism.

57. See Israeli-Palestinian Economic Agreement, signed in Paris Apr. 1994; and Israel Foreign Ministry, "Economic Survey," Feb. 6, 1996.

58. Danny Rubinstein, "Recipe for Delusion," *Ha'aretz*, Sept. 4, 1995, p. B1.

59. See Guy Bechor, "We Were Enemies, We Became Strangers," *Ha'aretz*, Nov. 1, 1995, p. B2. Jordanians with modems are already working for Israeli computer companies. Ibid.

60. One example of the flow of ideas: "changing the curricula of both [Israeli and Syrian schools] to teach mutual coexistence and acceptance." Natan Sharanksy, "Demand Rights, Demand Compliance," *Jerusalem Report*, Feb. 23, 1995, p. 35.

61. See Itamar Rabinovich, "The Palestinian Right of Return," Occasional Paper Series, American Academy of Arts and Sciences (Oct. 1990), p. 26.

62. Article XIV.

63. Article XIX. Freedom of movement between the West Bank and Gaza, and to and from Egypt and Jordan, as well as other international crossings, are addressed in Oslo II's Annex I, Appendix 5. Annex II contains the protocol regarding elections. See also Ra'ed Abdul Hamid, *Legal and Political Aspects of Palestinian Elections* (Jerusalem: Israel/Palestine Center for Research and Information, 1995).

64. See Henry J. Steiner and Philip Alston, *International Human Rights in Context: Law, Politics, Morals* (Oxford: Clarendon Press, 1996), pp. 563–706; and Louis Henkin et al., *International Law: Cases and Materials*, 3rd ed. (St. Paul, MN: West Publishing Co., 1992), pp. 1026–40, for descriptions of these existing regional human rights implementation systems.

65. Eric Rouleau, "The Middle East After the Advent of Peace," in *Palestinian Statehood: A Special Report* (Washington, DC: Center for Policy Analysis on Palestine, Mar. 1994), pp. 31, 32. Rouleau believes that with equal rights and equal treatment, "the Arab citizens of Israel will become a very positive factor of mutual understanding with the rest of the Arab world." Ibid., p. 32.

66. In the words of Palestinian journalist Daoud Kuttab (brother of attorney Jonathan Kuttab): "While in some Arab regimes there are no rules, the Palestinian people have gotten used to guidelines. They question authority. They do it every day as a result of the Intifada." Nevertheless, he also acknowledges that because of the Israeli occupation, every Palestinian has been imbued with an understanding of due process of law. "When people are fighting for their rights," Kuttab adds, "they become much more aware of the need for democracy and accountability, to protect them." Isabel Kershner, "The People Behind the Politics," *Jerusalem Report*, May 5, 1994, pp. 22, 28.

67. See the bibliographical essay at the end of this book for a discussion of sources relevant to the topic of democratic institutions and the rule of law. The establishment of a Palestinian law school would be an important step in this area.

68. See *Palestine Report* 1 (Dec. 1, 1995), p. 33.

69. See Thomas M. Franck, "The Emerging Right to Democratic Governance," *American Journal of International Law* 86 (1992), p. 46. See also the biblio-

graphical essay at the end of this book for a discussion of sources relevant to the topic of other human rights standards.

70. See, among numerous essays and articles on this topic, David Horovitz, "Israel Fights for its Soul," *Jerusalem Report*, Dec. 14, 1995, p. 14; Natan Sharansky, "We've Lost More than a Leader," *Jerusalem Report*, Nov. 30, 1995, p. 19. On the liberalization of Israeli society as an outgrowth of peace, see Yoav Peled, "From Zionism to Capitalism: The Political Economy of Israel's Democratization of the Occupied Territories," *Middle East Report* 25, no. 3/4 (May–June/July–Aug. 1995), p. 13.

71. See, for instance, John L. Esposito, *The Islamic Threat: Myth or Reality* (New York: Oxford University Press, 1992); and Donna E. Arzt, "The Treatment of Religious Dissidents Under Classical and Contemporary Islamic Law."

72. Ann Elizabeth Mayer, "Universal Versus Islamic Human Rights: A Clash of Cultures or a Clash with a Construct?" *Michigan Journal of International Law* 15 (Winter 1994), pp. 307, 373. See also Ann Elizabeth Mayer, *Islam and Human Rights: Tradition and Politics* (Boulder, CO: Westview Press, 1995).

73. Quoted by Douglas Jehl, "Three Leaders Angered by New Terrorist Attacks," *New York Times*, July 27, 1994, p. A8.

74. A typical example of such faulty analogies is John Quigley, *Palestine and Israel: A Challenge to Justice* (Durham, NC: Duke University Press, 1990). For a more accurate analysis, see David Kretzmer, *The Legal Status of the Arabs in Israel* (Boulder, CO: Westview Press, 1990).

75. "Israeli society is likely to become increasingly pluralistic when peace becomes a matter of concrete, reciprocal arrangements rather than a distant, abstract hope. If they feel less threatened, Israelis will also be less prone to view themselves as victims of aggression, and their positive self-image will become more nuanced." Jeff Green, "Reading from Right to Left," *Jerusalem Post* magazine, Nov. 17, 1995.

76. On the proper basis for invoking these exceptional measures, see Alexandre Charles Kiss, "Permissible Limitations on Rights," and Thomas Buergenthal, "To Respect and to Ensure: State Obligations and Permissible Derogations," in Louis Henkin, ed., *The International Bill of Rights: The Covenant on Civil and Political Rights* (New York: Columbia University Press, 1981); and Joan Fitzpatrick, "Derogation from Human Rights Treaties in Public Emergencies," *Harvard International Law Journal* 22 (1981), pp. 1–52.

Conclusion: Accepting Reality

1. Rashid I. Khalidi, "The Palestinian Right of Return," Occasional Paper Series, American Academy of Arts and Sciences (Oct. 1990), p. 10. See also Rashid Khalidi, "The Palestine Refugee Problem: A Possible Solution," *Palestine-Israel Journal* 2, no. 4 (Autumn 1995), p. 72.

2. See Marianne Heiberg and Geir Ovensen, *Palestinian Society in Gaza, West Bank and Arab Jerusalem: A Survey of Living Conditions* (Oslo: FAFO Report 151, 1993), p. 13.

3. Quotes from Elia Zureik, "Palestinian Refugees and Peace," *Journal of Palestine Studies* 24, no. 1 (Autumn 1994), pp. 5, 16, and Lamis Andoni, untitled paper prepared for the Council on Foreign Relations study group entitled "The Shape of the Arab-Israeli Settlement: Demographic and Humanitarian Issues" (Feb. 1994), p. 13.

4. See Shlomo Gazit, "Name the Baby," *Jerusalem Post*, July 19, 1995, p. 6. Even Jewish settlers are beginning to accept the reality that with Palestinian self-rule, they are now "effectively exiled in the new West Bank." See Yossi Klein Halevi, "Reality Bites," *Jerusalem Report*, Feb. 22, 1996, p. 8. See also William Plaff, "Israel: The People Speak and the Signs Improve," *Israel/Palestine Center for Research and Information News* (Summer 1995), pp. 3–4, describing opinion poll data indicating less intransigence in regard to issues such as Jerusalem and borders on the part of both Israelis and Palestinians than is often assumed. "People see that second best solutions are all they are going to get." Ibid.

    Regarding Israeli rejection of Palestinians returning, see, for instance, Shlomo Gazit, "Toward 'Lesser Israel,'" *Jerusalem Post*, March 27, 1995, p. 6, stating Israel's two "minimum terms" are valid security arrangements and "no Palestinian 'return' of 1948 refugees inside Israel's borders." Earlier, Gazit stated: "The right of return is the only issue except Jerusalem on which there is a 100 per cent consensus in Israel. Allowing the return of the 1948 refugees or giving them the right to choose whether they want to return would be commiting suicide for us Israelis. You may call us idiots, but we are not going to commit suicide." *Promoting a Culture for Peace in the Middle East: An Israeli-Palestinian Dialogue* (U.N. Department of Public Information, May 1994), p. 62. Sales no. E.94.I.15. Even Shulamit Aloni of the left-wing Meretz party has recently stated that Israel cannot accept the return of refugees to "Israel proper" because "we have responsibilities to [Jewish] refugees from European and Arab countries." "Joint Discussion on Refugees," *Palestine Report* 1 (Feb. 2, 1996), p. 36—as if responsibilities to Jews were incompatible with responsibilities to Palestinians.

5. See *Population Growth and Our Caring Capacity* (New York: Population Council, 1994).

6. An unnamed Jordanian official predicts what would happen if the Palestinian refugees are not given a square deal: "They would become radicalized, they'd support Hamas, there'd be infiltrations and reprisals from Israel." Jordan would have to crack down, he notes, while the radicals could call on extremist patrons in Iran and Afghanistan. "It's a potential Lebanon." Isabel Kershner, "Home Away From Home," *Jerusalem Report*, Jan. 13, 1994, pp. 28, 29.

7. This is a reference to the series of CSCE (Conference on Security and Co-operation) agreements of the mid-1970s through 1990s, described in chap-

ter 5, which were designed for the very purpose of allowing the two sides of the Cold War to keep a check on each other. See also Michael Gordon, "U.S.–North Korea Accord Has a 10-Year Timetable," *New York Times*, Oct. 21, 1994, p. A8: "One of the distinctive features of the new accord is that it is based on a foundation of mutual mistrust."

8. Isabel Kershner, "The People Behind the Politics," *Jerusalem Report*, May 5, 1994, p. 22.

Bibliographical Essay

T his essay is intended to provide direction for anyone interested in
pursuing further the chief aspects of the question of Palestinian
refugees, within the broader context of the effort to achieve peace
and human rights in the Middle East. It is not a comprehensive survey
but rather a review of sources (primarily English language) that were
most useful to the author. While every effort has been made to include
multiple perspectives, in regard to some topics it is more difficult to
achieve a balance.

After covering a few introductory topics, the essay generally tracks
the chapter-by-chapter structure of the book. It concludes by listing
other useful resources that are likely to be available to most readers,
particularly those outside the Middle East. Although most of the material deals with the Palestinian-Israeli conflict, references to resettlement experiences involving refugees from other regions of the world,
along with human rights standards developed in other contexts,
are offered as sources of comparative study. Also included is a note
on the problematic quality of the existing demographic information on
Palestinians.

General Background and Overview

The Palestinians, the Arabs, and the Israelis

Journalistic accounts that can serve as introductions for the general
reader include David Shipler, *Arab and Jew: Wounded Spirits in a
Promised Land* (New York: Times Books, 1986); Danny Rubinstein, *The
People of Nowhere: The Palestinian Vision of Home* (New York: Times
Books, 1991); Yossi Melman, *The New Israelis: An Intimate View of a
Changing People* (New York: Carol Publishing Company, 1992); David
Lamb, *The Arabs: Journeys Beyond the Mirage* (New York: Random
House, 1987); Mahmoud Darwish, *Victims of the Map* (London: Saai
Books, 1984); and Milton Viorst, *Sandcastles: The Arabs in Search of the
Modern World* (New York: Alfred A. Knopf, 1994).

More academically oriented studies include the many books by Don
Peretz, particularly *Palestinians, Refugees and the Middle East Peace
Process* (Washington, DC: United States Institute of Peace Press, 1993);

two books by Rosemary Sayigh, *Palestinians: From Peasants to Revolutionaries* (London: Zed Press, 1979) and *Too Many Enemies: The Palestinian Experience in Lebanon* (London: Zed Books, 1994); plus the collections of essays in Khalil Nakhleh and Elia Zureik, eds., *The Sociology of the Palestinians* (New York: St. Martin's Press, 1980), and Milton Esman and Itamar Rabinovich, eds., *Ethnicity, Pluralism and the State in the Middle East* (Ithaca, NY: Cornell University Press, 1988).

More personalized accounts include Fawaz Turki, *The Disinherited: Journal of a Palestinian Exile* (New York: Monthly Review Press, 1972) and *Exile's Return: The Making of a Palestinian American* (New York: Free Press, 1994); and Meron Benvenisti, *Intimate Enemies: Jews and Arabs in a Shared Land* (Berkeley: University of California Press, 1995);

The Road to Peace

Two short books describe the regional stage-setting of the 1990s: Muhammad Faour, *The Arab World After Desert Storm* (Washington, DC: United States Institute for Peace Press, 1993); and Walid Khalidi, *The Middle East Postwar Environment* (Washington, DC: Institute for Palestine Studies, 1991). A summary of the actual Israeli-Palestinian negotiations, by a *Jerusalem Post* journalist, David Makovsky, is titled *Making Peace with the PLO: The Rabin Government's Road to the Oslo Accord* (Boulder, CO: Westview Press, 1996). Memoirs by key participants in the process include Shimon Peres, *Battling for Peace: Memoirs* (London: Weidenfeld & Nicolson, 1995), and Hanan Ashwari, *This Side of Peace: A Personal Account* (New York: Simon & Schuster, 1995). See also Ziva Flamhaft, *Israel on the Road to Peace: Accepting the Unacceptable* (Boulder, CO: Westview Press, 1996); Jane Corbin, *The Norway Channel: The Secret Talks that Led to the Middle East Peace Accord* (New York: Atlantic Monthly Press, 1994); Willem-Jan van der Wolf and Marianne van de Pas, *Shalom, Salaam, Peace: The Long and Winding Road to Peace in the Middle East* (Boxtel, the Netherlands: Global Law Association, 1994); and Mohamed Heikal, *Secret Channels: The Inside Story of the Arab-Israeli Peace Negotiations* (New York: Harper Collins, 1996).

Numerous authors themselves laid the groundwork for the peace negotiations by endorsing and describing the contours of a binational solution to the conflict. One of the earliest such endorsements by an Israeli is Mark A. Heller, *A Palestinian State: Implications for Israel* (Cambridge, MA: Harvard University Press, 1983). See also the earlier work by Richard J. Ward, Don Peretz, and Evan M. Wilson, *The Palestine State: A Rational Approach* (Port Washington, NY: Kennikat Press, 1977). Others, in no particular order of significance, include: Penny Rosenwasser, *Voices from a "Promised Land": Palestinian and Israeli Peace Ac-*

tivists Speak Their Hearts (Willimantic, CT: Curbstone Press, 1992); Deborah J. Gerner, *One Land, Two Peoples: The Conflict Over Palestine* (Boulder, CO: Westview Press, 1991); Harvey Sicherman, *Palestinian Autonomy, Self-Government & Peace* (Boulder, CO: Westview Press, 1993); Mark A. Heller and Sari Nusseibeh, *No Trumpets, No Drums: A Two-State Settlement of the Israeli-Palestinian Conflict* (New York: Hill and Wang, 1991); Ann Mosely Lesch et al., *Transition to Palestinian Self-Government: Practical Steps Toward Peace: Report of a Study Group of the Middle East Program, Committee on International Security Studies, American Academy of Arts and Sciences* (Bloomington: Indiana University Press, 1992); Robin Twite and Tamar Hermann, *The Arab-Israeli Negotiations: Political Positions and Conceptual Frameworks* (Tel Aviv: Papyrus Publishing House, 1993); and Muhammad Muslih, *Toward Coexistence: An Analysis of the Resolutions of the Palestine National Council* (Washington, DC: Institute for Palestine Studies, 1990).

Israel, Palestine, and U.S. Foreign Policy

Three recent books deal with the role of the United States in the Arab-Israeli conflict: Donald Neff, *Fallen Pillars: U.S. Policy Towards Palestine and Israel Since 1945* (Washington, DC: Institute for Palestine Studies, 1995); Camille Mansour, *Beyond Alliance: Israel in U.S. Foreign Policy* (New York: Columbia University Press, 1994); and David Schoenbaum, *The United States and the State of Israel* (Oxford: Oxford University Press, 1993). See also the older volumes, Nadav Safran, *Israel: The Embattled Ally* (Cambridge, MA: Harvard University Press, 1978), and Ann Mosely Lesch and Mark Tessler, *Israel, Egypt and the Palestinians: From Camp David to Intifada* (Bloomington: Indiana University Press, 1989).

History

The Origins of the Palestinian People

See Baruch Kimmerling and Joel S. Migdal, *Palestinians: The Making of a People* (Cambridge, MA: Harvard University Press, 1994); Henry Cattan, *Palestine, The Arabs and Israel: The Search for Justice* (London: Longmans, 1969); Edward Said, *The Question of Palestine* (New York: Vintage Books, 1979); Don Peretz, "The Historical Background of Arab Nationalism in Palestine," in Ward, Peretz, and Wilson, *The Palestine State*; and Tad Szulc, "Who Are the Palestinians?" *National Geographic* (June 1992), pp. 84–92; which variously trace the Palestinians back to the mid-nineteenth century or even to the time of the Philistines in the thirteenth century B.C.E.

The counterargument, namely that the Palestinians did not exist as a group distinguishable from other Arabs until very recently, is raised by Joan Peters, *From Time Immemorial* (New York: Harper & Row, 1984). But the Peters book has been widely discredited, even by Jewish authors such as Norman G. Finkelstein, in "Disinformation and the Palestine Question: The Not-So-Strange Case of Joan Peters' From Time Immemorial," in Edward Said and Christopher Hitchens, eds., *Blaming the Victims: Spurious Scholarship and the Palestinian Question* (New York: Verso, 1988). See also Kimmerling and Migdal, *Palestinians*, pp. xvi–xvii, 323 n. 5, on the Peters book.

New Historiography on the Origins of the Refugee Problem

Beginning in the late 1970s, archives in Jerusalem, London, and Washington concerning the 1948 war were declassified, leading to a new Israeli historiography of the origins of the state. Some of the more notable new English-language publications include two books by Benny Morris, *The Birth of the Palestinian Refugee Problem* (Cambridge, UK: Cambridge University, 1987), and *1948 and After: Israel and the Palestinians* (New York: Oxford University Press, 1990); Ilan Pappe, *The Making of the Arab-Israeli Conflict* (New York: St. Martin's Press, 1992); and Simha Flapan, *The Birth of Israel: Myths and Realities* (New York: Pantheon, 1987); and Kimmerling and Migdal, *Palestinians*. Benny Morris's more recent work includes "Falsifying the Record: A Fresh Look at Zionist Documentation of 1948," *Journal of Palestine Studies* 24, no. 3 (Spring 1995), pp. 44–62.

Similar new works by non-Israelis include Fred Khouri, *The Arab-Israeli Dilemma* (Syracuse, NY: Syracuse University Press, 1985); Mark Tessler, *A History of the Israeli-Palestinian Conflict* (Bloomington: Indiana University Press, 1994); and Laurence J. Silberstein, ed., *New Perspectives on Israeli History: The Early Years of the State* (New York: New York University Press, 1991). For discussions and summaries of the new historiography, see Jerome Slater, "Lost Opportunities for Peace: Reassessing the Arab-Israeli Conflict," *Tikkun* 10, no. 3 (1995), p. 59; Ilan Pappe, "The New History and Sociology of Israel: A Challenge to the Old Version," *Palestine-Israel Journal* 2, no. 3 (1995), p. 70; and the special Spring/Summer 1995 symposium issue entitled "Israeli Historiography Revisited" of the journal *History & Memory*.

The most comprehensive Arab works on the years 1946 to 1949 are the six volumes by Aref el-Aref, *The Disaster* (Beirut: Al Maktabel al Asriya, 1956–1960); and the two volumes by Robert John and Sami Hadawi, *The Palestine Diary* (New York: New World Press, 1970). See also Nafez Nazzal, 1948: *The Palestinian Exodus From Galilee* (Beirut: Institute for Palestine Studies, 1978); Sami Hadawi, *Bitter Harvest: A Modern History of Palestine* (London: New World Press, 1967); and Nur Masalha, *Expulsion of the Palestinians: The Concept of "Transfer" in Zionist Political Thought, 1882–1948* (Washington, DC: Institute for Palestine Studies, 1992).

On UNRWA

In addition to UNRWA's own publications, including its annual report to the United Nations and materials published by its Public Information Department, see Milton Viorst, *Reaching for the Olive Branch: UNRWA and Peace in the Middle East* (Washington, DC: Middle East Institute, 1989); Benjamin N. Schiff, *Refugees Unto the Third Generation: UN Aid to Palestinians* (Syracuse, NY: Syracuse University Press, 1995); Edward H. Buehrig, *The UN and the Palestinian Refugees: A Study in Non-territorial Administration* (Bloomington: Indiana University Press, 1971); Howard Adelman, "Palestine Refugees, Economic Integration and Durable Solutions," in Anna C. Bramwell, ed., *Refugees in the Age of Total War* (London: Unwin Hyman, 1988), pp. 295–311; and W. Pinner, *The Legend of the Arab Refugees: A Critical Study of UNRWA's Reports and Statistics* (Tel Aviv: Economic and Social Research Institute, 1967). See also Neil Caplan, *The Lausanne Conference, 1949: A Case Study in Middle East Peacemaking* (Tel Aviv: Moshe Dayan Center, 1993); Pablo de Azcarate, *Mission in Palestine: 1948–1952* (Washington, DC: Middle East Institute, 1966); and David P. Forsythe, *United Nations Peacemaking: The Conciliation Commission for Palestine* (Baltimore: Johns Hopkins University Press, 1972).

Demography and Sociology

Existing Sources

The most comprehensive recent source is probably the aforementioned Peretz, *Palestinians, Refugees and the Middle East Peace Process*. An overview of relevant demographic trends is Kevin F. McCarthy, "The Palestinian Refugee Issue: One Perspective," RAND Corporation Greater Middle East Studies Center, DRU-1358-GMESC (Mar. 1996). Other studies of Palestinians in one of more states or territories include Marianne Heiberg and Geir Ovensen, *Palestinian Society in Gaza, West Bank and Arab Jerusalem: A Survey of Living Conditions* (Oslo: FAFO Report 151, 1993); Laurie Brand, *Palestinians in the Arab World: Institution Building and the Search for State* (New York: Columbia University Press, 1988); Kitty Warnock, *Land Before Honour: Palestinian Women in the Oc-*

cupied Territories (New York: Monthly Review Press, 1990); A. Plascov, *The Palestine Refugees in Jordan, 1948–1957* (London: F. Cass, 1981); S. N. Ghabra, *Palestinians in Kuwait: The Family and the Politics of Survival* (Boulder, CO: Westview Press, 1987); the numerous articles by Rosemary Sayigh, usually published in *Journal of Palestine Studies* and collected in her 1994 book, *Too Many Enemies*; fact sheets and booklets published by the Center for Policy Analysis on Palestine; and the publications of UNRWA's Public Information Office.

On the region as a whole, see Colbert Held, *Middle East Patterns: Places, People and Politics*, 2nd ed. (Boulder, CO: Westview Press, 1994); and A. Richards and J. Waterbury, *A Political Economy of the Middle East: State, Class and Economic Development* (Boulder, CO: Westview Press, 1990).

Note on the Quality of Existing Demographic Information

A comprehensive survey of existing demographic sources on the West Bank and Gaza Strip written by Dr. Hisham Awartani of An-Najah National University, the West Bank, has recently been published by the United Nations Conference on Trade and Development: *Sources of Economic and Social Statistics on the West Bank and Gaza Strip* (Geneva: United Nations, 1996), UNCTAD/ECDC/SEV/10. It concludes that despite two decades of efforts, the situation is "still seriously deficient."

Because Palestinians are today scattered over at least 16 Middle Eastern countries and no official census of even the West Bank and Gaza has been taken since the end of 1967, most present-day figures are inevitably derived from the highly contested "magic number" of Palestinian refugees who fled Israel in 1948. See chapter 1 of this book. Without consensus on the original number of refugees, and with Palestinian growth rates varying from a low of 2.3 percent to a high of 5.2 percent annually (the latter in the Gaza Strip, which is probably the highest or second highest known rate of natural increase in the world), contemporary figures can deviate dramatically with a variation in the 1948 numbers of as little as 50,000 or 100,000. But assuming consensus could somehow be reached on the "magic number," current estimates should be calculated easily with the standard demographer's formula [Population at present − (Pop. at T) plus (Births at $T + N$) minus (Deaths at $T + N$) plus (Net Migration at $T + N$), where T equals the number at base period and N equals the number of years since the base period].

But even this calculation is not necessarily reliable. Even if the agreed starting point is the 1.3 million total number of Palestinians who probably resided in pre-1948 Palestine, the demographer is stymied in calculating a contemporary figure when there is no definitive data on death rates, birthrates, or even migration rates. Families are reluctant to report deaths if it means a loss of benefits, and neither have births been uniformly recorded. Moreover, the statistics are muddled by conflicting data on students, laborers, and others who have left a particular territory, returned, or overstayed an exit visa.

As noted in chapter 1, the figure used by UNRWA has the advantage of falling in almost the exact center of the spectrum of "magic numbers": 726,000 refugees. Moreover, because the organization operates on the ground in a wider scope of territory than any other organization working with Palestinians, UNRWA's contemporary figures are assumed to be the most comprehensive. However, its registry of who is a Palestinian refugee is subject to the criticism that it is both overinclusive (it does not accurately register deaths or migrations and may be padded in other ways) and underinclusive (it does not include Palestinians who have lost their means of livelihood but not their homes, as well as the reverse). See Hadawi, *Bitter Harvest*, p. 139.

"As early as 1950, the UNRWA discovered that births were always registered for ration purposes, but deaths were frequently concealed so that the family could continue to obtain the rations of the deceased," states Mitchell Bard in "Homeless in Gaza," *Policy Review*, no. 47 (Winter 1989), p. 36. In 1964, UNRWA estimated that less than half the refugees could be considered destitute. "The relief rolls continued to expand, however, because refugees who had at least partially integrated themselves into their host countries and no longer needed aid were unwilling to give up their ration cards or their refugee status." Bard, "Homeless in Gaza," pp. 39–40. According to Tessler, *A History of the Israeli-Palestinian Conflict*, p. 279, the heads of refugee households and U.N. administrators deliberately exaggerated the numbers of refugees in order to justify receipt of additional funds. UNRWA itself notes that its statistics "are based on figures of registration with the Agency and do not necessarily reflect the true population figures, mainly because of unreported deaths and duplicate registration." (See UNRWA General Commissioner's Report, 82/83.) In addition, in some cases, particularly in Lebanon, non-Palestinian Arabs may have registered with UNRWA, either because they were working in Palestine in 1948 and also fled, or because they were otherwise destitute and wanted to take advantage of UNRWA benefits. See Nawaf A. Salam, "Between Repatriation and Resettlement: Palestinian Refugees in Lebanon," *Journal of Palestine Studies* 24, no. 1 (Autumn 1994), pp. 18, 19.

As to underinclusiveness, it is important to understand that UNRWA's definition of who is a Palestinian refugee is narrower than that of the Palestine National Covenant, which does not require that a refugee has lost both his home and his means of livelihood. It is also likely that as many as 12 percent of what even UNRWA would define as 1948 refugees may never have registered with the agency. Some, including those who fled to Egypt or to other North African states, could not register because UNRWA did not operate there. See Schiff, *Refugees unto the Third Generation*, p. 24.

Despite UNRWA's self-criticisms, a FAFO study considers the agency's data quite promising for social science research purposes. See Lena C. Endresen and Geir Ovensen, *The Potential of UNRWA Data for Research on Palestinian Refugees: A Study of UNRWA Administrative Data* (Oslo: FAFO, 1994). Nevertheless, UNRWA is not always willing to make all its data available to researchers, as was the case with the author of the present book, who was given access to, but not allowed to draw citations from, the agency's publication, *Basic Data on UNRWA and Palestine Refugees* (Vienna: UNRWA Public Information Office, October 1992). Both researchers and peace planners will therefore need to wait until a more definitive data base is compiled by the Norwegian delegation to the Refugee Multilateral Working Group, the Palestinian Authority's Bureau of Statistics, or other emerging sources.

International Law

On refugee law and the law of freedom of movement generally, see Guy S. Goodwin-Gill, *The Refugee in International Law* (Oxford: Clarendon Press, 1990); James Hathaway, *The Law of Refugee Status* (Toronto: Butterworths, 1991); Hurst Hannum, *The Right to Leave and Return in International Law and Practice* (Dordrecht, the Netherlands: Martinus Nijhoff, 1987); Jean-Marie Henckaerts, *Mass Expulsion in Modern International Law and Practice* (The Hague, the Netherlands: Martinus Nijhoff Publishers, 1995); Louis B. Sohn and Thomas Buergenthal, eds., *The Movement of Persons Across Borders* (Washington, DC: American Society of International Law, (Oct. 1992); Warren Freedman, *The International Right to Travel, Trade and Commerce* (Buffalo, NY: William S. Hein, 1993); Analysis of the Current Trends and Developments Regarding the Right to Leave Any Country Including One's Own and to Return to One's Own Country, and Some Other Rights or Considerations Arising Therefrom, Final Report by Special Rapporteur C. L. C. Mubanga-Chipoya, to the Sub-Commission on Prevention of Discrimination and Protection of Minorities, Fortieth Session, Item 5(e) of the Provisional Agenda, U.N. Doc. E/CN.4/Sub.2/1988/35 (June 20, 1988); and Luke Lee, "The Right to Compensation: Refugees and Countries of Asylum," *American Journal of International Law* 80 (1986), p. 532.

On nationality (citizenship) law, see the classic work, P. Weis, *Nationality and Statelessness in International Law* (Westport, CT: Hyperion Press, 1979, reprinting the 1956 Stevens edition). Other older works include Nissim Bar-Yaacov, *Dual Nationality* (New York: Praeger, 1961), and Daniel Turack, *The Passport in International Law* (Lexington, MA: Lexington Books, 1972). More recent treatises include Ruth Donner, *The Regulation of Nationality in International Law*, 2nd ed. (Irving on Hudson, NY: Transnational Publishers, 1994), and Rogers Brubaker, *Citizenship and Nationhood in France and Germany* (Cambridge, MA: Harvard University Press, 1992). Two recent books that deal with the political and social implications of nationality policy are Jeff Spinner, *The Boundaries of Citizenship: Race, Ethnicity and Nationality in the Liberal State* (Baltimore: Johns Hopkins University Press, 1994), and Peter Fitzpatrick, ed., *Nationalism, Racism and the Rule of Law* (Aldershot, England: Dartmouth Publishing Co., 1995).

Many of the numerous books and articles on the legal aspects of the Palestinian refugee question, as well as the Arab-Israeli conflict generally, are cited in Donna E. Arzt and Karen Zughaib, "Return to the Negotiated Lands: The Likelihood and Legality of a Population Transfer Between Israel and a Future Palestinian State," *New York University Journal of International Law and Politics* 24, no. 4 (Summer 1992), pp. 1399–1513. See also, among numerous others, Paul J. I. M. De Waart, *Dynamics of Self-Determination in Palestine: Protection of Peoples as a Human Right* (Leiden: E. J. Brill, 1994); and Eyal Benvenisti, *The International Law of Occupation* (Princeton, NJ: Princeton University Press, 1993), pp. 107–48. Specific resources on compensation for Palestinian refugees include Don Peretz, "The Question of Compensation," in *Palestinian Refugees: Their Problem and Future* (Washington, DC: Center for Policy Analysis on Palestine, Oct. 1994), p. 15; and Eyal Benvenisti and Eyal Zamir, "Private Claims to Property Rights in the Future Israeli-Palestinian Settlement," *American Journal of International Law* 89 (April 1995), p. 295.

Implementation Issues

Repatriation, Resettlement, Integration, and Rehabilitation

At the request of the Canadian government, convenor of the Refugee Multilateral, the York University Centre for Refugee Studies has compiled and published *Annotated Bibliography on Themes Identified at the Middle East Peace Negotiations, Working Group on Refugees*, with subsections on Child Welfare; Development of Social and Economic Infrastructure; Human Resource Development; Public Health; Vocational Training and Job Creation; and additional lists of documents, data bases and organizations.

For the Lawyers Committee for Human Rights guidelines on repatriation described in chapter 5, see Arthur Helton, "Repatriation or Refoulement," *Refugees*, no. 90 (July 1992), pp. 38–40. On involuntary resettlement, see Michael M. Cernea, *Involuntary Resettlement in Development Projects* (Washington, DC: World Bank Technical Paper No. 80, 1988); and Christy Ezim Mbonu, "Human Rights Dimensions of Population Transfer, Including the Implantation of Settlers and Settlements," U.N. Doc. E/CN.4/Sub.2/1991/47, June 15, 1991. See also Philip Shenon, "Rearranging the Population: Indonesia Weighs the Pluses and Minuses," *New York Times*, Oct. 8, 1992, p. A12, on one such case. Other sources on the legal and policy aspects of refugee movements, voluntary and involuntary, are cited in Donna E. Arzt and Karen Zughaib, "Return to the Negotiated Lands: The Likelihood and Legality of a Population Transfer Between Israel and a Future Palestinian State," *New York University Journal of International Law and Politics* 24, no. 4 (Summer 1992), pp. 1399, 1440–74.

Relevant case studies of recent refugee repatriation and resettlement movements in Africa and Asia are recounted in Gaim Kibreab, *Refugees and Development in Africa: The Case of Eritrea* (Trenton, NJ: Red Sea Press, 1987); Judy A. Mayotte, *Disposable People? The Plight of Refugees* (Maryknoll, NY: Orbis Books, 1992); Leonard Davis, *Hong Kong and the Asylum-Seekers from Vietnam* (New York: St. Martin's Press, 1991); Alan Nichols and Paul White, *Refugee Dilemmas: Reviewing the Comprehensive Plan of Action for Vietnamese Asylum Seekers* (Manila, the Philippines: LAWASIA Human Rights Committee, 1993); and Zonke Majodince, "Dealing with Difficulties of Return to South Africa: The Role of Social Support and Coping," *Journal of Refugee Studies* 8 (1995), pp. 210–227. See generally Gil Loescher, *Beyond Charity: International Cooperation and the Global Refugee Crisis* (New York: Oxford University Press, 1993); and UNHCR, *The State of the World's Refugees: In Search of Solutions* (Oxford: Oxford University Press, 1995).

Special issues of *Refugees* (the magazine of the UNHCR) devoted to repatriation, resettlement, and other regional solutions include no. 75 (May 1990), no. 94 (Dec. 1993), no. 96 (II-1994), and no. 99 (I-1995). The Forced Migration Projects of the Open Society Institute, established in 1993, publishes an electronic newsletter, *Forced Migration Monitor*, which has reported on repatriation movements in Abkhazia, Georgia; the Crimea, Ukraine; and the former Yugoslavia, among others. See "Other Relevant Resources/Organizations," below, for further information.

Citizenship, Minorities and Freedom of Movement

In addition to the works cited in "International Law," above, see Patrick Thornberry, *International Law and the Rights of Minorities* (Oxford: Clarendon Press, 1991); Robert A. Goldman et al., eds., *Forging Unity Out of Diversity: The Approaches of Eight Nations* (Washington, DC: American Enterprise Institute, 1989); and Hurst Hannum, *Documents on Autonomy and Minority Rights* (Dordecht, Boston: M. Nijhoff, 1993). On the CSCE process, see Bloed, ed., *Conference on Security and Cooperation in Europe*. In addition to the reports cited in chapter 5, many of the other publications of the New York–based nongovernmental organization Human Rights Watch focus on abuses of the rights of minorities. The new scholarly periodical *International Journal on Group Rights* and the new report, *International Human Rights Reports*, are additional sources of developing norms on minority rights.

Other Human Rights Standards

Pages 68–94 of De Waart's book, *Dynamics of Self-Determination in Palestine*, cited earlier, contains a "Code of Conduct on Self-Determination" that describes 14 standards applicable both to Israeli and Palestinian governments as well as other peoples, individuals, states, and international organizations: Democratic Society; Principles of International Law; Prohibition of Secession; Prohibition of the Use of Force by States; Prohibition of Terrorism by Liberation Movements; Peaceful Settlement of Disputes; Right to Development; International Bill of Human Rights; Derogation; Limitation; People's Participation; International Humanitarian Law; Non-international Armed Conflicts; and Occupied Territories.

With the proliferation of new states in the wake of the demise of the Soviet Union, both the United States and the European Union (European Community, at the time) developed guidelines on which to base determinations of formal recognition. In October 1991 the United States articulated five principles, including safeguarding human rights, based on full respect for the individual and including equal treatment of minorities; and respect for international law and obligations, especially adherence to the CSCE body of documents, including the Helsinki Final Act and the Charter of Paris. See U.S. Department of State, *Foreign Policy Bulletin* 2 (Nov./Dec. 1991), pp. 39, 42; and *Foreign Policy Bulletin* 2 (Sept./Oct. 1991), pp. 39, 44. The European Union guidelines of December 1991 require, among other points: respect for the provisions of the Charter of the United Nations, the Helsinki Final Act and Charter of Paris, and guarantees for the rights of ethnic and national groups and minorities, in accordance with the CSCE framework. See *International Legal Materials* 31 (1992), pp. 1485–87.

More detailed guidelines for the new states that emerged out of the former Yugoslavia are contained in the report of the European Community's Conference on Yugoslavia Arbitration Commission, 31 *International Legal Materials* 1488 (1992). In addition, the U.N. Secretary-General's Report on the International Conference on the Former Yugoslavia, Nov. 11, 1992, appearing at *International Legal Materials* 31 (1992), pp. 1549, 1566–68, contains standards for three categories of human rights: civil and political rights; minority rights; and economic, social, and cultural rights. The minority rights provisions include the "obligation to maintain group balance in governmental decision-making bodies as well as in the various central and provincial civil, police and other services (or, at the minimum, strict non-discrimination)." A list of human rights treaties to be incorporated by reference into the Constitution of Bosnia-Herzegovina is also included, pp. 1589–93.

Most recently, the peace agreements between the parties to the conflict in Bosnia-Herzegovina contain relevant standards. In September 1995, the governments of Bosnia, Croatia, and Yugoslavia (representing the Bosnian Serbs) pledged their full support, starting immediately, for: "a) freedom of movement, b) the right of displaced persons to repossess their property or receive just compensation, c) freedom of speech and of the press, and d) protection of all other internationally recognized human rights in order to enhance and empower the democratic election process." See "A Framework for Bosnia: Excerpts from Accord by 3 Governments," *New York Times*, Sept. 27, 1995, p. A10.

The Dayton Peace Agreement, adopted Nov. 21, 1995, began with a preamble in which the same three governments, "Recogniz[e] the need for a comprehensive settlement to bring an end to the tragic conflict in the region; [and] Desir[e] to contribute toward that end and to promote an enduring peace and stability." Article VII stated: "Recognizing that the observance of human rights and the protection of refugees and displaced persons are of vital importance in achieving a lasting peace, the parties agree to and shall comply fully with the provisions concerning human rights set forth in Chapter One of the agreement at Annex 6, as well as the provisions concerning refugees and displaced persons set forth in Chapter One of the Agreement at Annex 7." See "Text of Framework Peace Accord," *Agence France Presse*, Nov. 23, 1995; Warren Christopher, "No Troops, No Peace," *New York Times*, Nov. 27, 1995, p. A15. Among other provisions, these annexes establish a Human Rights Commission, which includes an ombudsman and a chamber (court), incorporates a list of preexisting human rights treaties, and creates a Commission for Displaced Persons and Refugees.

Although only indirectly related to human rights, the Middle East Peace Facilitation Act, U.S. legislation that authorizes continued U.S. dialogue with and financial support for the Palestinian Authority, requires the Palestinian Authority to: disavow and nullify the articles of the Palestinian National Covenant that call for destruction of Israel; establish institutions for apprehending, prosecuting, convicting, and imprisoning terrorists; cooperate with Israel to prevent and punish terrorism; confiscate unlicensed weapons; refrain from providing financial or material assistance or training to terrorist groups; exclude terrorists from participating in the Palestinian Authority; refrain from operating offices in Jerusalem; and cooperate with U.S. government investigations on U.S. victims of PLO terror. See Section 583 [a] of the Foreign Relations Authorization Act, Fiscal Years 1994 and 1995 [P.L. 103–236].

On the Palestinian Authority's record, through 1995, on compliance with human rights standards, see Amnesty International, "Israel and the Occupied Territories Including the Area Under the Jurisdiction of the Palestine Authority: A Year of Shattered Hopes," AI Index: MDE 15/07/1995 (May 1995); Human Rights Watch/Middle East, "The Gaza Strip and Jericho: Human Rights Under Palestinian Partial Self-Rule" 7, no. 2 (Feb. 1995); Amos Perlmutter, "Arafat's Police State," *Foreign Affairs* 73, no. 4 (July/Aug. 1994), pp. 8–11; Joel Greenberg, "Palestinians Conduct Closed Military Trials," *New York Times*, Apr. 13, 1995; Khaled Abu Toameh and Isabel Kershner, "Hot on the Presses," *Jerusalem Report*, June 15, 1995, pp. 32–33; Serge Schmemann, "Palestinian Christians Feeling Like a Minority," *New York Times*, Dec. 31, 1995, p. E5; and Bassem Eid, "Arafat's Justice," *New York Times*, Jan. 19, 1996.

Democratic Institutions and the Rule of Law

Examples of the legal and political transition to democracy in other new and transitional states can be found in the three-volume collection edited by Neil J. Kritz, *Transitional Justice: How Emerging Democracies Reckon with Former Regimes* (Washington, DC: United States Institute of Peace Press, 1995). Much has been written on the recent changes in South Africa, including Peter Gastrow, *Bargaining for Peace: South Africa and the National Peace Accord* (Washington, DC: United States Institute of Peace Press, 1995); Stephen Ellmann, *In a Time of Trouble: Law and Liberty in South Africa's State of Emergency* (Oxford: Clarendon Press, 1992); Stephen Ellmann, "The New South African Constitution and Ethnic Division," *Columbia Human Rights Law Review* 26 (1994), p. 5; and the March 1995 *New Internationalist* magazine's special issue on South Africa. The case of Namibia, a new state that emerged belatedly out of the League of Nations mandate system, provides an even closer model for Palestinians. See Human Rights Watch/Africa, "Accountability in Namibia: Human Rights and the Transition to Democracy" (Aug. 1992); Joshua Bernard Forrest, "Namibia—The First Postapartheid Democracy," *Journal of Democracy* 5, no. 3 (July 1994), pp. 88–100. See generally Thomas M. Franck, "The Emerging Right to Democratic Governance," *American Journal of International Law* 86 (1992), p. 46.

On Palestinian efforts to build the institutions of democracy, see the *Law and Development Program Bulletin* 1 (Summer 1995) of the Israel/Palestine Center for Research and Information (address in "Other Relevant Resources/Organizations," below); Ra'ed Abdul Hamid, *Legal and Political Aspects of Palestinian Elections* (Jerusalem, Israel: Palestine Center for Research and Information, 1995); "Human Rights and Interim Palestinian Self-Government," (New York: Lawyers Committee for Human Rights, Jan. 10, 1994); Edy Kaufman, Shukri B. Abed, and Robert L. Rothstein, eds., *Democracy, Peace and the Israeli-Palestinian Conflict* (Boulder, CO: Westview Press, 1993); William B. Quandt, "The Palestinian Future: The Urge for Democracy," *Foreign Affairs* 73, no. 4 (July/Aug. 1994), pp. 2–7; Stanley Cohen, "Justice in Transition? Prospects for a Palestinian-Israeli Truth Commission," *Middle East Report* (May-June/July-Aug. 1995), pp. 2–5; and the Special Report on Palestinian steps toward building the rule of law, *American Bar Association Journal* (Feb. 1994), pp. 46–65. The Center for Palestine Research and Studies in Nablus, the West Bank, conducts opinion polls on Palestinian reactions to aspects of the peace process, including democratization. A recent article by the center's director, Khalil Shikaki, is "The Peace Process, National Reconstruction, and the Transition to Democracy in Palestine," *Journal of Palestine Studies* 25, no. 2 (Winter 1996), pp. 5–20.

University of Iowa law professor Adrien Wing has generated a considerable body of literature on the subject of Palestinian democracy. See her "Palestinian Democracy: Prospects and Impediments," in *Palestinian Statehood: A Special Report* (Washington, DC: Center for Policy Analysis on Palestine, March 1994), which outlines characteristics of Palestinian civil society such as the degree of educational attainment; political pluralization; communitarian vs. hierarchical social structures; distrust of authority; a multilayered legal regime; human rights aspirations; influence of the *intifada*; and the role of fundamentalism, religion, and custom. See Wing's other articles on the evolution of Palestinian legal traditions, such as "Legal Decision-Making During the Palestinian *Intifada*: Embryonic Self Rule," *Yale Journal of International Law* 18 (1993), p. 95; and "Legitimacy and Coercion: Legal Traditions and Legal Rules During the *Intifada*," *Middle East Policy* 2, no. 2 (1993), p. 87; as well as her "Communitarianism v. Individualism: Constitutionalism in Namibia and South Africa," *Wisconsin International Law Journal* 11 (1993).

Other Relevant Resources

Documentary Collections

Collections of official documents on the Arab-Israeli conflict and the peace process have been published in English by the American Society of International Law (the four-volume *Arab-Israeli Conflict* edited by John Norton Moore) and the Institute for Palestine Studies (including the series *U.S. Official Statements* [see particularly *The Palestinian Refugees*] and *United Nations Resolutions on Palestine and the Arab-Israeli Conflict*). The Israeli Ministry of Foreign Affairs has published English-language versions of each of the recent peace agreements, together with all annexes and maps. See also individual issues of *Journal of Palestine Studies* and *Mideast Mirror*.

English-Language Periodicals

Jerusalem Report (biweekly), *Journal of Palestine Studies* (quarterly), *Palestine-Israel Journal* (quarterly); *Middle East Report* (bimonthly), *Mideast Mirror* (daily). Almost the entire issue of vol. 2, no. 4 (August 1995) of *Palestine-Israel Journal* is devoted to the topic of refugees.

The Internet

Israel Foreign Ministry
 gopher://israel-info.gov.il
 or http://www.israel-mfa.gov.il

Americans for Peace Now
 http://www.peacenow.org/Resources/resources.html
  FAFO (Norway):
 http://www.fafo.no.:80/engelsk/

Institute for Global Conflict and Cooperation (project on the Middle East multilateral peace process)
 http://www-igcc.ucsd.edu/igcc/memulti/

FOFOGNET and Palestinian Refugee Research Net:
 http://www.facl.mcgill.ca/MEPP/PRRN/prfront.html

Miscellaneous Palestinian websites
 http://www.cs.TU-Berlin.de/~ishaq/pal/palestine/palestine.html
 http://www.alquds.org/www/frames/map.html
 http://aic.netquake.net/
 http://www.charity.org/anera.html

U.N. sites relating to Palestinians
  http://pappsrv.papp.undp.org/public_html/status33.html
  gopher://gopher.undp.org:70/11/unearth/organizations/unrwa

Organizations

Americans for Peace Now
27 West 20th Street, Ninth Floor
New York, NY 10011
Tel. 212-645-6262
Fax 212-645-7355

Center for Policy Analysis on Palestine
2435 Virginia Avenue, N.W.
Washington, DC 20037
Tel. 202-338-1290
Fax 202-333-7742

FAFO (Fagbevegelsens senter for forskning, utredning
og dokumentasjon) (Norwegian Institute for Social
Science Research)
Fossveien 19
N-0551, Oslo, Norway
Tel. 47-22-716-000
Fax 47-22-716-060

Forced Migration Projects
Open Society Institute
888 Seventh Avenue, Suite 1901
New York, NY 10106
Tel. 212-887-0655
Fax 212-489-8455
email: (refugee@sorosny.org)

Institute for Palestine Studies
3501 M. Street, N.W.
Washington, DC 20007
Tel. 202-342-3990 and 800-874-3614

International Development Research Center
Middle East Initiatives
250 Albert Street
Ottawa K1G 3H9, Canada
Tel. 613-236-6163
Fax 613-563-0815

Israel Government Press Office
Beit Agron
Hillel Street 37
Jerusalem, Israel
Tel. 972-2-233-385

Israel/Palestine Center for Research and Information
P.O. Box 51358
Jerusalem, Israel 91513
Tel. 972-2-274382
Fax 972-2-274383
email: ipcri@zeus.datasrv.co.il

Jerusalem Media and Communications Center
Nashashibi Street 18
East Jerusalem, Israel
Tel. 972-2-819-776
Fax 972-2-829-534

Revue d'Etude Palestinian
7 rue Bernard-Palissy
Paris, France 75006
Tel. 443-93927
Fax 454-48236

Shaml (Palestinian Diaspora & Refugee Center)
P.O. Box 38152
Jerusalem, Israel 97800
Tel. 972-2-9957537
Fax 972-2-9956538
email: shaml@netvision.net.il

UNHCR (U.N. High Commissioner for Refugees)
Public Information Service
P.O. Box 2500
1211 Geneva 2 Depot, Switzerland
Tel. 022-739-8502
Fax 022-739-8449
or
1775 K. Street, N.W.
Suite 300
Washington, DC 20006

UNRWA (U.N. Refugee and Works Administration for Palestinians)
Public Information Office
East Jerusalem, Israel
Tel. 972-2-890-409
Fax 972-2-322-842

WOJAC (World Organization for Jews from Arab Countries)
118a Ben-Yehuda Street
Tel Aviv, Israel 63401
Tel. 972-3-524-0173
Fax 972-3-524-0174

See the York University *Annotated Bibliography*, cited earlier, for other organizational listings.

Documentary Appendix

United Nations General Assembly Resolution 194(III)

11 December 1948

The General Assembly

Having considered further the situation in Palestine,

1. *Expresses* its deep appreciation of the progress achieved through the good offices of the late United Nations Mediator in promoting a peaceful adjustment of the future situation of Palestine, for which cause he sacrificed his life; and
   Extends its thanks to the Acting Mediator and his staff for their continued efforts and devotion to duty in Palestine;

2. *Establishes* a Conciliation Commission consisting of three Member States of the United Nations which shall have the following functions:
   (a) To assume, in so far as it considers necessary in existing circumstances, the functions given to the United Nations Mediator on Palestine by the resolution of the General Assembly of 14 May 1948;
   (b) To carry out the specific functions and directives given to it by the present resolution and such additional functions and directives as may be given to it by the General Assembly or by the Security Council;
   (c) To undertake, upon the request of the Security Council, any of the functions now assigned to the United Nations Mediator on Palestine or to the United Nations Truce Commission by resolutions of the Security Council; upon such request to the Conciliation Commission by the Security Council with respect to the remaining functions of the United Nations Mediator on Palestine under Security Council resolutions, the office of the Mediator shall be terminated;

3. *Decides* that a Committee of the Assembly, consisting of China, France, the Union of Soviet Socialist Republics, the United Kingdom and the United States of America, shall present, before the end of the first part of the present session of the General Assembly, for the approval of the Assembly a proposal concerning the names of the three States which will constitute the Conciliation Commission;

Highlighting in text is the author's.

4. *Requests* the Commission to begin its functions at once, with a view to the establishment of contact between the parties themselves and the Commission at the earliest possible date;

5. *Calls upon* the Governments and authorities concerned to extend the scope of the negotiations provided for in the Security Council's resolution of 16 November 1948 and to seek agreement by negotiations conducted either with the Conciliation Commission or directly with a view to the final settlement of all questions outstanding between them;

6. *Instructs* the Conciliation Commission to take steps to assist the Governments and authorities concerned to achieve a final settlement of all questions outstanding between them;

7. *Resolves* that the Holy Places—including Nazareth—religious buildings and sites in Palestine should be protected and free access to them assured, in accordance with existing rights and historical practice; that arrangements to this end should be under effective United Nations supervision; that the United Nations Conciliation Commission, in presenting to the fourth regular session of the General Assembly its detailed proposal for a permanent international regime for the territory of Jerusalem, should include recommendations concerning the Holy Places in that territory; that with regard to the Holy Places in the rest of Palestine the Commission should call upon the political authorities of the areas concerned to give appropriate formal guarantees as to the protection of the Holy Places and access to them; and that these undertakings should be presented to the General Assembly for approval;

8. *Resolves* that, in view of its association with three world religions, the Jerusalem area, including the present municipality of Jerusalem plus the surrounding villages and towns, the most Eastern of which shall be Abu Dis; the most Southern, Bethlehem; and the most Western, Ein Karim (including also the built-up area of Motsa) and the most Northern, Shu'fat, should be accorded special and separate treatment from the rest of Palestine and should be placed under effective United Nations control;
   Requests the Security Council to take further steps to ensure the demilitarization of Jerusalem at the earliest possible date;
   Instructs the Conciliation Commission to present to the fourth regular session of the General Assembly detailed proposals for a permanent international regime for the Jerusalem area which will provide for the maximum local autonomy for distinctive groups consistent with the special international status of the Jerusalem area;
   The Conciliation Commission is authorized to appoint a United Nations representative who shall cooperate with the local authorities with respect to the interim administration of the Jerusalem area;

9. *Resolves* that, pending agreement on more detailed arrangements among the Governments and authorities concerned, the freest possible access to Jerusalem by road, rail or air should be accorded to all inhabitants of Palestine;

Instructs the Conciliation Commission to report immediately to the Security Council, for appropriate action by that organ, any attempt by any party to impede such access;

10. *Instructs* the Conciliation Commission to seek arrangements among the Governments and authorities concerned which will facilitate the economic development of the area, including arrangements for access to ports and airfields and the use of transportation and communication facilities;

11. **Resolves that the refugees wishing to return to their homes and live at peace with their neighbours should be permitted to do so at the earliest practicable date, and that compensation should be paid for the property of those choosing not to return and for loss of or damage to property which, under principles of international law or in equity, should be made good by the Governments or authorities responsible;**
     Instructs the Conciliation Commission to facilitate the repatriation, resettlement and economic and social rehabilitation of the refugees and the payment of compensation, and to maintain close relations with the Director of the United Nations Relief for Palestine Refugees and, through him, with the appropriate organs and agencies of the United Nations;

12. *Authorizes* the Conciliation Commission to appoint such subsidiary bodies and to employ such technical experts, acting under its authority, as it may find necessary for the effective discharge of its functions and responsibilities under the present resolution;
     The Conciliation Commission will have its official headquarters at Jerusalem. The authorities responsible for maintaining order in Jerusalem will be responsible for taking all measures necessary to ensure the security of the Commission. The Secretary-General will provide a limited number of guards for the protection of the staff and premises of the Commission;

13. *Instructs* the Conciliation Commission to render progress reports periodically to the Secretary-General for transmission to the Security Council and to the Members of the United Nations;

14. *Calls upon* all Governments and authorities concerned to cooperate with the Conciliation Commission and to take all possible steps to assist in the implementation of the present resolution;

15. *Requests* the Secretary-General to provide the necessary staff and facilities and to make appropriate arrangements to provide the necessary funds required in carrying out the terms of the present resolution.

Text of Security Council Resolution 242, November 22, 1967

The Security Council,

Expressing its continuing concern with the grave situation in the Middle East,

Emphasizing the inadmissibility of the acquisition of territory by war and the need to work for a just and lasting peace in which every State in the area can live in security,

Emphasizing further that all Member States in their acceptance of the Charter of the United Nations have undertaken a commitment to act in accordance with Article 2 of the Charter.

1. *Affirms* that the fulfillment of Charter principles requires the establishment of a just and lasting peace in the Middle East which should include the application of both the following principles:

    (i) Withdrawal of Israeli armed forces from territories occupied in the recent conflict;

    (ii) Termination of all claims or states of belligerency and respect for and acknowledgement of the sovereignty, territorial integrity and political independence of every State in the area and their right to live in peace within secure and recognized boundaries free from threats or acts of force;

2. *Affirms further* the necessity:

    (a) For guaranteeing freedom of navigation through international waterways in the area;

    (b) **For achieving a just settlement of the refugee problem;**

    (c) For guaranteeing the territorial inviolability and political independence of every State in the area, through measures including the establishment of demilitarized zones;

3. *Requests* the Secretary-General to designate a Special Representative to proceed to the Middle East to establish and maintain contacts with the States concerned in order to promote agreement and assist efforts to achieve a peaceful and accepted settlement in accordance with the provisions and principles in this resolution;

4. *Requests* the Secretary-General to report to the Security Council on the progress of the efforts of the Special Representative as soon as possible.

Text of Security Council Resolution 338,
October 22, 1973

The Security Council

1. *Calls upon* all parties to the present fighting to cease all firing and terminate all military activity immediately, no later than 12 hours after the moment of the adoption of this decision, in the positions they now occupy;

2. *Calls upon* the parties concerned to start immediately after the cease-fire the implementation of Security Council Resolution 242 (1967) in all of its parts;

3. *Decides that*, immediately and concurrently with the cease-fire, negotiations start between the parties concerned under appropriate auspices aimed at establishing a just and durable peace in the Middle East.

Multilateral Working Group on Refugees
Opening Remarks by Eli Sanbar for
the Palestinian Side of the Joint
Palestinian-Jordanian Delegation
Ottawa, May 13, 1992

The Palestinian refugee problem has long been the human core of the Palestinian-Israeli conflict and its continued non-resolution has constituted one of the main sources of instability in the region. In our view, this instability is rooted in Israel's continued refusal to implement U.N. resolutions relevant to the question of Palestine, and in the silence of the world community over this continued bypassing of international legality.

Not surprisingly, the Palestinian refugee camps have been the cradle from where the Palestinian political claim to self-determination has reemerged after the Catastrophe of 1948. The refugee camps, whether in the Occupied Palestinian Territories (OPT), or in Exile, have been the embodiment of the unity of the Palestinian people, of its capacity to survive while transcending the fragmentation imposed on it.

The international consensus which materialized in Madrid, at the opening of this process, has made it possible to undertake the work of solving all at once the Palestinian refugee problem and the wider issue of the Arab-Israeli conflict of which it constitutes the very root, by satisfying the demands for Palestinian self-determination while responding at the same time to the Israeli demand for secure boundaries and recognition within the Middle Eastern community of nations.

We have expressed, in Madrid as well as in Washington bilateral negotiations, orally as well as in written documents, our position vis-à-vis the short- and long-term objectives of our participation. We have entered this process on the basis of specific terms of reference, which are contained in the letters of invitation to the Peace Conference sent to the parties by the co-sponsors, dated October 18, 1991. U.N. Security Council Resolution 242, passed some weeks after the June 1967 war, which stipulates the inadmissibility of the acquisition of territory by war, and establishes the principle of "land for peace," is the basic frame of reference for the whole peace process. Resolution 242 also explicitly requires the provision of "a just solution of the refugee problem." The basis for this "just solution" lies in the implementation of basic U.N. resolutions on Palestinian refugees, in particular Resolution 194.

The Palestinian Refugee Problem

The uprooting and forcible displacement and dispossession of which the Palestinian people have been the victim is undoubtedly one of the greatest tragedies of the contemporary era. The Palestinian refugee problem was created during the war of 1948, when the majority of Palestinians, urban dwellers and peasants were uprooted by force from their homeland. Part of them found refuge in what later became known as the West Bank of the Jordan River and the Gaza Strip, while others were dispersed over the neighboring Arab countries and elsewhere. Tens of thousands also became refugees inside Israel when their lands, their villages and even their homes were seized and destroyed or confiscated by the nascent State of Israel. It is important to note here that the vast majority of those Palestinians were expelled in the period between November 1947 (the Partition Plan) and January 1949 (the Rhodes Armistice agreement).

A second wave of refugees was created by the war of June 1967 in which the remaining parts of Arab Palestine, in addition to the Syrian Golan Heights and the Egyptian Sinai Peninsula, came under Israeli occupation. An additional quarter of a million refugees escaped, or were made to leave, from the newly occupied territories, and they became a further burden on the strained economies of the host countries of Jordan, Lebanon and Syria.

During the 25 years of Occupation, a systematic pattern of land confiscation and economic hardships have resulted in displacing thousands of Palestinians within the Occupied Palestinian Territories (OPT), and from there to neighboring countries. Much of the confiscated land was placed at the disposal of Israeli Jewish settlers (and non-Israeli Jewish immigrants), in the avowed design to prevent the return of their rightful owners. A series of laws were enacted by Israel (including the Law on Absentee Property and the Israeli Law of Return—which gives privileged treatment to Jewish immigrants over those enjoyed by Arab citizens of Israel and Arab refugees from Israel, and were also meant to ensure that land and property thus acquired became non-accessible to Palestinians).

We should here mention the fact that Israeli settlement activities in the OPT, which have universally been recognized as illegal, continue to constitute an insurmountable obstacle to peace, and that their immediate cessation is a condition for the success of the peace process. Settlement activities, with their double aspect of explosion and exclusion, of land and water confiscation and apartheid, are indeed at the root of the whole conflict, and of the refugee problem in particular. Hence the centrality of the issue of Israeli settlement activities in all our negotiations.

Basic Definitions

Let us examine who is included in the categories of those Palestinians that can be designated as refugees, and thus are entitled to demand the implementation of U.N. resolutions concerning the Right of Return.

The Palestinian refugees are all those Palestinians (and their descendants) who were expelled or forced to leave their homes between November 1947 (Partition Plan) and January 1949 (Rhodes Armistice agreement), from the territory controlled by Israel on that later date. This, by the way, coincides with the Israeli definition of "absentees," a category of Palestinians meant to be stripped of its most elementary human and civil rights.

This definition does not apply only to camp-dwellers, and certainly not only to those recognized refugees who enjoyed formal registration by UNRWA, since the latter never exercised jurisdiction over more than a segment of the total refugee problem.

Such a definition does not include the emigrants who left Palestine before 1947, but it includes all those displaced, even inside the territory that became the State of Israel in the 1948–49 period. It also includes all the 1967 and post-1967 displaced persons, for whom we have already demanded immediate and unconditional return to the OPT within the framework of the establishment of the Palestinian Interim Self-Governing Authority.

It also includes the residents of "border villages" in the West Bank, who lost their agricultural lands in the war of 1948, and therefore the source of their livelihood, but remained in their villages. It includes residents of the Gaza Strip refugee camps, who were either relocated to the Rafah side of the Egyptian border, or who found themselves separated from their families and kin as a result of border incarceration after the Camp David Accords between Israel and Egypt. It finally includes Palestinian Bedouins who were forcibly removed from their grazing lands within the State of Israel, as well as those who were induced to abandon the West Bank and relocate in Jordan.

Although some of the above categories may not be regarded as refugees in the technical sense (for example, deportees, or residents of "border villages") they nevertheless share the hardships and fate of most refugees who fall in the first categories. At the core of their status is alienation and the denial of return to their country.

The State of Israel has been, and continues to be, responsible for the process through which the refugee problem was crafted (through violence against civilian populations in times of war, and through expropriation of their lands and homes after the war). Yet Israel persists in disclaiming responsibility for these acts, and in denying the right of the Palestinians to return to their homeland (including the right of return to the territories occupied in 1967).

A Just and Lasting Settlement of the Refugee Problem

The fundamental legal framework for a just solution to the Palestinian refugee problem is the U.N. General Assembly Resolution 194. Its strength is derived essentially from its consensuality: the fact that in 1949, the U.S., and even more so Israel (at that time eager to be admitted to the U.N. as a full member-state), voted in favor of that resolution. In fact, both the Partition Plan [Resolution 181], which asserts the principle of self-determination, and the return of refugees [Resolution 194] constituted the foundations for the State of Israel itself, for their implementation was a condition for Israel's admittance into the community of nations [Resolution 273]. Hence the strong and special Israeli obligation towards these two resolutions in the spirit and letter of international law.

Without the solemn recognition of the refugees' right of return, the refugee problem will remain unsolved. Such a recognition is also necessary to alleviate the impact of prolonged refugee presence in the host countries, and thus to facilitate harmonious relations with the latter during the period of forced exile.

It must, however, be clear that our people have consistently refused all the schemes of resettlement and naturalization into the host countries, and have expressed in all possible ways their will to solve their problems within the context of a national solution of the Palestinian people as a whole.

The current condition of Palestinian refugees, whether inside or outside refugee camps, cannot be ameliorated by "humanitarian" projects aimed at improving the condition of their living (although we fully favor upgrading their health, welfare and educational standards). What is more needed, more urgently today than ever, is a comprehensive political settlement based on the recognition of the right of return and self-determination. Refugees are not merely slum dwellers who need an improvement in the quality of life. The refugee question is a national question. Its humanitarian aspects are a consequence of the refugee status, not its essence.

Improvement of the refugees' living conditions is a moral obligation for the world community, in addition to the core of the political aspect of the conflict and the urgency for a just and durable political settlement. It is an inherent human right, not a subject of *quid pro quo*, nor the subject of negotiation. The right of the refugees cannot be exchanged for any political advantage.

To contribute to a lasting and just settlement, the world community is invited to support a settlement based on the application of the U.N. resolutions pertaining to this issue and which:

—Guarantees the implementation of international legality, that is to say allows the exercise of the refugees' right of return as embodied in U.N. General Assembly Resolution 194, and all subsequent relevant international resolutions.

—Expresses the political aspirations of the parties concerned. The refugees' basic aspiration to live in dignity indicates their fundamental demand, which they share with the rest of the Palestinian people: self-determination.

Conclusion

The logic of racial, religious or ethnic homogeneity, or "purity," often used to justify the denial of the Palestinian right of return, is repugnant to the ethics of our age. It mocks the very concept of coexistence which motivates our present endeavors. Peaceful coexistence among the people and states of the Middle East cannot be built on societies which find plurality intolerable or threatening.

To conclude, I would like to appeal directly to the Israelis. We know they are listening to us, even though their delegation has decided to boycott this session, because of the mere fact of our presence.

To the Israelis we shall say that the real condition of sustainable peace is to achieve, beyond the treaties and agreements between states, reconciliation between peoples. This requires that men and women, at given crucial moments of their history, have the courage to take a look at themselves in order to be able to see, and at last understand the adversary.

To the Israelis we shall say that reconciliation passes through the moral recognition of the immense injustice inflicted upon our people 44 years ago.

To the Israelis we say: Is it not clear that the security which you claim to pursue will not come from your military might and territorial assets, but from a just peace based on the recognition of the rights of the Palestinian people?

To the Israelis we also say: In order for us to offer you the solution of the two states, mutually recognized and accepted, the people of Palestine have had to inflict a great violence upon themselves. Indeed, for unlike war, peace is always a tormenting victory of one's own self. And the time has come for you to take this decisive step and recognize the rights of our people.

Multilateral Working Group on Refugees Opening Remarks for Israel by Prof. Shlomo Ben-Ami Ottawa, November 11, 1992

The Multilateral Conference on Refugees in the Middle East is a historic endeavor. It is the vindication of an old aspiration expressed by successive Israeli governments. Indeed, a central chapter in the Israeli peace initiative of May 1989 has explicitly called for such an international effort to solve the refugee problem. Based on a deep moral conviction that a nation of refugees like ours must be actively involved in the search for humane solutions to the plight of

refugees and on the persuasion that the peace we are now negotiating in the bilateral track needs to be accompanied and sustained by an international effort
of human improvement and social rehabilitation, we have come to this conference with many illusions, much good will and, we believe, creative ideas.
Hence, our peace policy today is inspired by a dream that there must be a way
to reconcile peace with justice and security.

Arab and Jewish Refugees

The wave of refugees in the Middle East, which started towards the end of
1947, was the direct result of the Arab effort to prevent by force the implementation of the United Nations resolution of November 29, 1947, to partition
Palestine into a Jewish and an Arab state. Following upon the declaration of
Israel's independence on May 14, 1948, Arab armies launched an all-out war
against reborn Israel with the purpose of establishing exclusive Arab control in
the whole of Palestine. The war, as is tragically the case in most wars in
recorded history, swept in its wake large segments of the civilian population.
The Arab exodus was initiated by the wealthy and the powerful Arab families
who left the masses insecure and leaderless. The mass escape that ensued was
inflamed by the horrors of war and by the hope of a speedy return to an Arab
Palestine once the victorious Arab armies had completed their task. The escape
affected not only those Palestinians who lived in the land for generations but
also tens of thousands of very recent legal and illegal Arab immigrants to Palestine from neighboring countries. A land of contention, Palestine had attracted
both Jewish and Arab immigrants. The latter flocked into the country especially
during periods of prosperity. Indeed, in recognition of the very recent origin of
many of the refugees—inaccurately represented as part of a "millenarian"
Palestinian population—the United Nations was later moved to describe as eligible for refugee status any Arab who had lived in Palestine for a minimum of
two years.

It is a travesty of historical truth to present the Palestinian refugee problem
as the result of mass expulsion. There is no denying, however, that once the
Jews, who for thousands of years waited with humility for their redemption,
made their reencounter with history as a sovereign nation, they had to assume
the inherent immorality of war. The suffering of the civilian population will always be a burden on the conscience of any nation at war. The Arab-Israeli conflict has no monopoly on this maxim. Clearly, the Palestinians were a major
victim of the Arab-Israeli conflict. The Palestinian refugee problem was born
as the land was bisected by the sword, not by design, Jewish or Arab. It was
largely the inevitable by-product of Arab and Jewish fears and the protracted
bitter fighting.

On the other hand, the Middle East witnessed a virtual exchange of population as hundreds of thousands of Jewish refugees were forced to evacuate their
places of residence and find a haven in Israel. The 1948 War of Independence
climaxed centuries of discrimination against, and even repression of, the de-
fenseless Jewish minorities in some Arab countries. The war bequeathed a

refugee problem to both parties as the Jewish communities of the Arab world were virtually liquidated during the period 1948–1952 and their property was all but lost. Indeed, when we reach a stage where peace may require the termination of Jewish and Arab claims, Israel will present the case for due compensation for all the havoc, destruction, the loss of life and properties of the Jews in the Arab lands. Ideally, one would expect that a system be devised of mutual compensation with the full participation of the international community.

While Jewish refugees were warmly integrated into Israel, Arab refugees were subjected to an abuse of their plight. Since World War II, over 100 million people have become refugees, virtually all of whom have been integrated into the host societies. In the case of the Palestinian refugees, pawn politics and indifference were the two foci of a problem of tragic and human dimensions. Their fate was to be denied resettlement and be consigned to camps in dismal conditions of hopelessness and destitution. The notion that nothing should be done to rehabilitate the refugees as long as a political settlement has not been achieved is morally wrong.

The Government of Israel views an agreed-upon solution of the refugee problem as an essential component of the historical reconciliation between the Palestinian people and Israel.

A New Approach — Rehabilitation

The philosophy of welfare and relief, important as it certainly is, must give way to one of rehabilitation. More than once in the past the need was voiced for large-scale productive investments in the host Arab countries in order to create sources of employment for the refugees and facilitate their rehabilitation. But the Arab countries nipped in the bud this approach and continued to insist on the most unrealistic solution possible: repatriation.

It is our endeavor, together with others, to join efforts in order to resolve the refugee and displaced persons problems. It is also our position that this noble enterprise should avoid references to cumulative one-sided U.N. resolutions adopted hitherto, for we would then run the risk of converting this working group into a replica of the U.N. General Assembly. I trust that this was not exactly the intention of the initiators of this conference.

Israel has always maintained that a multinational effort to dignify living conditions in the refugee camps does not have to await a political solution or indeed to substitute for it. The treatment of the humanitarian problem is not aimed at prejudging the bilateral discussions and the future political settlement. It is doubtful whether the existence of refugees makes the case for Palestinian political rights any stronger. Palestinian refugees can live in better conditions while the search for peace continues. The rewards of peace can be shared by all while we build its political foundations.

Israel is fully aware not only of the necessity to redeem the plight of the refugees of 1948 but also of those who were displaced by the 1967 war. As early as 1949, Israel initiated a Family Reunification Scheme, which made possible the return to Israel by 1967 of about 50,000 and to the territories by 1991 of an additional 93,000. The Family Reunification Scheme is an ongoing system inspired by humanitarian considerations; it is not an instrument for radical demographic movements. It is our contention that this working group was not convened to decide about the movement of people; it is rather a historic attempt to bring about a movement of resources and ideas in order to improve the living conditions of people.

An Agreed Database

The need for an agreed database on refugees in the Middle East is clear. It is obviously not only a question of figures—some of the statistics and definitions may be in discrepancy with socioeconomic realities—but also, or perhaps mainly, of living conditions. An agreed and reliable database is an essential instrument of socioeconomic policy. Israel would be willing to join any group of experts that might be formed to prepare by consensus a reliable system of categorizing and cataloguing the data and of finding methods to increase data accessibility.

Projects for the Refugees

Israel is ready to participate in the implementation of projects ranging from global designs of total reintegration in the host countries and in the administered territories, leading eventually to the dismantlement of all the refugee camps throughout the region, down to more specific and modest enterprises of improving health services, child welfare, development of human resources, vocational training and job creation and the development of a social and economic infrastructure. A comprehensive plan that would demonstrate that the fruits of peace exceed the spoils of war should ideally replace funds which have prolonged the refugee status of the Arab refugees by aid in conjunction with development, in a way that would ensure self-support and respect. The program should be offered without prejudice to the political negotiations. If the idea of a Reintegration Fund sounds revolutionary to some of us, I should recall that precisely such an approach was endorsed in the early 1950s by UNRWA (the Blandford Plan) only to be later undermined by the Arab countries. Forty-five years of mass deprivation and fatalistic frustration of two entire generations of refugees on the one hand, and the promising prospects of an Arab-Israeli peace on the other, should hopefully lead us to inaugurate a new phase in refugee rehabilitation.

Israel is willing to participate in, and to facilitate, any partial solution that would lead to an alleviation of the plight of the refugees and improve the quality of life in the camps. We are ready to work with each Arab country on a bilateral basis and with other concerned parties on a multilateral basis.

Israel is ready to propose a program of housing, infrastructure and basic services for the refugee camps in the territories and in the refugee camps in Arab countries as well. Based on the experience and conclusions drawn from the ongoing rehabilitation program implemented in the Gaza District that has already housed 12,000 families of refugees comprised of about 100,000 persons, all of whom were given an opportunity to acquire land and build their houses as they wished, in the camps or adjacent to them, our proposal is designed for a time span of five to eight years, and will affect 45,000 families.

If such a comprehensive program sounds too ambitious, we are ready to submit detailed project proposals for the improvement of living conditions in each and every refugee camp throughout the territories with the understanding that similar projects would be applied to refugee camps in Arab countries as well. Israel would collaborate in carrying out the program whether it is endorsed in its totality or only on one of several of its components, however modest they may be.

Simultaneously, or alternatively, we would consider submitting a pilot project for the rehabilitation of one particular refugee camp in the territories and one in an Arab country. Sharing problems and experience that could turn such a project into an instrument of regional cooperation.

A Regional Research Center

All the nations of the Middle East share common problems of refugees and mass dislocation. To better understand and share our respective experience in this field and in order to work out better solutions to the problems, we propose that a Regional Research Center be established to conduct applied investigation into the human and material problems of refugees. Such an institute could act as a regional think tank that would serve the peace process in the field of refugee rehabilitation. It may even be instrumental in facilitating a policy consensus on a regional basis. The Center should employ experts from Israel, Arab countries, Palestinians and experts from outside the region.

Israel is ready to join an initiative of developing human resources through vocational training, and submit its own proposals. The experience in this field—about 85,000 young men and women have so far acquired new professions in the territories—should be expanded; the lessons of its achievements and shortcomings can be shared in the context of regional cooperation. A program in this particular field should start, we believe, with the survey of the pressing needs in terms of skills, vocation and the needs of the different economies of the region. The project could be elaborated and led by a steering committee of experts that would also coordinate its implementation with the countries hosting the refugee camps, monitor its developments and evaluate its results.

A Time for Peace

Israel is not a homogeneous society; it is one of the richest ethnic mosaics possible, adding to that the fact that 20 percent of our population consists of an

Arab minority enjoying full citizenship. These are the same Palestinian Arabs who remained on their land during the exodus of 1948 that condemned their brethren to a hopeless life of destitution and despair in refugee camps throughout the region. Our society is fully aware of the vital necessity to reach a historic compromise with the Palestinian people while recognizing its legitimate rights for a life of freedom and dignity. The tragedy of the Israeli-Palestinian conflict stems from discrepant historical rhythms. The history of our modern national movement has been characterized by realistic responses to objective historical circumstances; the Palestinians have consistently fought for the solutions of yesterday, those they had rejected a generation or two earlier. This persistent attempt to turn back the clock of history lies at the root of many of the misfortunes that have befallen the peoples of the region. Now it is time for all of us to overcome dire memories and look forward. Neither the physical nor the rhetorical war of images will bring us any closer to peace and reconciliation. No one has a monopoly on the mythology of suffering and atrocities. In this tragic dispute, we have all committed acts of violence that we ought not to be proud of. To the Palestinians we say: we are excited to be sitting with you for the first time in the troubled history of our relations in order to shape our dreams of peace. Let us then join hands in asking the world which has been watching, perplexed at, and sometimes even fueling our wars to mobilize its resources for the benefit of our peoples.

We are all entangled in a seemingly insoluble conundrum. We know that unless your and our wounds are healed, peace—not only the political peace but also that of the mind and the conscience—would not be complete. Yet, at the same time we realize that the total satisfaction of our respective dreams or presumed rights will lead us to perdition. Hence, it is incumbent upon us to devise realistic ways that would heal without opening new wounds, that would dignify our existence as free peoples without putting into jeopardy the collective existence of each other. I believe that at the end of the road we shall find such an ideal compromise, while banishing the sword from this Land of God.

Excerpts:
Declaration of Principles on Interim
Self-Government Arrangements
September 13, 1993

The Government of the State of Israel and the Palestinian team (in the Jordanian-Palestinian delegation to the Middle East Peace Conference) (the "Palestinian Delegation"), representing the Palestinian people, agree that it is time to put an end to decades of confrontation and conflict, recognize their mutual legitimate and political rights, and strive to live in peaceful coexistence and mutual dignity and security and achieve a just, lasting and comprehensive peace settlement and historic reconciliation through the agreed political process.

Accordingly, the two sides agree to the following principles:

Article I—Aim of the Negotiations

The aim of the Israeli-Palestinian negotiations within the current Middle East peace process is, among other things, to establish a Palestinian Interim Self-Government Authority, the elected Council, (the "Council") for the Palestinian people in the West Bank and the Gaza Strip, for a transitional period not exceeding five years, leading to a permanent settlement based on Security Council Resolutions 242 and 338.

It is understood that the interim arrangements are an integral part of the whole peace process and that the negotiations on the permanent status will lead to the implementation of Security Council Resolutions 242 and 338.

Article V—Transitional Period and Permanent Status Negotiations

1. The five-year transitional period will begin upon the withdrawal from the Gaza Strip and Jericho area.
2. Permanent status negotiations will commence as soon as possible, but not later than the beginning of the third year of the interim period, between the Government of Israel and the Palestinian people representatives.
3. **It is understood that these negotiations shall cover remaining issues, including: Jerusalem, refugees, settlements, security arrangements, borders, relations and cooperation with other neighbors, and other issues of common interest.**
4. The two parties agree that the outcome of the permanent status negotiations should not be prejudiced or preempted by agreements reached for the interim period.

Article XII—Liaison and Cooperation With Jordan and Egypt

The two parties will invite the Governments of Jordan and Egypt to participate in establishing further liaison and cooperation arrangements between the Government of Israel and the Palestinian representatives, on one hand, and the Governments of Jordan and Egypt, on the other hand, to promote cooperation between them. **These arrangements will include the constitution of a Contin-**

uing Committee that will decide by agreement on the modalities of admission of persons displaced from the West Bank and Gaza Strip in 1967, together with necessary measures to prevent disruption and disorder. Other matters of common concern will be dealt with by this Committee.

Excerpts:
Treaty of Peace between the State of Israel and the Hashemite Kingdom of Jordan October 26, 1994

Preamble

The government of the Hashemite Kingdom of Jordan and the government of the State of Israel:

Bearing in mind the Washington Declaration, signed by them on 25 July 1994 and which they are both committed to honor;

Aiming at the achievement of a just, lasting and comprehensive peace in the Middle East based on Security Council Resolutions 242 and 338 in all their aspects;

Bearing in mind the importance of maintaining and strengthening peace based on freedom, equality, justice, and respect for fundamental and human rights: thereby overcoming psychological barriers and promoting human dignity;

Reaffirming their faith in the Charter of the United Nations and recognizing their right to live in peace with each other as well as with all states, within secure and recognized borders;

Desiring to develop friendly relations and cooperation between them in accordance with the principles of international law governing international relations in times of peace;

Desiring as well to ensure lasting security for both their states and, in particular, to avoid threats and the use of force between them;

Bearing in mind that in their Washington Declaration of 25 July 1994 they declared the termination of the state of belligerency between them;

Deciding to establish peace between them in accordance with this treaty of peace;

Have agreed as follows:

Article 1 — Establishment of Peace

Peace is hereby established between the Hashemite Kingdom of Jordan and the State of Israel (the parties) effective from the exchange of the instruments of ratification of this treaty (henceforth—ratification).

Article 2—General Principles

The parties will apply between them the provisions of the Charter of the United Nations and the principles of international law governing relations between states in times of peace. In particular:

    a.   They recognize and will respect each other's sovereignty, territorial integrity, and political independence.

    b.   They recognize and will respect each other's right to live in peace within secure and recognized boundaries.

    c.   They will develop good neighborly relations of cooperation between them to ensure lasting security, will refrain from the threat or use of force against each other, and will settle all disputes between them by peaceful means.

    d.   They respect and recognize the sovereignty, territorial integrity, and political independence of every state in the region.

    e.   They respect and recognize the pivotal role of human development and dignity in regional and bilateral relationships.

    f.   **They further believe that within their control, involuntary movements of persons in such a way as to adversely prejudice the security of either party should not be permitted.**

Article 8—Refugees and Displaced Persons

1.   Recognizing the massive human problems caused by both parties by the conflict in the Middle East, as well as the contribution made by them towards the alleviation of human suffering, the parties will seek to further alleviate those problems arising on a bilateral level.

2.   Recognizing that the above human problems caused by the conflict in the Middle East cannot be fully resolved on the bilateral level, the parties will seek to resolve them in appropriate forums, in accordance with international law, including the following:

    a.   **In the case of displaced persons, in a quadripartite committee together with Egypt and the Palestinians;**

    b.   **In the case of refugees,**

        (i) **in the framework of the work of the Multilateral Group on Refugees;**

        (ii) **in negotiations, in a framework to be agreed, bilateral or otherwise, in conjunction with and at the same time as the permanent status negotiations referred to in Article 3 of this Treaty.**

3.   **Through the implementation of agreed United Nations programs and other agreed international economic programs concerning refugees and displaced persons, including assistance to their settlement.**

Article 11—Mutual Understanding and Good Neighborly Relations

1. The parties will seek to foster mutual understanding and tolerance based on shared historic values, and accordingly undertake:
   a. To abstain from hostile or discriminatory propaganda against each other, and to take all possible legal and administrative measures to prevent the dissemination of such propaganda by any organization or individual present in the territory of either party;
   b. As soon as possible, and not later than three months from the ratification, to repeal all adverse or discriminatory references and expressions in their respective legislation;
   c. To refrain in all government publications from any such reference or expressions;
   d. To ensure mutual enjoyment by each other's citizens of due process of law within their respective legal systems and before their courts.
2. Article 1(a) is without prejudice to the right to freedom of expression as contained in the International Covenant on Civil and Political Rights.
3. A joint committee shall be formed to examine incidents where one party claims there has been a violation of this article.

Declaration on the Human Rights of Individuals Who are Not Nationals of the Country in Which They Live
December 13, 1985

The General Assembly

Considering that the Charter of the United Nations encourages universal respect for and observance of the human rights and fundamental freedoms of all human beings, without distinction as to race, sex, language or religion,

Considering that the Universal Declaration of Human Rights proclaims that all human beings are born free and equal in dignity and rights and that everyone is entitled to all the rights and freedoms set forth in that Declaration, without distinction of any kind, such as race, colour, sex, language, religion, political or other opinion, national or social origin, property, birth or other status,

Considering that the Universal Declaration of Human Rights proclaims further that everyone has the right to recognition everywhere as a person before the law, that all are equal before the law and entitled without any discrimination to equal protection of the law, and that all are entitled to equal protection against any discrimination in violation of that Declaration and against any incitement to such discrimination,

Being aware that the States parties to the International Covenants on Human Rights undertake to guarantee that the rights enunciated in these Covenants will be exercised without discrimination of any kind as to race, colour, sex, language, religion, political or other opinion, national or social origin, property, birth or other status,

Conscious that, with improving communications and the development of peaceful and friendly relations among countries, individuals increasingly live in countries of which they are not nationals,

Reaffirming the purposes and principles of the Charter of the United Nations,

Recognizing that the protection of human rights and fundamental freedoms provided for in international instruments should also be ensured for individuals who are not nationals of the country in which they live,

Proclaims this Declaration:

Article 1

For the purposes of this Declaration, the term "alien" shall apply, with due regard to qualifications made in subsequent articles, to any individual who is not a national of the State in which he or she is present.

Article 2

1. Nothing in this Declaration shall be interpreted as legitimizing the illegal entry into and presence in a State of any alien, nor shall any provision be interpreted as restricting the right of any State to promulgate laws and regulations concerning the entry of aliens and the terms and conditions of their stay or to establish differences between nationals and aliens. However, such laws and regulations shall not be incompatible with the international legal obligations of that State, including those in the field of human rights.

2. This Declaration shall not prejudice the enjoyment of the rights accorded by domestic law and of the rights which under international law a State is obliged to accord to aliens, even where this Declaration does not recognize such rights or recognizes them to a lesser extent.

Article 3

Every State shall make public its national legislation or regulations affecting aliens.

Article 4

Aliens shall observe the laws of the State in which they reside or are present and regard with respect the customs and traditions of the people of that State.

Article 5

1. Aliens shall enjoy, in accordance with domestic law and subject to the relevant international obligations of the State in which they are present, in particular the following rights:
    (a) The right to life and security of person: no alien shall be subjected to arbitrary arrest or detention; no alien shall be deprived of his or her liberty except on such grounds and in accordance with such procedures as are established by law;
    (b) The right to protection against arbitrary or unlawful interference with privacy, family, home or correspondence;
    (c) The right to be equal before the courts, tribunals and all other organs and authorities administering justice and, when necessary, to free assistance of an interpreter in criminal proceedings and, when prescribed by law, other proceedings;
    (d) The right to choose a spouse, to marry, to found a family;
    (e) The right to freedom of thought, opinion, conscience and religion; the right to manifest their religion or beliefs, subject only to such limitations as are prescribed by law and are necessary to protect public safety, order, health or morals or the fundamental rights and freedoms of others;
    (f) The right to retain their own language, culture and tradition;
    (g) The right to transfer abroad earnings, savings or other personal monetary assets, subject to domestic currency regulations.
2. Subject to such restrictions as are prescribed by law and which are necessary in a democratic society to protect national security, public safety, public order, public health or morals or the rights and freedoms of others, and which are consistent with the other rights recognized in the relevant international instruments and those set forth in this Declaration, aliens shall enjoy the following rights:
    (a) The right to leave the country;
    (b) The right to freedom of expression;
    (c) The right to peaceful assembly;
    (d) The right to own property alone as well as in association with others, subject to domestic law.
3. Subject to the provisions referred to in paragraph 2, aliens lawfully in the territory of a State shall enjoy the right to liberty of movement and freedom to choose their residence within the borders of the State.
4. Subject to national legislation and due authorization, the spouse and minor or dependent children of an alien lawfully residing in the territory of a State shall be admitted to accompany, join and stay with the alien.

Article 6

No alien shall be subjected to torture or to cruel, inhuman or degrading treatment or punishment and, in particular, no alien shall be subjected without his or her free consent to medical or scientific experimentation.

Article 7

An alien lawfully in the territory of a State may be expelled therefrom only in pursuance of a decision reached in accordance with law and shall, except where compelling reasons of national security otherwise require, be allowed to submit the reasons why he or she should not be expelled and to have the case reviewed by, and be represented for the purpose before, the competent authority or a person or persons specially designated by the competent authority. Individual or collective expulsion of such aliens on grounds of race, colour, religion, culture, descent or national or ethnic origin is prohibited.

Article 8

1. Aliens lawfully residing in the territory of a State shall also enjoy, in accordance with the national laws, the following rights, subject to their obligations under article 4:

   (a) The right to safe and healthy working conditions, to fair wages and equal remuneration for work of equal value without distinction of any kind, in particular, women being guaranteed conditions of work not inferior to those enjoyed by men, with equal pay for equal work;

   (b) The right to join trade unions and other organizations or associations of their choice and to participate in their activities. No restrictions may be placed on the exercise of this right other than those prescribed by law and which are necessary, in a democratic society, in the interests of national security or public order or for the protection of the rights and freedoms of others;

   (c) The right to health protection, medical care, social security, social services, education, rest and leisure, provided that they fulfil the requirements under the relevant regulations for participation and that undue strain is not placed on the resources of the State.

2. With a view to protecting the rights of aliens carrying on lawful paid activities in the country in which they are present, such rights may be specified by the Governments concerned in multilateral or bilateral conventions.

Article 9

No alien shall be arbitrarily deprived of his or her lawfully acquired assets.

Article 10

Any alien shall be free at any time to communicate with the consulate or diplomatic mission of the State of which he or she is a national or, in the absence thereof, with the consulate or diplomatic mission of any other State entrusted with the protection of the interests of the State of which he or she is a national in the State where he or she resides.

Index

Abandoned Areas Ordinance, 16
Absentees' Property Law, 16
Absorption plan, 3, 5, 7, 122; and citizenship law, 84, 86–87, 89–90; and compensation, 85–87, 94–100; and current needs and preferences, 92–95; and the dynamics of permanent absorption, 102–7; and the enforcement and extinguishment of claims, 99–100; and funding sources, 95–99; for non-Middle Eastern states, 90; and norms of implementation, 101–23; overview of, 83–100; targets for, 85, 87–92
Adelman, Howard, 103
Affirmative action, 51
Afghanistan, 31, 101
Africa, 6, 46, 53, 67. *See also* specific countries
African Americans, 118
Agreement on the Gaza Strip and the Jericho Area (1994), 116
Aleppo, 48
Algeria, 53, 110
Aliyah, 1, 17–18
Allah, 31
Al-Nakba, 1
Americans for Peace Now, 196–97
Amman Economic Conference, 115
Annotated Bibliography on Themes Identified at the Middle East Peace Negotiations, Working Group on Refugees 190–91, 199

APG (All-Palestine Government) documents, 56
Arab Higher Committee, 15
Arab-Israeli war (1948), 1, 8, 21–25, 31–32. *See also* Dispersal of 1948
Arab League, 55, 77–78, 117
Arafat, Yasser, 29, 54
Armenia, 75, 110
Asia, 6, 25, 46, 67, 122. *See also* specific countries
Aussiedler, 111
Australia, 46, 58

Bahrain, 53, 74
Balfour Declaration (1917), 50, 134n51, 150n89
Baltic states, 6, 107–8
Basic Law, 51, 111
Bedouins, 17, 49, 129n8
Beersheva, 34, 37
Beilin, Yossi, 27
Beirut, 32, 47
Beisan, 34
Ben-Gurion, David, 18–19, 131n21, 133n43
Bernadotte, Folke, 21
Bethlehem, 19, 40
Bible Triangle, 50
Bisan, 37
Black September (1970), 44
Bosnia, 5, 75
Brand, Laurie, 32–34; identification of four Palestinian-Jordanian groups by, 45; on the status of Palestinians in Egypt, 56